O9-BTZ-795

Wilderness

Other books by Rutherford Platt

THIS GREEN WORLD

THE WOODS OF TIME

AMERICAN TREES, A BOOK OF DISCOVERY

1001 QUESTIONS ANSWERED ABOUT TREES

THE RIVER OF LIFE

Wilderness

THE DISCOVERY OF A CONTINENT OF WONDER

by Rutherford Platt

WITH ILLUSTRATIONS BY FRANCES ELLIS

Dodd, Mead & Company, New York, 1961

COPYRIGHT © 1961 BY RUTHERFORD PLATT

ALL RIGHTS RESERVED

NO PART OF THIS BOOK MAY BE REPRODUCED IN ANY FORM

WITHOUT PERMISSION IN WRITING FROM THE PUBLISHER

LIBRARY OF CONGRESS CATALOG CARD NUMBER: 61-8308

PRINTED IN THE UNITED STATES OF AMERICA

CONTENTS

Wilderness

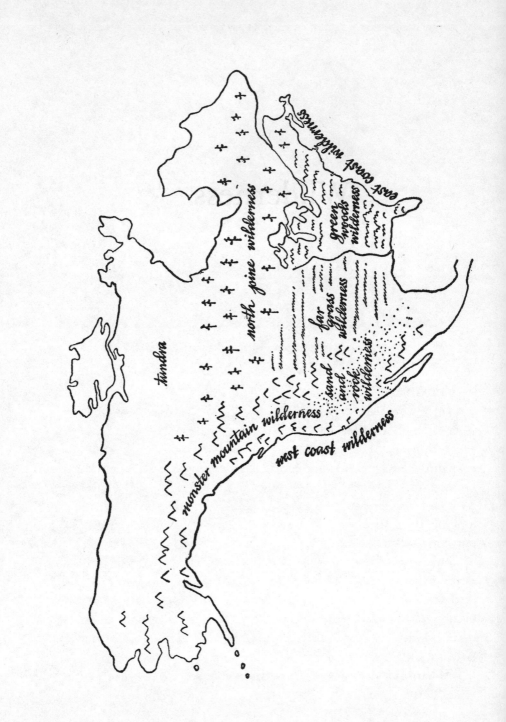

CHAPTER I

THIS SURPRISING CONTINENT

AMERICA was the biggest surprise in the history of man.
Nobody at the time of its discovery believed that another
great continent lay beyond the western horizon. They thought
that all the continents in the world were Europe, Asia, and Africa.
Because of this belief, nobody ever set sail to discover America.
The idea was so far from people's thinking that even when men,
looking for a short cut to Asia, stumbled over America, they did
not know what they had found.

Columbus, who is called the discoverer of the New World, may
never have set foot on the continent of North America, and he
died without ever hearing of the New World. His greatness lies in
blazing a westward trail and dispelling fears, myths, and superstitions, so that on the heels of Columbus many men crossed the
Atlantic.

It is hard for us to imagine how awesome was the mystery of the ocean when Columbus disappeared into the sunset. Most people still believed that the world was flat, and they could not imagine another shore to the ocean. Their thoughts were probably colored by the ancient belief that the ocean was an uncrossable stream of water, flowing around the lands of the world and blending with the sky. Dante, whose books were widely read in that day, told in his *Inferno* how Ulysses sailed out of sight across the ocean to die. Without any facts to go on, the general opinion was that lands beyond the ocean, if any, were unnatural lands, peopled by giants and monsters.

Seafaring men, who are often superstitious, especially felt this awe and fear of what they called "The Ocean Sea." During the fifty years before Columbus, sailors had ventured far enough to discover the Madeira Islands, the Canary Islands and the Azores, which were known as "the end of the inhabited West." Those islands lay off familiar coasts, and doubtless some fearless sailors of whom there is no record, burning with curiosity, must have headed west on their own and disappeared like Ulysses into the setting sun. Those who returned reported endless horizons, furious empty seas, where day after day a ship became more helpless until the terror-stricken crew was forced to put about and return to a known port.

This explains why America was not discovered until so late in history and why it was such a tremendous surprise.

The first white men who leaped ashore on the beaches of America simply could not imagine the size and nature of this land mass. They saw only mangrove swamps, strips of sand, rocky shores, and the faces of forests. For a long time they dared not go inland. Weary and beaten after weeks at sea, they clung to the Atlantic frontier. For a hundred years they pushed into the continent, step by step, in the south and in the north. Everything was queer and surprising. It took almost two hundred years after the first landings before French explorers reached the Mississippi River, less than a third of the way across the continent. It was more than three hundred years after Columbus when the first explorers went from the Mississippi all the way across to the west coast.

Yet these long trails were merely lines across the immense continental wildernesses. Between these, and to the north, vast mysterious regions have continued to astonish and surprise people even to our time.

AMERICA! The word has a ring. It comes from Amerigo, a unique word with the four major vowels in alphabetical order. That word was sheer luck. It was not chosen by any explorer, including Amerigo Vespucci himself. It was not chosen by any king who was planting his flag in the New World. That sort of naming came later, when parts of America were called New France, New Spain, New England. The name America was coined in a tiny village in the Vosges Mountains near the borders of France and Germany. It happened through an extraordinary chain of events involving a big scientific error, a little printing press, a letter to a gentleman in Florence, and a group of bright young poets and artists.

The scientific error kept Columbus from naming the new world. If he had known that he had discovered, not the east coast of Asia, but a brand-new continent, our country would probably be named Columbia. But neither the Spanish monarchs nor Columbus thought there was any new land to be named. He was made Admiral of the Ocean Sea. His islands became known as the West Indies, and the ten scared redmen whom he brought back to Spain were known as Indians. All this stemmed from the great error in calculating the size of the earth as half the size that it actually is. Columbus was given this information eighteen years before his famous voyage, and he never lived to see it corrected.

When Columbus was growing up, his imagination was stirred by exciting news from a great scholar in Florence named Toscanelli, who said that the earth was round. People generally, who were

3

carrying on their humdrum, everyday lives, thought that this was ridiculous—anybody can see that the earth is flat. But Toscanelli, who belonged to a family made rich by trading with the Orient, had done a lot of thinking. He was an expert in mathematics and geography. He spent his time talking about astronomy, voyages, the form of the earth, and the limits of the sea. He argued that it was possible to sail west and bring back quite easily in a ship the pearls, gold, and spices of the Orient and thus avoid the long, dangerous, overland caravan route to and from the East.

A small printing press is next in the chain of events which led to the naming of America.

During the half century after Gutenberg invented printing with movable type, printing was a great art. Few men had the skill and patience to cut the letters and set the mold and adjust the press. The Bibles and illustrated books printed in that day are among the world's great art treasures.

It is astonishing that a tiny village named Saint-Dié, hidden among the pine trees in the hills of Lorraine, should have acquired a printing press in 1507. Here were an old church, a cloister, a few houses surrounded by a stone wall. The duke of Lorraine was a peaceful, quiet little man with an energetic secretary named Vautrin Lud. Lud was supervisor of the mines from which the king got his income. He was also head of the monastery and served as mayor and judge in the community. He built a new chapel, sang in the choir, and led processions. He also had a keen wit and enjoyed good fellowship. Saint-Dié was a wide-awake place.

A nephew of Vautrin's, a young man in his early twenties named Nicholas, lived in a stone house close to the church in the center of the town. Nicholas had a startling idea. Saint-Dié should have a printing press! He offered his house for it.

In those days Europe had only a few printing presses, and these were located in the great centers. For example, Venice was famous for its printing because it was Europe's biggest center for sea-borne traffic, trading with the Orient, and it had many industries. Western

Germany was famous for its printing, because Gutenberg had lived there. Mainz had experts in cutting type, making lead molds, and applying pressure with the big levers.

Printing presses were located also in the great capitals of Europe. Rome, Paris, London, Madrid, Brussels—these were the centers of art and culture where rich monarchs were supporting armies, building cathedrals, and sponsoring expeditions to make themselves richer. Each of these had to have a printing press for his prestige and to spread his fame.

Clearly, Nicholas Lud's idea for a printing press in Saint-Dié, an almost invisible hamlet far from the centers of power and learning, was preposterous. Lorraine was a petty province of France ruled by a mere duke. He was hardly more than a good-natured country gentleman who agreed to everything that his secretary suggested. But Vautrin's energy and imagination were equal to the occasion. So the day came when a printing press was installed in Saint-Dié.

It drew like a magnet young men who were typographers, proofreaders, and pressmen trained in Germany. The group included a poet and a writer who had been in Venice and Paris. The oldest was a man named Waldseemüller, a man of thirty who was an artist and map maker trained under Dürer, the most famous painter and engraver in Europe at the time. A key man in the group was a young poet named Ringmann.

They had much fun. Vautrin said, "Not all our time can be devoted to serious matters. We must have a little amusement." So they turned out *The Picture Book Grammar* in which all definitions are drawings. A noun was a priest, the masculine gender a boy, the feminine a girl, and a bench on which the pupils sat was the neuter gender.

But the little group and their printing press at Saint-Dié would hardly be known in history and would have vanished among their pines in the remote mountain valley except that Columbus' trip had suddenly thrown Europe into great confusion over what the world was actually like.

They must have had many lively discussions at Saint-Dié, and then all agreed that they would make a new book about the world. It would be called *Introduction to Cosmography*. Cosmography is the science of the universe, including astronomy, geology, and geography. It would feature a map of the world, but it would also tell about the stars and the elements. It would have pictures of the great navigators wearing fancy Florentine hats and frilly sleeves and gold chains around their necks with crosses dangling from them. It would have ships sailing over rippling seas, blown along by cherubs with fat cheeks. The exciting history of the day would be told in pages of poetry and philosophy.

Strange as it sounds, a man who lived in Alexandria, Egypt, in 100 A.D., named Ptolemy, was still the world's top authority on astronomy and geography when Columbus sailed in 1492. Ptolemy said the earth was like a fixed platform in the center of the universe. It stood still while the sun, moon, and stars revolved around it.

Europe was greatly excited by the reports from the Portuguese explorers who sailed around Africa to the Far East and by the big news that Columbus had found a short cut to Asia by sailing west. Yet educated people were not ready to throw Ptolemy overboard. The group at Saint-Dié said that their *Introduction to Cosmography* would be merely a revised edition of Ptolemy.

The most important feature of *Introduction to Cosmography* was to be a map of the world based on the amazing news that the earth was round. Waldseemüller drew this beautifully with the skill of an excellent artist. It was printed in flat pages in segments shaped so that, if cut out along lines indicated, they would fit together when pasted on a solid globe.

One page of this ingenious book—the most famous map in history—shows a coast line facing Africa. The land mass is as long and narrow as a fish. What lay to the west of the coast line is a complete mystery. That area is labeled with three Latin words, *Terra Ultra Incognita*—Unknown Land Beyond.

Was this the continent of Asia? If Columbus had found Japanese

6

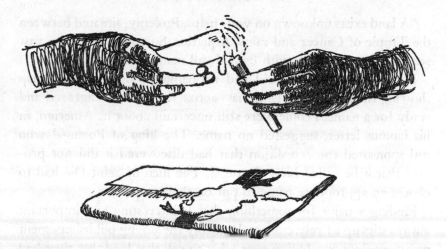

islands or islands of the Malay Peninsula, as he said he had, this should be labeled Asia. But an astonishing piece of news had just arrived from Florence. Lorenzo the Magnificent had received a letter from Amerigo Vespucci in which he said, "We reached a new land which we discovered to be mainland . . . which according to my navigation is the fourth part of the world."

This was the first hint of a fourth continent, but it did not say so positively. It was probably Asia; but then another letter from Amerigo arrived—"In days past I wrote you of my return from those lands which we have sought and discovered, and which I can lawfully call the *New World* . . . we learned that that land is not an island but a continent because it extends along far stretching shores that do not encompass it and it is populated by innumerable inhabitants."

This exciting letter was copied countless times and translated into all the European languages. It introduced an unknown quarter of the globe to the people of Europe.

Young Ringmann, the poet, had come to Saint-Dié with the phrase *New World!* ringing in his thoughts. It had inspired a little poem which he dashed off before they started work on *Introduction to Cosmography:*

7

"A land exists unknown on your maps, Ptolemy, situated between the Tropic of Cancer and rainy Aquarius. Surrounded by the vast sea. In this land ablaze with light dwell many naked peoples."

But still the New World had no name. Waldseemüller's map showing the fish-shaped land mass across the sea was engraved and ready for a name. People were still uncertain about it. Amerigo, in his famous letter, suggested no name. The king of Portugal who had sponsored the expedition that had discovered it did not propose that it be called New Portugal. The men of Saint-Dié had to choose an appropriate name to put on their map.

Finding a name for something that is interesting and important always stirs up a lively contest. Probably the young publishers spent many evenings squabbling over what to call that land that they had drawn on their globe. Was it or was it not a new continent? We can be sure that Ringmann said it was, but some of the others may have shaken their heads and pointed out that Columbus was certain it was Asia.

In Venice the land which Amerigo saw had been referred to as "the land of parrots." People had been dazzled as much by the marvelous blue and yellow parrots as they were by the red skins of the naked Indians which Columbus brought back, but the phrase about the parrots was used only in conversation. It was not a good name at all for that mysterious land mass which was now drawn on a map of the world for the first time, especially if it was in fact a fourth part of the world, a *New World*.

One day a messenger from Paris galloped into Saint-Dié with an envelope for the duke. It contained a copy of a letter, perhaps the most historic letter ever written, which Amerigo Vespucci was assumed to have sent from Lisbon in 1504 to Pieri Soderini, Gonfaloniere (a majestic Italian name for the Mayor of Florence). Amerigo saluted the Gonfaloniere as "Your Magnificence." The whole first paragraph was devoted to exalting the magnificent lord to whom it was written and belittling the part which the humble writer had played, saying that the contents of this letter would be trifling compared to the affairs of the sublime Republic of Florence.

This way of writing was according to the custom of the times. People were not trying to save minutes and seconds. The biggest news in the world could wait for much bowing and many flowery words of greeting. Soderini, of course, recognized it for what it was. Dazzling news. A new continent was discovered!

Others in the room when the Gonfaloniere opened the letter probably stared at it and then all talked at once, clapped each other on the back, and ordered up wine.

The letter was promptly released over the news services of Europe. This consisted of calling in the translators and copyists, stopping the presses in Venice, and getting the letter set up in type, which took a month or two. As fast as copies were made or printed, they were shot out by boat and horseback. Some traveled through the Pillars of Hercules (the Straits of Gibraltar) and then north along the coast to England. According to legend, the Pillars of Hercules bore the inscription *Non plus ultra*—Nothing more beyond. That legend was now out of date.

Copies of the Soderini letter were dispatched on horseback over the post roads of Europe to Rome, Paris, Brussels, and other capitals. In the course of weeks and months more copies radiated from these capitals to monasteries, castles, and cities wherever there were people of importance and learning to receive them.

It was two years after the letter was written when the French translation of it reached Saint-Dié. There could have been no more opportune time for its arrival. Ringmann immediately set to work translating it into Latin, the language of scholars.

As the astonishing words were read, the form of a new hemisphere emerged from the shadows of the unknown. Waldseemüller may have been the first to stand up in meeting and proclaim that the map which he had drawn was indeed the New World. But the

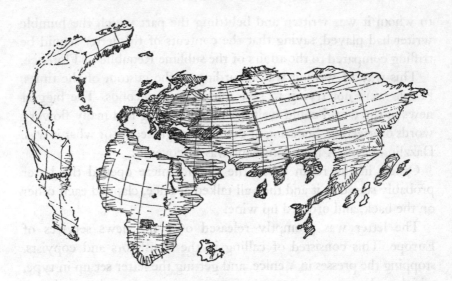

question still remained, "What was its name?" The up-to-date map in the *Introduction to Cosmography* must above all be authoritative and accurate.

We do not know which one of the men suggested that they use the first name of Amerigo Vespucci, but it is a good guess that it was Ringmann. It was he who had been so excited about the New World letter that it inspired his poem the year before. Later, when *Introduction to Cosmography* came off the press, it bore this prose poem by Ringmann:

"But now that these parts of the world have been widely examined and another fourth part has been discovered by Americu Vesputiu (as will be seen in the following), I see no reason why we should not call it America, that is to say, land of Americus, for Americus its discoverer, man of sagacious wit, just as Europe and Asia received in days gone by their names from women."

Elsewhere in the margin appears this comment, "It is fitting that this fourth part of the world, inasmuch as Americus discovered it, be called Amerigo, or let us say, land of Americi, that is: AMERICA."

The day came when the plate for the page of the mysterious land mass was mounted on the press. The printer ran his ink roller over the type, pulled on the lever, giving just the right pressure against the parchment. The page was taken out of the press carefully and carried over to the window where they studied it for any little defect. The name *America* appeared clearly printed for the first time on a map!

Doubtless the group at Saint-Dié were very proud of their work. It looked well. It was a good piece of printing.

The year after they completed printing *Introduction to Cosmography*, the Duke of Lorraine died. His successor was not interested in the enthusiasms of the Saint-Dié group and their printing press. Suddenly the creative, happy group vanished. They would have sunk unknown into the river of time—except that by sheer lucky chance the geography part of the work turned up in Strassburg in 1522. There it was reprinted and distributed throughout Europe. Coming then from such an important center as Strassburg, scholars paid attention to it. From that time on the name *America* has appeared in all the atlases of the world.

Who was this man whose first name became known to more people in the world than that of any other man who ever lived? Because the naming of America happened in such a surprising and unplanned way and seemed to snatch some laurels from Columbus, some historians have looked on Amerigo as a kind of impostor.

The records of that time, 450 years ago (quite recent in the history of the world), are plentiful, and they were not written to impress us. They detract not at all from Columbus, the bold pioneer who blazed the trail across the Atlantic and shook the world. Only a man with Columbus' character could have succeeded. He was a man of few words, stern, always calm in the face of panic. His crew respected and feared him. They did not love him. Nothing could shake his belief that he was on the way to India.

His tired, snarly crew, jammed into a little boat, were in a dangerous mood by the time they reached the middle of the

Atlantic. There they saw the seaweeds of the Sargasso Sea and sea-gulls feeding among them. This was a sign of land.

Ignorance helped history at this point. Sargassum weed is not a sign of shallow water—the sea was four miles deep under their keel.

Columbus buried his terror deep inside himself when he saw that the magnetic needle pointed farther and farther from true north as they sailed westward. He did not know about the magnetic pole and the variation of the needle. After more dreary days they saw whales and boobies diving for fish. These seemed to be more signs of shallow water. Then the sea grew calm and a drizzly rain set in. This was the first time that men had been in the middle of the ocean. They did not know that whales and birds can feed there and that drizzly rains and calms exist also in the middle of the Atlantic.

Columbus said little but only growled his orders to his sulky men, and they held their course.

Columbus had greatness. The Spanish monarch bestowed on him

the majestic title of "Admiral of the Ocean and Sea and Viceroy and Governor of the Islands that had been discovered in the Indies." But in those times especially greatness made a man very insecure in a jealous world. A few years later when it was found that he had not discovered a route to the gems and spices of India, Columbus fell out of favor. He was even put in irons. He was baffled and heartbroken when he died.

In contrast to Columbus, Amerigo Vespucci was a little man with no prestige and power. He knew Columbus and respected him, but things happened to Amerigo not because he was competing with Columbus and the other great explorers, or because he was out for fame and glory, but because he was an adventurer at heart.

Amerigo's imagination was stirred when he was working in Spain with the firm which was outfitting Columbus' ships. He was connected with the merchants who handled the picking of crews; the purchase of ships' stores, the stocks of sea biscuits, wine, flour, oil, vinegar, cheese; who contracted for cannon, lances, and swords. In this connection he came to know everybody and everybody knew him. This included the kings of Spain and Portugal, Christopher Columbus, and the biggest bankers in town, down to the truckmen who delivered the ships' stores and the riggers who put on the sails. People trusted him and liked him and called him by his first name.

Columbus was seldom called Christopher by his friends; on the other hand, Vespucci was always called Amerigo. The name echoed on the water fronts of Spain's busy ports, in the wineshops where people were discussing the new expeditions which were being planned to follow up Columbus, and in the chartrooms where pilots were consulting about courses across the Ocean Sea.

In his four years as an employee of the merchants who were outfitting expeditions, Amerigo had come to know ships and how they are built and what they can do. He had a feel of sails and he had learned their rigging and how to handle them. He had talked with sailors and knew their language and their ways. He was

familiar with the old Ptolemy charts and thought them very old-fashioned compared with the "modern" charts of Toscanelli which Columbus used. He saw the outlines of islands across the Ocean Sea where Columbus drew them after his first voyage. Above all, Amerigo was interested in the stars and how navigators used the stars to know the position of their ship when no land was in sight.

Amerigo was overcome by curiosity. What *was* that land which Columbus had seen? Were those islands really offshore Asia? What lay beyond them? Perhaps he could find rivers there and sail up them where no man had ever been before. He wanted to meet the people and ask them questions. What kind of trees were there? What animals and birds? Amerigo Vespucci was the first man ever to think in terms of a New World wilderness. He had a strong sense of wonder of all nature.

He decided that no longer would he stand on the shore and watch ships disappear in the sunset. He had interviewed the men on those ships. He had checked their weapons and their food. He had secured charts for the pilots and advised them on their courses. Now he suddenly had a chance to join an expedition himself!

Amerigo's famous letter to Soderini, Gonfaloniere of Florence, tells about this opportunity. Amerigo came to Spain as a trader. During four years he noticed that people who deal in worldly goods and have ambitions to be rich and powerful are often knocked down by the blows of fortune. "At one moment Fortune places a man at the top of her wheel and at another casts him down and strips him of the possessions we may call borrowed." So Amerigo, a true explorer at heart, decided to give up all that and go see the world and its wonders. To him adventure was the best reward.

He writes in the Soderini letter: "The opportunity was afforded me at a most timely moment and conjunction for the King, Don Ferdinand, needing to send out four ships to discover lands to the West, I was chosen by His Highness to go with the fleet and help in the discovery."

Columbus had returned from his second voyage still asserting that it was Asia that he had found, but he had brought back no gems, no spices. He had not found the palaces and the wealth which Marco Polo had told about. People were beginning to question the whole business. Columbus' popularity was waning—when he wanted to get an interview with the king, he was kept waiting four months.

Perhaps the queen said to the king, "Isn't there somebody we

can trust whom we can send as our agent to tell us what is over there? To see whether this is really Asia or some other place?" Whatever the words, when Columbus was beseeching the king to help him make a third voyage, Amerigo was already sailing along the Mexican coast, discovering the mainland of the New World. He was in a special expedition of four ships. The name of the man in command is not known, but there is strong intimation that Amerigo was confidential investigator for the Spanish monarch. We know that he stood at the rail thrilled with what he saw. In the months following, he was to sail along twenty-five hundred miles of the South American coast. He saw the people and their ways. He explored the rivers. He noted the trees and birds.

When he came back, he made his report to Don Ferdinand. It disappeared. After all, it was a confidential report.

As time passed, Amerigo wished that he had a copy of that report, but the king would not let him have it back, so Amerigo tried to recall every detail of what he had said in his original letter to the king. Six years after his return these recollections were written in the famous letter to Soderini. They show that Amerigo was a good writer and that he had a sense of the excitement and interest of little things. For example, he mentions the hammocks which the people in the New World slept in. "These big nets made of cotton and swung in the air . . . although this fashion of sleeping may seem uncomfortable, I tell you it is pleasant to sleep in them and we preferred them to our blankets."

He reported not only facts but feelings. He told how a person feels when confronted by a wilderness where everything is strange.

This first report of a New World became the biggest adventure story in Europe. Amerigo was not concerned with conquest or obtaining riches for the king and himself. It never occurred to him that the New World should bear his first name. Amerigo's letter to Soderini was a fresh and stirring report. It was copied into all the languages of Europe and everybody was talking about it, while Columbus' reports were all but forgotten.

Here are some sentences from Amerigo's letter:

"We anchored our ships off land. We cast off our boats laden with men and arms. We proceeded toward land and sighted many people who were walking along the shore. We found them to be a naked race. They showed fear of us, I think because they saw us clothed and of an appearance different from theirs. All withdrew to a mountain and in spite of signs of peace and friendship we made to them, they would not come to converse with us.

"At another place we leaped ashore, full forty well-equipped men. The people still showed themselves shy. They would not come to talk with us until we gave them bells, mirrors, glass beads, and other trash that made them confident and they came to converse. The next day we saw hordes of people on the beach. They had with them their wives and children all laden with their possessions. Before we reached land, many of them dove and came to meet us a crossbow shot out to sea, for they were great swimmers.

"Men and women alike go about naked. They are of medium stature, very well-proportioned. Their skin is of a color that inclines to red like a lion's mane. If they were clothed they would look like white people, like ourselves. They have long black hair which renders the women beautiful. They have broad faces, so that their appearance is like that of the Tartar. [This shows Amerigo's keen observation. The Tartars are Mongolian people. It is now known that the Indians of North and South America were descended from Mongolians.]

"Their weapons are bows and arrows, very well made except that they have no iron or hard metal. In place of iron they put animals' or fishes' teeth or a splinter of stout wood burnt at the tip. They are sure shots, for they hit wherever they please.

"It is not their custom to have any captain and they do not walk in an orderly array. Each man is master of himself.

"They speak little and with subdued voice. They use the same accents as ourselves because they form the words either on the palate or the teeth or the lips, except that they use other names for things.

"They live and are contented with what nature gives them. The wealth which we affect in Europe such as gold, jewels, pearls, and other riches they hold of no value at all.

"We leaped ashore and advanced along a path which led to the wood where we found huts. They had built fires and were roasting animals and fish of many kinds. They were roasting one beast which resembled a serpent except that it had no wings and was so ugly in appearance that we wondered greatly at its fierceness. [This was probably the giant New World lizard which we call iguana. This lizard, including the tail, may be six feet long. It is so fierce looking that iguana is often exhibited in side shows and circuses, where it is called 'Chinese dragon.']

"The land is filled with an infinite number of animals. Few are like ours except the lions, panthers, stags, boars, goats, and deer, and even these look different. They have no horses, mules, asses, dogs, sheep, oxen, but so numerous are other animals, and they are all wild, that they cannot be counted.

"What shall we say of the birds which are so numerous and colorful that it is a wonder to behold them?

"The land is full of huge forests and woods. The fruits are so many that they are beyond number and entirely different from ours.

"Many came to see us and marvelled at the whiteness of our complexions. They asked whence we came and we gave them to understand that we came from heaven and that we were going to see the world."

This shows how Amerigo Vespucci thought and felt about the New World wilderness and its people. He returned to Spain as the king's reporter and no more. He received no title of nobility from the king and no coat of arms. There is no record that he ever asked for or expected such honors.

However, the king named Amerigo Pilot-Major, put him in charge of training pilots, and ordered him to make a master chart for navigators. The king said, "There are many general charts drawn up by different shipmasters which vary greatly one from another." The king wanted a master chart that would show each point of land, each island, each river mouth, each bay and its proper location.

He ordered all pilots to come together and give Amerigo assistance in this project. His master chart was to be known as the Royal Chart "by which all pilots are to govern and guide themselves."

This must have made Amerigo happy because he loved the stars and adventure and he had a definite eyewitness picture in his mind of a continental coast across the Ocean Sea.

Amerigo died in 1512, content that he had founded a school for pilots. There is no record that he ever saw the Saint Dié map with his first name printed across the New World.

Ten years after Amerigo wrote his letter, the first white man ever to leave the coast and plunge deep into an American wilderness was struggling westward through a pathless jungle in Panama for the first crossing of the New World. Here was an impassable tropical rain forest where a way had to be picked through labyrinths of fallen timber. The light was dim. The air was filled with steam. Weird, harsh calls of birds and animals came through the ghostly surroundings.

Balboa and his men had to follow streams and gullies and animal trails, often crawling on hands and knees under masses of vegetation where deadly snakes hissed at them. The sky was completely hidden by the upper story of the jungle where, a hundred feet or more above their heads, the intertwining branches and vines supported a fierce population of birds and animals which hooted and screamed and banged when the men came along.

There was so little sight of the sky that their westward direction had to be checked often by someone expending great energy to climb a tall tree.

These men, far from looking like Spanish conquistadors in shining armor, must have become virtually jungle animals themselves, soaked and beaten by cloudbursts that came roaring down through the trees. If they felt relief when they saw sunlight and could look farther ahead at the opening of a pond or swamp, this would have been temporary when whirling clouds of mad mosquitoes hit them.

Balboa and his band kept on through this ferocious wilderness only because they noticed that the land under their feet was constantly rising. They followed streams up the ravines out of the steaming jungle until they could see the sky and watch the birds. Now the ground became dry underneath. The underbrush was scattered. Where there were rocks and sunlight there were also rattlesnakes, but they could see these and cope with them. They were less dangerous than the water moccasins in the black swamps below and the coral snakes that lay in the fallen branches.

At last they reached the crest of a mountain ridge.

Below them the steam was rising from the jungle through which they had passed. To the right and left a series of mountain peaks stretched as far as the eye could see. Ahead and below there was a little more jungle, but that suddenly ended at the shore of a blue ocean. White men were looking at the Pacific for the first time.

This was the one glorious hour of Balboa's life which history records. A year after that moment when Balboa was shading his eyes looking at the Pacific, he was accused of treason by a jealous official in Central America and beheaded.

So Balboa brought back news of a baffling inland wilderness in the New World—of deep, dark forests and tremendous mountains and valleys a mile deep. But this was not reported as a grand discovery. It is a good guess that Balboa and his men cursed the American wilderness. The big news of the day was that another ocean which they called the Western Sea lay just beyond, offering a broad, blue highway to the Orient. The New World was a miserable, jungly obstruction on the way to this, and some waterway must be found through it or around it.

It is easy to see how great a misunderstanding there was about the breadth of the New World. Balboa could not know that by chance he had crossed at the narrowest place. He could not know that the Isthmus of Panama, only some fifty miles wide, is to North America like the slender tail of a big kite. The New World was discovered, but the great wildernesses to the north were still undreamed of.

It would take hundreds of years to discover the north pine and the green woods, the west coast wilderness, the mountain forests of the west, the grass horizons of the prairies, the flowering sands of the deserts, the Appalachians, the Rockies, the Cascade Mountains. These fabulous wildernesses abounded with bear, bison, beavers, raccoons, skunks, deer, prairie dogs, and rattlesnakes—and all the rest of our dramatic American animals.

The wildernesses were all in their places. Mount Mazama, a volcano 12,000 feet high, had exploded, and its top one third had dissolved into a seething caldron, 4,000 feet deep, which had filled with water the color of purple ink as we see Crater Lake today. Water from the Great Lakes was roaring over Niagara Falls. Echo River was flowing in the black depths of Mammoth Cave. Old Faithful Geyser in Yellowstone Park was shooting a jet of steam and boiling water 150 feet in the air every hour, the steam unfurling in the breeze like a white flag on a watery pole. The Colorado River had cut its way one mile straight down through solid rock, creating the Grand Canyon. Tree trunks of a forest that had been buried three thousand feet underground where they had turned to solid stone had been uncovered by wind and rain and lay scattered across the Painted Desert, flashing with brilliant agate colors. A fireball from outer space, perhaps five hundred feet in diameter and weighing three million tons, had hit in northern Arizona, carving in one second the immense Meteor Crater in the desert sand. The deep waters of the Mississippi were rolling for two thousand five hundred miles through the middle of the continent. The big-tree sequoias, some one hundred feet in circumference around the base, were standing in their places in the High Sierras of California, many of them the same trees which we see today.

When white men first discovered America, not only were the wildernesses complete in every detail, not only were they filled with animals unlike animals anywhere else in the world, but also every-

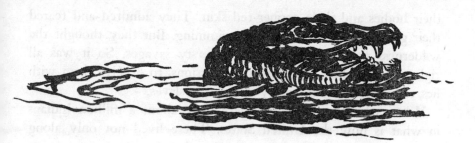

where in these wildernesses lived wilderness people.

Some of these people crowded the beaches when the first "white birds" arrived bringing white men heavily clothed in metal and cloth. Perhaps they were gods. When white men standing on the deck of the *Santa Maria* caught the first glimpse of the wilderness people, Columbus may have turned to the man next to him and muttered one word—"Indians."

White men donned their armor, took lances, crossbows, and cannons, boarded small boats to row ashore, and asked the red-skins to lead them to their emperor. The spices, silks, and gold of the Orient which Marco Polo had told about might be just around the corner. When the first landing parties started for the beach, the red men vanished. The green leaves of the forest was the armor of their naked skins. With spears and bows and arrows ready, they waited to see what would happen next. The moment was so tense that the cracking of a stick, the flash of a sword catching the sun-light, a splash in the water, a call from one man to another, would bring a hiss of arrows in the air, followed by a Spanish curse from a man with a shaft through his shoulder.

In fear the white men loaded their cannon and pulled the halyard. The roar shook the leaves of the trees where the redskins were hidden. The strangers who had just landed on the beach must be gods after all. They carried thunder in an elongated, heavy, black box. We know what Europeans thought of the wilderness people. They were utterly astonished at their nakedness. They feared the hissing, bloodletting arrows. They marveled at the strength of their bodies and their copper-red skin. They admired and feared their great skill in running and swimming. But they thought the wilderness people were also bloodthirsty savages. So it was all right to cheat them out of their possessions, to deceive them with lies, to kidnap them and carry them off as slaves.

When white men arrived, there were about a million Indians in what is now the United States. These lived not only along the east and west coasts, as it seemed at first, but they were everywhere across the continent. Their trails crossed almost every square mile. There were six hundred societies of Indians with six hundred dialects, but they used an international sign language. The six hundred societies were divided into countless family groups or tribes. These tribes were more or less at war with one another all the time. "War" was a word for a big family feud which started when somebody's father or brother was killed, or perhaps merely because the carcass of a deer was stolen in the dead of night. It was a case of revenge for crime where there were no laws except the laws of the wilderness.

When white men invaded the wilderness with guns and traps to take the game, they heard the war whoops and felt the sting of arrows. Sometimes they were pounced upon at their campfires and asleep in their blankets and their scalps were taken. No wonder the Indians were considered bloodthirsty savages, although they were acting according to tribal custom.

As we now look back on those wilderness people without fear of being scalped, we see how well they blended with their wilderness. They were as much a part of it as the trees, bushes, and grass, as the growling bear, the bugling elk, and the beaver building a dam, as the V of ripples from the muzzle of a moose swimming on the glassy surface of a lake, as a salmon leaping a waterfall, as a herd of bison grazing on the prairie, or a coyote wailing in the night. The people knew the spoor and signs of their wilderness.

They lived freely in their local worlds, without importing anything. Their shelters were caves or pueblos carved out of cliffs or adobe huts made by mixing sand and clay, or grass-thatched huts, or wigwams made from the skins of big animals—whatever the surrounding country gave them.

Wilderness people lived well off the land. All of them were hunters and trappers. Those in the forest stalked the prey or lay in wait with bow and arrow, or spears, using as skillful strategy and as keen a sense of sight, smell, and hearing as the wild animals themselves.

People who lived along the seacoast and by rivers and lakes were expert fishermen. Wherever there were open spaces in the forests and also on the plains, they were farmers. Their menu had a real American ring. They were raising corn, squash, sweet potatoes, melons, and beans; they also raised cotton and tobacco. Civilized people of Europe knew nothing about breathing in the smoke from a burning tobacco leaf. The ridiculous idea is mentioned by Columbus in his journal when he says that at an Indian settlement they had witnessed "the demonstration of a mystifying and unbelievable habit: *the natives drank smoke.*"

Men who are hunters, fishers, farmers must have tools, many kinds of tools and implements. The wilderness, generous with its people, provided all the materials needed to fashion these tools with their bare hands. Most important of all were the points, used for arrowheads and spear tips. The wilderness people must have used millions of these. They have been found everywhere with their remains, scattered over the ground from Alaska to the Atlantic Coast. They were made of flint, an ironlike stone that can be shaped and sharpened by chipping. Flint quarries are rare, but the Indians knew where they were and traveled many miles to get the special kind of stone for their points.

The shaft of an arrow must be slender, straight, and very tough. It cannot warp and fray and taper. The smoother it is, the less friction it will have, the faster and farther it will travel in the air. The green woods supplied arrow shafts like this with a small bush that it scattered all through the woods of eastern America. We call it viburnum, or arrowwood. For a few days in the fall its leaves turn bright purple, as though the wilderness were hanging a sign on it: Arrow shafts, come and get them!

A good bowstave is five feet long, a half inch thick, and two inches wide at the mid-point, tapering to the ends. It takes muscle to bend it, and then it suddenly snaps back to the straight position. For this the wilderness people liked shagbark hickory above all others. Ash and white oak also make fine bows. But to split the log and extract the bow wood, these mighty trees must be felled. This is a tough job with a stone ax, so the wilderness people burned the big tree down. First they surrounded the trunk with a heavy ring of wet clay about two feet above the ground. With this as a fire stop, they built a circular fire at the base. They blew on it until the fire had eaten through the trunk. When the tree was ready to topple, they simply pushed it over.

Sinews from the legs of deer made excellent bowstrings. But the finest bowstrings on the market came from the skin of a snapping turtle's neck cut spirally to make it long enough. Rolled and twisted, it made the toughest bowstring in the wilderness. It would not stretch or shrink.

Every Indian needed a hand knife—for shaping wood and bones, for cutting meat, for stripping sinews and fibers, for scraping skins and building snares and traps, and for scalping an enemy. The "crooked knife" is most famous, second only to the bow and arrow. The handle was a thick piece of wood shaped to fit the hand, which gripped it palm down. The blade was the front tooth of a beaver. This is curved and has a flat edge like a chisel. It is used by the beaver to cut down trees when building a dam.

Primitive people around the world have always been boatbuilders. Rafts and canoes were man's original vehicles for travel. But the American wilderness people who lived among the white birches of the north woods made the finest canoes of all time. Birch bark can be stripped in sheets. They are flexible, light and easily shaped to a frame. Overlapping edges are calked with pine resin. The white side is on the inside of the canoe with the yellow, corky surface on the outside. Such a canoe is so light it can be carried on a man's back and it shoots through the water at the stroke of a paddle. In contrast to this, the wilderness people in the west and south who had no white birch trees had to make their canoes by gouging out heavy logs.

The wilderness people were as purely nature as their trees, bushes, and grasses, as their animals, birds, and fishes. And just like all other life around them, they were in a continual struggle to live. They were always facing sudden death. They had to defend their territories as fiercely as the eagle and as bloodily as the bear. They could disappear among green leaves like a deer. They could vanish and turn up at another spot like a beaver. On a hunt they could follow a trail like a wolf.

These were the people called Indians by Columbus. They were the people met by every explorer in every American wilderness.

CHAPTER II

THE FOUNDATIONS OF THE WILDERNESS

WE must probe deep in the story told in rocks, to about one hundred and fifty million years ago, to find the foundations of the American wilderness. The outline of the continent is there, although it seems to be out of focus and different. It is bigger and smoother, standing out farther into the Atlantic. All of the offshore islands, including Newfoundland, are part of the mainland. The coast line is continuous, with no rivers flowing into the sea, no bays or headlands, no sandy beaches. The broad, smooth continental rock slopes gently into the ocean where the water is warm and shallow for many miles offshore.

The West Coast is vaguely familiar, for its outline is suggested by two large islands. That to the north includes British Columbia, Washington, and Oregon. The Cascade Mountains of Oregon are starting to push up, but they are still low. The island to the south became California; the coastal ranges are pushing up, and much land to the west is now under water. Large arms of the Pacific, several hundred miles wide, surround these islands. Their seas are shallow and warm. They lap the curving rock of the continent so as to form a coast line some eight hundred miles east of the Pacific coast line today.

As we look at that continent far away in time it suggests the broad, smooth back of a whale, rising out of the sea, shouldering off the waters. There are no mountains, no Great Lakes, no prairies and river valleys. It is a wide open space of rolling rock, uninterrupted across thousands and thousands of square miles.

The sun and moon rise and set. Day and night flash off and on. The years add up to centuries and the centuries pass over the land. Nobody is keeping track of years, but the rocks are recording the geologic calendar. The weather is pleasant. It is mostly sunny and dry. There are no violent storms. Moisture is carried across the continent in gentle rain; but there are no winters and summers as we know them, no snow and ice alternating with warm sunshine, blue water, and flowers. Although the thermometer may register degrees cooler in the north than in the south, there is no great difference. The same kind of weather prevails from the Arctic to the Gulf of Mexico.

It is the Age of Reptiles. Although the rock has not yet acquired a green cover of woods and grass, the harsh, stony, sandy land is coming alive. Along the coasts and around depressions where moisture gathers there are broad patches of green formed by mosses and ferns. Strangely this vast, low continent, rising slowly through millions of years, presents the most dramatic spectacle of animal life ever seen on the face of the earth.

The first animal inhabitants of the American continent did not arrive on its shores from somewhere else. They were created on the shores of the shallow seas that deeply penetrated the western half of the continent. They evolved on the fringes of the estuaries that extended four thousand miles along the Atlantic Coast from Greenland to Florida. All across the interior of America fresh-water swamps and lakes left over from the Coal Age were drying up. Mud was turning into soil.

New kinds of trees grew upon this new kind of dry land. Some of them had leaves like ferns and have survived to our day. We call them ginkgo trees and we plant them in our big city streets where they survive dry, glaring pavements as they did the dry, glaring land in America where they grew a hundred million years ago. And there was another tree with leaves ten feet long and a single cone in the center. Two small survivors of these strange trees still grow in the tropics. We call them cycads. They are curiosities in our botanical gardens. In some places there were tall straight trees that looked more familiar. They were the ancestors of our pine trees. Today we can see their remains scattered across the sand and rock wilderness of Arizona. These are the petrified trees turned to agate stone, lying around on a plateau in northeastern Arizona.

The trees were scattered. The ground between them was sun baked. There were no dark forests, no cool, moist ravines. There were no grass or herbs, no little animals digging in the soil—only big, coarse trees in a rocky, harsh world.

These conditions called forth the giant animals of the Age of Reptiles. They owned America without competition for a hundred million years. The reptile land animals browsed off the cycad and ginkgo trees and grew bigger and bigger as the trees grew taller. When the Age of Reptiles was at its height, some of the brutes were so hungry that trees alone did not satisfy them so they ate one another.

The reptiles were America's pioneer animals. They were presented with a whole uncrowded continent where they could spread out over endless new land. But that was no smiling continent; it was a vast monotonous wilderness of raw rock, raw sand, raw trees. And there was only one kind of animal that could live upon that land. This was the reptile which we call dinosaur, a Greek phrase which means "terrible lizard."

There were many varieties and sizes of dinosaurs. Some were no larger than chickens, and they ran along on two hind legs like chickens. Others were colossal, with much greater bodies than the later elephants and mammoths. The biggest animal ever to walk on the land was the American *brontosaurus*. The neck of this creature was longer than a giraffe's but it was round and shiny like a giant snake. Its mouth was huge, cut in almost to the back of its head; it had two beady eyes and a brain the size of a small apple. This was a living bulldozer for chewing up whole trees, giving the leaves and branches a crunch and then channeling them into the enormous cavern of the body.

Brontosaurus means "thunder lizard." He was given this name by astonished scientists who assembled the huge bones of the legs and feet. They thought that this animal must have sounded like thunder when it walked. Brontosaurus could never have lifted such a huge neck without having a tail equally heavy to balance it. The body in between stood on pillars like elephant legs, but brontosaurus weighed thirty to forty tons compared to Jumbo, P. T. Barnum's big elephant, which weighed six tons.

Brontosaurus was a vegetarian that ate only trees. If you'd been there staring at it, you would have been beneath its notice. The little eyes had poor eyesight, seeing only the silhouettes of trees against the sky.

Another dinosaur, almost as big as brontosaurus, was so terrible it can only be observed with safety through the long telescope of time. The name is *tyrannosaurus*. This brute represents the high peak of dinosaur evolution because it had acquired the ability to eat other animals instead of just trees. The tree-eating monsters had flat-topped block teeth like grindstones, for grinding up trees. But tyrannosaurus had long, vicious, sharp teeth suitable for tearing apart the bodies of other dinosaurs. These teeth protruded between drooling lips so that this terrible lizard never stopped grinning. And long talons protruded from his feet so that he could lay open the body of another giant lizard with one vicious slash.

We do not know what sounds brontosaurus and tyrannosaurus

made, but when they battled, if there had been any ear to hear them, the ground must have rumbled and there would have been an awful thud of flesh and crashing like that of falling trees. This would have been all the more terrifying if they did not roar but battled in a world of grim silence where there were no bird or other animal sounds.

A man standing in front of tyrannosaurus would hardly have reached the animal's knees. He would have looked up at the face of the monster and seen it grinning at him up there as high as a third-story window. Then if a talon hooked through him and lifted him up to that face, the fangs would have gone through the thickest part of the man's body with no more resistance than if it were a marsh-mallow.

Time stood still in the Age of Reptiles. The outline of the American continent was vaguely familiar, but without mountains and rivers, plains and lakes it was strange. The climate was mild and pleasant, but the face of the land consisted of raw rock from horizon to horizon, interwoven with vast forests of scattered trees that were coarse and weird. There were lagoons and marshes and shallow seas along the Atlantic and Pacific coasts, and the dinosaurs lurched out of these and strode across the land in the wake of the trees. The cycad and ginkgo trees were as coarse food as the plant kingdom has ever produced. In our world we do not think of such trees as good food, but the dinosaurs chewed them up and swallowed them like hay.

Besides the monsters that strode on the land there were many other reptiles which did not leave the water. Some of them had enormous snakelike bodies. Others were formed like giant turtles. One water reptile was shaped in the middle like a huge turtle through which a colossal snake was thrust, giving it a prodigious neck and tail. The bulkiest animal resembled a hippopotamus but was much more huge, being eighty feet long and weighing forty tons. Such a body could not get out of the water and walk on the land; it needed the water for the support of its big body, and so it stood submerged with only its head showing. This monster lived without swimming or running around, by staggering along only a few steps at a time while scooping in great mouthfuls of fish and small reptiles and browsing on giant weeds at the water's edge.

This was permanence. This was the end of time. For a hundred million years the climate and the face of the land stayed about the same way, a wilderness of almost brainless animals who lived by body bulk, sheer ferocity, naked force. There was no other animal to challenge them.

But ever since life first appeared on earth in the form of microscopic animals and plants, there has never been a final climax. It was written in the spheres that the timeless nightmare of the brainless monsters was doomed. While the brutes were ruling the raw wilderness, evolution was preparing entirely new kinds of plants and animals for a future age.

Evolution of life has no timetable. It does not depend on the number of times the earth spins on its axis or circles the sun. The rate of evolution depends on living conditions. If temperature and moisture remain the same, then life tends to remain the same. As evidence of this, ocean water, which has offered the same kind of living place throughout geologic time, has forms of life today exactly as they were in bygone ages. Horseshoe crabs looked the same three hundred million years ago. A weird little animal called Amphioxus still lurks in tropical waters, showing us what the first animals with spinal cords looked like some five hundred million years ago. Also in the ocean are seaweed plants similar to the first plants ever to grow on earth.

It took a tremendous change in climate to topple the empire of the giant reptiles. The new kinds of plants and animals that would overwhelm them had to be created by evolution going into high gear. This happened when the granite foundations of America, that had been immovable for such an eternal length of time, began to buckle. Tremendous heat waves rolled under the crust, causing part of it to rise and build the western mountains while the central part of the continent sank so that the great plains and the middle west were flooded by a big inland sea. Mountain ridges in the west were shaken by earthquakes and punctured by escaping hot gases so that the mountains were built even higher by cinders and lava. Lands rose and fell also on the east coast, where the State of Maine was under water, and heat and pressure also pushed up volcanoes. The streams of lava that cut through the granite can be seen like black dikes on the coast of Maine today where the pounding surf exposes them.

There came a time when the bottom of the inland sea of the primeval continent rose so that the water drained out of it. In the Mississippi Valley the land rose up like a table top being lifted, and this was to be our flat prairie. Then the continental table tipped up so that the land gradually rises from the prairies to a mile high at the foot of the Rockies, forming the famous high plains, buffalo country.

Such events caused enormous changes in climate. The high western mountains cut off winds bearing rain from the Pacific, so that areas that were wet became dry. Shallow seas that carried warm water from the Gulf of Mexico to the northern part of America disappeared and warm weather turned cold. Then summers were very hot and winters very cold. But in the northern part it got colder and colder. Glaciers rose in the mountains and in Canada, gradually spreading until half of the continent was buried under ice.

The Big Ice, in some places thousands of feet deep, killed all that it touched. But an astonishing thing happened. Indirectly the glaciers brought the Green Woods Wilderness of eastern America and the Indians and animals of all the wildernesses, as we shall see.

One day a college professor named Louis Agassiz had an uncomfortable experience riding on a train between Boston and Springfield, Massachusetts. His notes of the trip said, "The rapidity of the locomotion is frightful. There is something infernal in the power of steam carrying such heavy masses along with swiftness of lightning . . . you cry out in dismay." This did not prevent Agassiz from looking out the window, where he saw the sand hills and boulders of New England. He had been studying the boulders and sediments around glaciers in the Alps. All of a sudden he knew what made the New England landscape that way. "All along the road are ancient moraines and polished rocks. No one who has seen these upon the track of glaciers could question how these masses that cover the country were transported."

Now we know that Agassiz was right, that the sand hills and boulders were left there by torrents of water that poured off a melting glacier. This was taking place only a few thousand years ago, at the height of the last Ice Age. These events changed the face of the land. Glaciers widened and carved out valleys in the western mountains. They left big waterfalls like the one in Yosemite; they formed rivers and lakes from coast to coast and set the boundaries of the North Pine Wilderness and the Green Woods Wilderness. The Great Lakes and Niagara Falls were created by the Big Ice. The thousands of beautiful lakes in Canada, Wisconsin, and Michigan, in upper New York State, and all of New England, are big puddles left by the retreating ice.

Before the ice the mountains of New England were twice as high and snow-capped and rugged like the Rocky Mountains. The ice went over these like a giant grindstone, wearing down sharp peaks and rounding the mountains. The sediments from this operation were carried down to the coast and even out to sea, where they were piled up. This created Cape Cod, Long Island, Martha's Vineyard, Nantucket, changing the coast of North America to the way it is today. Moreover, these glacial sediments were spread deeply and became the cradle for the seeds of the Green Woods Wilderness.

We are still living in the Ice Age. If anybody thinks that such a big glacier is a fairy tale, remember it is possible to see a continental glacier in Greenland right now. The dome of ice that burdens the land there is two miles deep. It slants off to a depth of two thousand feet at its edges, below which great icebergs break off from the fingertips of glaciers where they touch the sea and float away like dazzling white ships.

After the smashing of the dinosaur empire, the continent had been transformed in three major ways. First, the land was re-molded when heat power deep within the earth heaved up the mountains, and the Mississippi and other big river valleys and the Great Lakes were left when the ice melted back. Echoes of the western mountain building can be heard today when earthquakes rumble on the coasts and the underlying rock suddenly shifts. This destroyed San Francisco in 1906, and it happened again near Yellowstone Park in 1959; the terrible earthquakes and rise of volcanic mountains in Chile in 1960 are part of the same series of age-old events.

The second major change was in the plant life. Instead of monotonous one-color pine trees with no ground cover except fallen needles, there were entirely new kinds of plants which brought red, blue, purple, and yellow flowers to the land. Fragrance and fruits, butterflies and bees and grasses which pack enormous energy into their tiny grains were created. These new plants are called *encased-seed* plants.

The third major change was the animal life. The giant reptiles, which moved clumsily or stood up to their necks in water, chew-

ing trees and each other, were all gone. The air was filled with birds and the green woods and prairies with the wonderful new kind of animal that could run, jump, and follow a scent through the bushes, that could climb trees, hang on limbs, dig in the ground, that could bark, bugle, growl, yelp, and snarl. These new types of animals are called *mammals*.

When the ice was at its height, it did not cover the northwest shore of the continent. That was the part of Alaska facing Bering Strait. It is here that America is separated from Asia by only fifty miles of water. However, the two continents are joined just below the surface of Bering Sea. If the water level was reduced only a hundred and fifty feet, you could walk from Asia to America over dry land.

In the recent Ice Age the levels of the seas all over the world were lowered about three hundred feet. This was because water, evaporating from the sea and deposited as rain or snow on the land, became locked up in the glaciers. It took so much water to build the glaciers that sea level dropped. Then for thousands of years grass grew on the land between Siberia and Alaska. There were blueberry and crowberry bushes; rabbits and lemmings burrowed in the soil, and migrating sea birds nested there. This amazing land appeared when Ice Age glaciers grew to a certain size, and it disappeared when they melted and the water returned to the sea, raising its level.

Thus at the height of the Ice Age people (as well as animals) could come from Asia to America over a land bridge. They did not just pack their belongings and decide to migrate. They had no belongings to pack. They were nomads, always on the move, always looking for better hunting. They followed the animal tracks eastward across the bridge. Different tribes came at different times. Some of them remained in the north and became ancestors of the Eskimos. Others followed the Pacific coast line south. There is evidence that a principal route was eastward along the shore of the Arctic Ocean to the Mackenzie River delta. From there the nomadic Arians turned south, going up the great Mackenzie River valley. This brought them into the heart of the continent where they fanned out to become the ancestors of the American Indians in the North Pine Wilderness, the Green Woods Wilderness, and along the Atlantic seaboard.

It is misleading to call this connection between the continents a bridge. It must have looked as wide as a continent itself to men who were hunting across it on foot and to the tribes who camped on it. A hunter will always turn in the direction where the most game is to be found. Ahead of these people to the east and south lay vast American wildernesses, literally teeming with game; thus they were drawn on and on, eastward and southward, generation after generation.

The width of the land bridge varied in different Ice Age periods. Geologists tell us that at one time glaciers were so big the land bridge was a thousand miles wide. People and animals did not come over such a bridge from Asia in single file!

Those ancestors of the American Indian who were the first people ever to look upon the wildernesses of this continent were not following dinosaur trails. All that was left of the dinosaurs were their bones buried deep under the sediments of the Ice Age and under the lavas of the mountains. Gone also were the ginkgo and cycad trees. And the old ancestors of the pines had turned to stone millions of years before and were buried under the Arizona sands. The Asians who chased the animals across the land bridge entered wildernesses similar to American wildernesses today.

The land bridge between Asia and America was closed only about ten thousand years ago when water from melting glaciers of the last Ice Age raised the sea level until the ocean flowed over the bridge. This happened a short time before man's written history began, but the bridge is no myth. It wrote a history of its own in which we can read about the people and animals that passed back and forth on it. Their trails are seen on the approaches to the land bridge on each side of Bering Strait. Buried just below the surface of the ground are the charcoal remains of their campfires with their stone axes, hammers, spear points, and the bones of animals which they were hunting and eating.

Soundings in Bering Strait and the waters around it show that it is very shallow and that a broad rock ridge connects the continents. When these discoveries are drawn on paper, they make a map of that part of the world as it looked when America was first discovered. A picture emerges of the surface of the land bridge and events taking place there in a period which began about twenty-five thousand years ago and lasted until water flowed over the bridge.

This picture shows a landscape like a wide valley with mountains laden with glaciers in the far distance. The "valley" is the surface of the land bridge. It is covered with vegetation of fairly continuous spruce and fir forests and open spaces of grassy meadows and clumps of blueberry and crowberry bushes.

A group of people is gathered around a campfire where a stew is simmering in a stone pot. The men have long hair and beards. Their legs and upper parts of their bodies are bare. A woman holds a baby and a boy has a crude bow and arrow in one hand, while the other is busy with a thong tied around the neck of a wild dog that is straining to get at the stew.

All the people wear the hides of heavy-furred animals such as bear or musk ox around their waists. In the background the hide of a bear is shown stretched and fastened on the face of a boulder.

It may take a few months for this fresh hide to be completely dried by the sunlight and made ready to wear, but these people are not in a hurry and they have no timepieces. They are part of the timeless rhythm of the wilderness. It is a safe guess they are thinking about the stew on the fire and also that their thoughts are occupied with the wonderful hunting all around them and with planning what animals they will stalk the next day. They must have pondered how to make better tools and how far the wilderness and its animals extended in the direction of the rising sun. Perhaps they would reach the end of this great hunting country the next day and then they would turn around and go toward the setting sun, back to the land which they had left.

This is a picture of the final chapter of the land-bridge story when the ancestors of the American Indian were coming over the bridge. With them came the animals of the Ice Age, bison, bear, musk ox, reindeer, moose, mountain goats, antelope, yak. At this time also, and for thousands of years before the men came, little animals had been using the bridge to become part of our wildernesses. There were moles, shrews, beavers, rabbits, jumping mice, squirrels, chipmunks, and skunks. There was plenty of soil on the land bridge for the diggers to dig in. Also, runners of the dog family such as wolves and foxes must have been chasing back and forth on the land bridge for centuries.

At this time other animals from Asia had been living in the American wildernesses for millions of years. At some unknown time in the past elephants and mastodons arrived in our continent,

also camels and an extinct bison with horns reaching out six feet. The largest and most ferocious member of the cat family, the saber-toothed tiger, came to hunt in the American wilderness. So did a huge ground sloth, a relative of the rhinoceros.

All these animals used the Bering land bridge. They were here when the people and the Ice Age animals arrived. We find flint points from the spears and arrows of the Indians mixed with their bones. This indicates that they disappeared from America only a short time ago, between the time of the Indians and the arrival of the white men from Europe.

It is a great mystery what caused the disappearance of the mammoths and mastodons, of the camels and wild horses, of the giant beavers and ground sloths.

The horse is a special mystery because it is a truly native American animal. It evolved in this continent from tiny horses the size of a terrier dog to the full-sized horses that we know. But there were no wild horses left when Europeans discovered America. The Indians got their horses later from the Spaniards.

Besides the horse there are other animals which evolved in this continent and did not use the land bridge to get here—raccoons, prairie dogs, pocket gophers, kangaroo rats, porcupines, and the pronghorned antelope are all ancient Americans which are still living here. But what happened to the horses and the other animals that disappeared?

We know that the advancing glaciers made a lot of trouble. It drove animals and people southward. When the ice was at its height, the north pines and the green woods were crowded together between the southern Appalachians and the Gulf of Mexico. Then the area of Florida must have looked like a big zoo with saber-toothed tigers, wolves, horses, camels, monster tapirs, and giant tortoises trying to live together in that area.

Perhaps areas where the animals took refuge became so over-crowded that they fought and destroyed one another. Then, too, the newly arrived men may have destroyed some of them because they were terribly dangerous. Forest fires and prairie fires may have had something to do with it. Out west there were tremendous volcanic eruptions. Finally conditions such as these may have caused epidemics among the animals which killed them off in large numbers.

But the America which comes into focus in our history is a land which has newly recovered from the staggering blows of the Ice Age. When the white man discovered America, this surprising continent had fresh vigor and the greatest variety of living wilder-nesses on the face of the earth.

CHAPTER III

THE VIKINGS VISIT
BIG LAND TO THE WEST

FIVE hundred years before Columbus electrified Europe with the discovery of the east coast of "Asia" and staged a circus parade of redskins and blue, yellow, and red parrots in the streets of Seville, tough, bearded Vikings were exploring the northeast coast of America.

What they found was not written for kings and scholars to read. They reported to each other in gruff tones about wonderful fishing and the whales and seals that filled stormy, foggy waters among icebergs and rocks. Some of the stories were collected by tribal chiefs and became the history of the Norsemen. These were not written in Latin; they were handed down in Anglo-Saxon spoken by a faraway people who were thought of as barbarians. Their sagas never became part of the main streams of European history and literature.

Also, the Vikings were not considered to be "discoverers" of

43

America because they did not think they were visiting a new world or another continent. It never occurred to the Norsemen that their journeys were unusual. By the same token, five hundred years later, nobody could possibly have imagined that the new Spanish colonies around the Gulf of Mexico were on the same coast of the same continent which the Vikings told about in their sagas.

The Norsemen were unconcerned about the spices and gold of the Orient. All they were doing was exploring for better fishing. In their eyes their own rock-bound country, which was mostly islands, extended westward on and on. It was not a new world but the same world with familiar fogs and storms, dangerous reefs where the thunder of surf gave them warning in the fog and where in clear weather white foam could be seen in the distance. Here rose the steep, rocky headlands of their homeland, crowned with green grass and lush meadows on the lower slopes. There were clumps of spruce forest in deep valleys, indicating a good place to settle in the fall and wait for the frozen sea to break up in the spring.

There was good living in this world for Norsemen. Millions of birds squawked and circled above offshore islands. Their egg-filled nests were so close together among the rocks and along the shelves of cliffs that in some places a man could hardly walk without stepping on them. In summer blue water was made smooth by giant icebergs that paraded slowly southward and the seas around the islands teemed with cod. Whales spouted, and flocks of dolphins broke the water like turning wheels.

No wonder the Vikings kept right on going. They did not think of crossing the ocean. They were island hopping where there is no greater distance than two hundred and fifty miles between islands from Norway to Labrador via the Orkneys, the Faroes, Iceland, and Greenland.

The earliest report we have of a white man seeing the east coast of America concerns a man named Bjarni Herjulfson (call him Barney Hurlson). We cannot know about the men who vanished

over westward horizons and lost the gamble. Doubtless there were others lost at sea, wrecked on rocks, or some who, reaching the coast of America, were clubbed to death by Indians.

Bjarni was a bold and daring Viking, but not a reckless fool. He built his boat with great care, using extra-heavy timbers and the strongest construction in every part. In this fine boat Bjarni set sail for Greenland sometime around 995 A.D. to visit his friend, Erik the Red, who had gone to Greenland about ten years before and whose people had settled there permanently.

But Bjarni missed the way to Greenland and kept on going until he reached America. We do not know the details of what happened, as there was nobody aboard to write it down and men who are busy with oars and sails in a gale are grim and silent. Days must have passed for them like a bad dream. The recollection of such men begins with their landfall. They are mariners and chiefly interested in where the land lies and what the coast is like. Bjarni may have been driven off course by a northeast storm, or he may have steered west-southwest to skirt some ice floes off the southern coast of Greenland. He probably felt neither heroic nor scared, as this was no new and unusual adventure for a Viking and he knew his ship could take whatever the wind and sea had to offer.

After an unknown time Bjarni sighted land, possibly Cape Cod. From there he sailed northward along the coast of Maine. The coast of Maine is subject to severe fog. Tidal currents are strong, and small craft must go miles offshore to avoid the turbulent sea at the mouth of rivers during strong offshore winds. Mount Cadillac near Bar Harbor is the highest point on the coast, and this may have been Bjarni's landmark as he followed the coast line to Nova Scotia and from there along the coast of Newfoundland and out to sea, northeast to reach his friends in southern Greenland.

A strange circumstance of this strange voyage is that so little is known about it. Bjarni seems to have been a man with no curiosity and no sense of adventure. He was a great mariner without a compass; he was bound to get where he was going, and he made the sun, moon, and stars tell him how to get there.

During months on the way he must have made many landings along the American coast for water and supplies. He must have encountered Indians, because all the people that landed on that coast after Bjarni speak of the many bands of Indians. He must have seen animals and spruce forests and enjoyed fresh water from springs. Perhaps his men rested around a campfire while they roasted deer, rabbits, and birds for feasting. But on all these subjects Bjarni and his crew were silent.

Vikings in Greenland saw him sail in from the west instead of from the east, and then they saw the boatload of tired men tumble ashore. There is no record of any greetings. Perhaps Bjarni was very serious and did not smile, as this was all in the day's work.

There are few sand or pebble beaches along the shores of Greenland's fjords, but Bjarni's heavy ship could be carried up over

the smooth rocks at high tide. When the tide went out, the bottom could be scraped clean of seaweed and barnacles.

Viking ships were famous, not only because of their long, slender, speedy lines, but because their sails could be manipulated for sailing against a wind. The Viking boat was also propelled by long oars called sweeps, each one pulled by two or three men. There might be sixteen of these oars on each side. This explains why the Norsemen had no trouble in crossing the North Atlantic, where they had to buck head winds.

Europeans who poured across the South Atlantic five hundred years later used high-decked ships with square sails, sailing mostly before the wind. They could do this on a southern course by using the trade winds from the east which brought them to the West Indies and South America, and then pick up the westerly winds a little farther north for returning to Europe.

Greenland is so far to the west that it is part of America geographically. The big island is one of the wonders of the world because it still carries a huge cargo of ice left over from the Ice Age. The glacier makes a dazzling, white dome of solid ice from compressed snow extending from the Arctic Sea southward more than a thousand miles. The coast line of Greenland is formed by high mountains like the rim of a colossal cup which holds the massive, continental ice. Deep fjords cut through these mountains with steep cliffs that rise over a mile high. Fingers of the interior ice reach into the fjords, and in summer their tips break off so that icebergs parade majestically down the fjords and out into the ocean.

In southern Greenland the big glacier has retreated from the coast and here are a few hundred square miles of ice-free land with green meadows in the valleys and a few spruce trees scattered around ponds on the westward side. This was the land which had been discovered by Erik the Red ten years before Bjarni arrived there from the American coast. At that time about two thousand Norsemen were living in two towns. They were farmers with herds of cattle and they had vegetable gardens. That was almost a thousand years ago, when the weather was warmer in Greenland. Today there are no meadows for grazing herds and there is no ground where vegetable crops can be grown outdoors. But then Greenland was an important part of Viking land and it was the threshold for their many visits to the northeast coasts of America.

Let us look back in the Norse sagas and see the interesting characters and series of events that led to this first discovery of America by European people.

In 985, according to the legend, Erik the Red disappeared over the western horizon as a fugitive who was in a lot of trouble and who wanted to find an island where he could live in peace with his family.

As a young man in his twenties, Erik was good looking and up-and-doing. He was such an expert swordsman that the monarch of Norway, Earl Haakon, picked him to be a member of his bodyguard. Things were going well with Erik until one night there came a pounding on his door when a foot messenger arrived. Erik's father was on his boat hiding in a secret cove down on the coast because he had accidentally killed a man. He asked Erik to follow the messenger and come and help him. Erik promptly buckled on his sword, joined his father on the boat, and they sailed away to Iceland with a few slaves and some cattle.

Erik and his father built a stone house in a remote corner in the north of Iceland. But the pasture was poor, and when his father died, Erik went to the south of Iceland to live with the other people. There he became a popular and prosperous farmer. He built a fine house with beautifully carved wood columns.

He was all set to lead a happy life when a peculiar accident happened. His slaves were prying out building stones on a high cliff when some of the rocks tumbled and fell on the buildings of a farmer below. The farmer saw the roofs of his barns caved in, and in a towering rage he killed the slaves. The two men talked louder and louder until they got into a terrible quarrel in which Erik, in turn, killed the farmer.

There were no manslaughter laws in those tough days, so according to custom, the family of the farmer hired a professional killer to challenge Erik to a duel. Erik had kept secret his past life before he came to Iceland, and the professional killer did not know he had challenged one of the most expert swordsmen in Haakon's bodyguard. Erik quickly disposed of the man and then found himself a fugitive as his father had been before him. He was outlawed, without slaves, farm, or liberty, but he did have his ship, so he sailed with a few friends to a small island just offshore, where he could defend himself.

As time passed, the affair was more or less forgotten and Erik decided to return to his home. He found that somebody had stolen the beautiful carved wood columns and that they had been built into another man's house. He demanded their return, but this meant that the man would have to tear his house down. With no law to cover this situation, it had to be settled by a fight in which two of the man's sons were killed. So Erik was outlawed again, and he was completely fed up with hard luck.

While he was marooned again on an offshore island he had a visit from an old wise man, named Gunnbjörn, the last survivor of the

first settlers of Iceland. The old man must have liked Erik, as he took the trouble to seek him out and whisper in his ear a rumor about land beyond the western horizon. Who told the old man about this nobody knows, but Erik responded heartily to the idea that he go and look for that land and settle there. He could take along his young wife and son and a few friends, and they could live their lives in peace. So while still in hiding, Erik and his friends got his boat ready and stocked it with provisions and sailed away. People in Iceland and Norway probably thought that was the last they would see of Erik the Red.

Three years passed and a sail appeared on the horizon off Iceland. Erik had returned with his friends, his wife and son and a new baby. The boat was scarred. Her sails were dirty and patched, but everybody aboard was in good shape.

In the surprise of his return all that had gone before was forgotten. When the people crowding around him asked where he had been, he told a tale which filled them with amazement. He had found an immense land with mountains thousands of feet high and beyond them in the distance a white wall of ice even higher than the mountains. Around this land there was a belt of broken sea ice in which were scattered huge icebergs, some of them a mile or two long.

For some days Erik had been carried southward by the pack ice until he was able to free his boat near the southern tip of Greenland. He rounded the cape and explored a little way up the west coast. There he found a milder climate, green fields and meadows, small trees and driftwood. The hunting was better than in Iceland, with fox and hare on the land and the coastal waters filled with seal, walrus, polar bear, and whales. The party was so delighted at the sight of green plant life in contrast to the lifeless ice they had been looking at for many days that Erik called the land Greenland.

Erik had been on his own. The land had not been claimed in the name of a king, and so, according to Viking custom, Erik owned Greenland. Land for grazing herds in Iceland was scarce; so, when Erik invited people over to Greenland, they responded with enthusiasm.

In the summer of 986 A.D. thirty-five sleek, fat ships with an average of thirty-five Vikings in each, plus horses, cattle, feed, farm implements, and household goods, set sail from Iceland westbound. The fleet soon ran into tragic storms. Twenty-one ships were destroyed and some six hundred people were lost. Fourteen vessels survived, and their people became the first white settlers on the west side of the Atlantic Ocean. In the course of time the population of Greenland grew to several thousand people.

Thirteen years later, in 999 A.D., Erik's oldest boy, Leif Erikson, was twenty years old and, like his father, was full of zest for adventure. He begged Erik to let him take a boat and crew. Bjarni was then living in Greenland, having returned from his trip to Cape Cod and the coast of Maine, and his strong boat was lying in the harbor. Erik and Bjarni were the chief men of the colony and evidently they were good friends, because it was finally agreed that Leif could take Bjarni's ship, hire some of his crew, and see what he could find over in America.

In 1003 A.D. Leif Erikson set sail from Greenland, headed for the spot on the American coast from which Bjarni had departed. His description of the place is identified as Newfoundland. From there he headed southwest, and his next landing was on a rocky coast with heavy spruce forest thought to be near Halifax, Nova Scotia. He found no inhabitants but only trees and decided to take a long trip down the coast. After some days they arrived at Nantucket, so it seems, on a fine summer day. The blue water, sandy beaches and good fishing put them in high spirits. They headed over to the mainland and waded ashore on the south coast of Cape Cod. Their first morning was a fine, clear day with little wind, and they were amazed at the heavy dew sparkling on the grass of the fields. They passed their fingers through the grass and then put them in their mouths and licked off the clean water. Salmon were leaping in a small lake nearby, and altogether this arrival of Leif Erikson and his party sounds like a happy landing on the New England coast.

They decided it was good enough to stay there permanently, so they felled some trees from the wonderful forest of pitch pines that covered the cape and built a cluster of log cabins.

While this was going on, a faithful old servant of the Erik family, who had come along to help Leif, disappeared from the camp for a few hours. His name was Tyrk, and Leif called him by the affectionate nickname "foster father." People were not supposed to leave camp without permission, so Leif was worried and ordered out a search party to find Tyrk. They met him when he was on his way back with a big smile on his face, and Leif called out to him through the trees, "What did you find, foster-father?"

Tyrk said that he had found vines of wild grapes which were wonderful for eating and for making wine. Then with Tyrk leading the way, they all went over and picked grapes.

Because of the grapes, the good weather, and the friendliness of the shore, Leif decided that this was a better land than anybody had

said. They should launch their boats and go back home to tell the other people about it.

When they got home and told their story, Leif was called "Leif the Lucky" and the land which he had found was called Vinland because of the grapevines. Soon after his return his father, Erik the Red, died and Leif became head of the Greenland colony. This left his younger brother, Thorwald Erikson, to plan the next family expedition to America.

Thorwald thought that Leif had not explored enough of the land which he found. He had not looked along the coast much beyond the place where he built his houses, and he made his men stay around close to the camp. Leif agreed with this opinion, and he offered Thorwald his boat and thirty men and told him to go use his houses in Vinland.

Thorwald spent the next winter in Leif's houses on Cape Cod and early next spring explored westward along the coast of Long Island Sound, returning to spend a second winter in Leif's houses. The following summer they pointed northeast along the New England coast, but they had hardly started when a fierce storm came up and their boat was driven into the breakers and tossed up on the beach. They had no other way of getting around, so they were delayed a long time repairing their boat, including cutting a new keel. When ready to go to sea again, Thorwald climbed a small hill and planted the old keel upright as a monument at the top. He said, "We will call this spot Keelness." The best guess is that this was at the tip of Cape Cod where the Pilgrim monument stands today.

Then Thorwald sailed many days across the Gulf of Maine, following the coast northeast. They came to a fine headland covered with a forest overlooking a deep fjord. Thorwald exclaimed, "Here it is beautiful. Here I will make my home!" The place is supposed to be Somme Sound, near Bar Harbor, and the promontory would be Cadillac Mountain, one thousand seven hundred feet high.

But tragic events awaited the men on shore:

"We saw three little mounds on the sandy shore inside the head-

53

land. When we got closer, we saw three skin canoes with three men sleeping underneath each one." The Indians were probably not sleeping as the white men thought, but lying in wait for game. When they were surprised by the white men, they must have thought they were being attacked, for they sprang to their feet and began to shoot. The result was a fight in which the Norsemen killed eight Indians while one escaped. Later they saw "more mounds, farther up the fjord, which they took to be human dwellings." However, the mounds were far away and they "became very drowsy and all fell asleep." They were awakened by a whoop above them. They sprang to their feet and shouted, "Awake, Thorwald, if you value your life. Return to your ship and hurry away from this land with all of your speed." While regaining their ship, they saw countless canoes coming toward them, so they set up battle flakes, wicker hurdles made of withes woven together and laid along the rail of a ship to fend off arrows.

After the savages had shot at them a while, they disappeared in the woods, looking around to see if anyone had been hit. Thorwald was seen holding up his arm with blood flowing out of a wound. He said, "An arrow flew between the gunnel and the hurdle and hit me under the arm. Here it is. It will be my death. I advise you to leave this place as quickly as possible. But first take me to the headland which I found so pleasing for a home. It seems I spoke the truth when I said I would stay there. Bury me there."

They carried out their leader's orders and buried him on the headland. Then they returned to Leif's camp on Cape Cod where they stayed the winter. In the spring, after gathering grapes, they all sailed back to Greenland.

The third and youngest son of Erik the Red, named Thorstein, was living in Greenland, and when he heard of his brother's death he vowed he would go to America and find the body. So, in 1008 A.D., Thorstein set sail with a girl he had just married and thirty men. He had the fire and dash and strength of the other sons of Erik, but he did not have the seamanship. Contrary winds drove him back toward Iceland, and then south toward Ireland, then north, and finally some weeks later he arrived back on the west Greenland coast, about two hundred miles north of the place from which he had set sail. Thorstein died soon after, so he never saw America.

During the next hundred years the people in Greenland kept in touch with their friends back in Iceland and Norway. At that time the Christian religion was introduced into Greenland, and the pope appointed the Bishop of Iceland to be the Bishop of Greenland. One of the last reports from the colony said that the bishop had sailed to Vinland in the fall of 1107 A.D., but nothing was ever heard from him again. There was no more news from Greenland, and the colonies vanished. There is no record of anyone going to look for the people in Greenland until four hundred years later. Then all they found were the stone foundations of their houses and barns, which anyone who goes there can see today.

There are many guesses as to what happened to the people of Erik the Red's exciting colony. They may have been massacred by Eskimos, but their bones have never been found. Perhaps a severe cold spell set in which destroyed the pasture and their herds. Those people were more farmers than they were fishermen, and they could not maintain themselves without their animals and their crops. The descendants of the original settlers may have climbed into boats and escaped to America. If so, the American wildernesses swallowed them up.

A few doubtful and unexplained signs seem to support this theory. For instance, in the middle of the city of Newport, Rhode Island, stands a circular stone tower built with rough stones and having the proportions of a Norse lookout tower. It has no roof today, but there it stands, keeping its secret, with pigeons nesting in its niches. That this was a Norse tower built by settlers who came perhaps three or four centuries before the English colonists arrived at Plymouth has never been proved. About 1960 a skin diver reported his discovery of the wall of another circular stone tower with the same dimensions as the one in Newport under the water near Watch Hill, Rhode Island. About nine hundred years ago this second would have stood on a point of land when the level of the sea is known to have been much lower than it is today. Norsemen driven out of Greenland about that time may have gone first to Leif Erikson's houses in Vinland, and from there a short distance farther to the Rhode Island coast, preferring to settle on a high, rocky shore rather than a low, sandy beach on Cape Cod.

Similar puzzling relics have turned up scattered through Quebec, Ontario, and Minnesota. They consist of unexplained parts of swords, battle axes, implements, mooring stones, and campsites. On the coast a mooring stone had been found near what is supposed to be the site of Leif's houses on Cape Cod. On Monhegan Island, off the coast of Maine, a stone is buried almost out of sight in the floor of the woods. Strange markings attracted attention, and these are said to be Runic letters carved in the face of the stone. Runic was an ancient German alphabet used by the Vikings who did not use the Latin alphabet. A similar stone has been discovered on Pemaquid Point near Boothbay Harbor, Maine. It is a wonder that any such relics turn up after nine hundred years. Doubtless many more have disappeared forever, and others may yet be discovered.

From these tantalizing objects rises a vision of Norse people making many trips back and forth between the Greenland colonies and the American coast nine hundred years ago.

If any Vikings were left living in America's East Coast Wilderness after their home base in Greenland disappeared, they could not have survived long. The wilderness was at that time at the height of its power as a natural empire of its animals and wilderness people. At that time it was able to destroy strangers who were few in number and who did not have gunpowder to scare the natives. With their big swords, beards, and voices individual Vikings could take care of individual Indians, but the Indians were backed up by an impenetrable, hostile wilderness, harboring thousands of warriors that could smother small bands of intruders with showers of deadly arrows.

So the East Coast Wilderness would promptly have disposed of any Vikings who may have settled there. After that the wilderness remained untouched and unknown for four hundred years while European history was boiling over.

CHAPTER IV

THE EAST COAST WILDERNESS

WHEN merchants in London became excited and alarmed by the news that Columbus had found a short cut to the Orient, and the Spanish and Portuguese had quickly followed up with many more voyages by which they claimed all the rights to trade with the "Oriental" lands which they were reaching, Englishmen forthwith planned voyages of their own with all speed.

At that time the Italians were the experienced overseas navigators, while the English had worked their vessels close to the shores of Europe only. It so happened that when the merchants of London and Bristol were looking for a man to take charge of their overseas project, an Italian named Giovanni Caboto (translated into English, this means "John the Skipper") and his three sons were visiting in England. The man was a merchant of Venice who had the new maps of the world and was familiar with the great circle of navigation. He was already famous as a geographer and for his knowledge of navigation.

They changed his name to John Cabot and offered to finance his expedition. So Caboto, now Cabot, and his three sons petitioned King Henry VII for Letters of Patent to carry the English flag across the sea, promising that if this was granted, they would pray to God the rest of their lives for the king's prosperity and long life. In 1496 the Letters of Patent were handed to Cabot, and their words reveal the kind of places which the English thought Cabot might discover: "Iles, Countreyes, Regions, Provinces of Heathens and Infidels which have been unknown. And set up the king's banners in every village, towne, castel, or main land. . . . And may subdue, occupy, and possess such townes, cities, castels, and iles . . ."

These words were to lead to the sovereignty of England in America, although neither the king nor Cabot imagined such a thing. Also, it was agreed that the English merchants who financed the trip would get 80 per cent of the profits and the king 20 per cent. The purpose of the trip was to get gold, jewels, spices, and silk from the Orient. But events turned out differently.

Because the Spanish and Portuguese monopolized the southern routes, Cabot proposed to sail northwest, believing that he could reach Asia that way. In this he showed great boldness and daring because he faced unknown stormy north seas.

In May 1497 Cabot set sail with two sons in a small vessel named *Matthew*. He headed northwest, leaving the friendly trade winds far to the south and daring the cyclonic storms, contrary winds, and high waves of the North Atlantic. But luckily Cabot encountered fair weather, although he must have had fog off Newfoundland where warm, moist winds of the Gulf Stream meet the cold water and air of the Labrador Current. He kept doggedly on his course, filled with faith that he was on a northwest route to India, until one day the dim outline of a mountain appeared on the horizon.

Where did Cabot make his landfall on the American coast? The accepted tradition is that it was the great headland of Cape Breton Isle, Nova Scotia. A highway has been hewn out of the rocky cliff there and named the Cabot Trail in honor of the discovery of America by Englishmen. But a careful comparison of Cabot's description of the land with features that are now well known in the area has led to the opinion that he sailed farther north, passed out of sight of Newfoundland, and his landfall was on the Labrador coast.

John Cabot told of rocky offshore islands, dangerous shoals, hidden granite reefs. As a good navigator, he made frequent soundings and charted the coast as best he could. He encountered impenetrable ice floes which drove him south. Fields of sea ice with icebergs sprinkled among them are released by spring melting of the polar seas, carried south on the Labrador Current, blocking the coast of Labrador in June. But there is no such sea ice off Nova Scotia that month. Without being able to land, Cabot sailed south, following the coast for about nine hundred miles, so he says. And then, without reporting any landing, he sailed back to England, convinced that he had found the continent of Asia!

He had only one small boat and he must have thought of this as a scouting expedition. He had proved that Asia could be reached by sailing northwest, and his report was received with enthusiasm by the English who had been outstripped by the Spanish in the rush to "Asia."

The following spring, 1498, John Cabot again headed northwest on the same course, this time with five vessels and several hundred sailors and volunteers. The size of the expedition shows how serious the English were about doing business with Asia. Two of the ships put about and went home, and another was lost with John Cabot. We have no details; sea tragedies were routine in those days. That left two ships in charge of Cabot's second son, Sebastian, who turned out to be as indomitable as his father. He fetched the North American east coast at Newfoundland and there, offshore, he saw an amazing sight. He says that he had hard work forcing his vessels through the fish!

This is a tall tale about America that we can check because the shallow waters of the Grand Banks have not changed much since Sebastian Cabot saw them. In springtime schools of capelin and herring, millions flashing silver, still drive toward the shore in panic, pursued by droves of cod. Seals follow the cod, leaping on their tails excitedly, and after the seals come the sharks and dogfish. Countless millions of fish may be drawn into the vortex of this fierce pursuit. So it was then—and so it is today with little change.

From Newfoundland, Sebastian first turned northwest under the spell of his father's belief that the way to the Orient skirted the land to the north. Silks and spices were more important to Sebastian than codfish. But again they were halted by the ice floes off Labrador.

Sebastian had no choice but to steer southward. He coasted around Newfoundland, along the shore of Nova Scotia, across the Gulf of Maine.

We are told that Sebastian was looking for a way through the land, so he must have had serious doubts that they were on the coast of Asia. They rounded Cape Cod, sailing on and on, an incredible voyage.

Sebastian seems to have felt no thrill of discovery. The wonderful East Coast Wilderness of America blocked his way. His determination to find a passage through this impossible land increased. He is supposed to have passed New Jersey, Maryland, Virginia, until finally in the vicinity of Cape Hatteras he gave up. Sebastian turned his ships toward England, greatly disappointed. He could find no way through to Asia.

It is hard to believe that the Cabots could have probed fifteen hundred miles of America's east coast, with its ever-changing water front, without feeling the thrill of discovering a new world. Why were they not fired with curiosity to see what lay behind those rocks and sand dunes that fronted the ocean? They must have gone ashore for water and food, but they do not report these routine matters. They do not speak of seeing wild turkey and heath hens or of eider nests by the thousands along the Maine coast or of the great auks that stared at them from offshore rocks.

The Cabots were men of the sea with no interest in wilderness wonders, so they stuck to their ships and kept going with one purpose in mind. They were looking for what was named in the contract—"Heathens and Infidels . . . villages, townes and castels."

But as a sailor, Sebastian brought home good news about the fishing off Newfoundland. If his reports did not thrill the merchants and the king, they were very exciting to English fishermen. Without realizing it, the Cabots had found the great wealth on the East Coast Wilderness of America, the cod, and their voyages and charts led to establishing future English claims to the mainland.

When the Cabots hailed America, great auks by the thousands lined the offshore islands from Newfoundland southward to Maine. The stately birds, almost three feet high, with black backs and broad white breasts, stood like beacons on the rocks.

A great auk held its head thrown back, its chin uplifted, pierced the water with its gaze looking for rock bass, perch, and cod. The big eyes seemed tremendous, with a large oval white spot in front of each. The wings were ridiculously little, mere stubs that could never lift such a giant body off the rock. When the great auk saw water colored by a school of fish, it stooped and dove into the swell of the sea as it was lifting over the rock. Then it used those

little wings, like fast propellers, swimming and darting after prey as quickly as a seal under water.

No more dignified and fearless bird has ever lived on earth. The great auk came straight out of the Ice Age, evolving amid salt spray tossed high by storms. A written description in the seventeenth century called the auk a gairfowl: "The gairfowl stands stately, its whole body erected, its wings short, flies not at all; lays its eggs upon the bare rock. . . . She is whole-footed [this means web-footed like a duck] and has the hatching spot upon her breast, a bare spot from which the feathers have fallen off with the heat in hatching. It comes without regard to any wind."

No man can say how great auks came through the storms when nor'easters lifted a tonnage of water out of the depths and sent it roaring and tearing over the rocks again and again for three days and nights. The big bird had a secret granite fortress, from which it would emerge after the storm and lay more eggs on the bare rock and scan the water for another dive.

Only it could not defend itself on a fair day from men who landed in long boats and clubbed it to death as it waddled around on its rock. Nature had made the great auk unconcerned about gales and swirling tides in icy water and crashing surf that shook the granite—so why be afraid of a raft of floating logs where men had placed some good fish ready to eat, to be reached when the bird placed its head through a plaited hair loop? Such a loop is invisible to eyes which were made to scan distant waters, and the loop can suddenly wring a neck.

The record tells us that a pair of great auks was taken off the coast of Iceland as late as 1844. With that the stately birds which knew no fear vanished from the earth.

Amazing as it seems, that dramatic, mysterious coast which Sebastian Cabot explored must have bored him. At least he did not return to America at the first opportunity to see what was there. The next we hear of Sebastian he is in the employ of the Spanish king in South America. He may have thought that the Spanish and

Portuguese had come closer in their southern lands to the spices and gems and gold-domed castles than he and his father who had found only ice, fog, rocks, sand dunes that reminded him of deserts, and endless black spires of spruces.

But the Cabot charts of the coast of North America, from Labrador to Cape Hatteras, worked like leaven, causing ideas to rise in the minds of other people. Ten years after Cabot a most imaginative king, Francis I, ascended the throne of France. He ordered his architects to design the ornate palace of the Louvre and surround it with the Tuileries Gardens. It took a lot of money to pay for such luxuries. "Perhaps," the king's treasurer may have whispered in the king's ear, "it would pay you, sire, to take a look at the lands across the western sea." The Cabots had said they were "just a wilderness," so the English had not followed up. But wealth was pouring back from the offshore waters, for by this time French, English, Irish, Portuguese, Spanish, and Italian fishermen, after cod, were encountering each other on the Grand Banks off Newfoundland. But —what about the land?

So the king of France set up an expedition headed by the top Italian navigator at the time, named Verrazano. This was the first man to look at the East Coast Wilderness of North America mile by mile.

Verrazano sighted Cape Fear, North Carolina, in March 1524. Presently he saw that astonishing elbow of sand, Cape Hatteras, thirty miles off the mainland. He put a boat ashore and saw Pamlico

Sound stretching westward to the horizon. He was struck by an odd illusion. The land which Cabot had seen was less than a mile wide! Just beyond, the sea stretched to the Orient. Moreover, there was no problem for a ship to sail on, for there were two or three entrances through this land. He was (like all the others before him) looking for a route to the Orient. This body of water, the other side of which he could not see, "is the one without doubt which goes about the extremity of India, China, and Cathay."

Verrazano was so excited that he did not even try to see the western side of Pamlico Sound but continued northward enthusiastically, sure that his expedition had been crowned with success in its first few days. Why hurry home? He could probably find other routes to the Orient which the English had missed.

So Verrazano continued feeling his way northward along the coast. He came to New York Harbor, sailed through the Narrows between Brooklyn and Staten Island. He saw the campfires of the Indians at the Battery. No use taking a chance by landing now and having his men lose their scalps. He ventured into the Hudson and sailed a few miles up and then turned around, probably marking his chart that here was another route to the Orient.

On and on, rounding Long Island, it was good sailing and they must have been in high spirits. Along the New England coast Verrazano kept well offshore, away from the rocks—it was good fishing there. And into the Gulf of Maine. They could now turn back. Verrazano had the New World in his pocket and he was ready to hand it over to King Francis I of France.

But first they should get some trophies; besides, they needed supplies. So they cautiously approached a high rock which has been identified as York Cliffs. They were extremely cautious. People who have already captured a new land should not take chances. Verrazano's report to the king says: "Found land high, full of thicke woods, trees were firres, cipresses, as wont to grow in cold countries. People full of rudeness and ill manners, so barbarous that by no signs that ever we could make, could we have any traffike with them . . . clothe themselves in bear and seal and other beastes skinnes. . . . If we desire to exchange for their commodities they come to shore on craggy rocks and we standing in our boats, they let down a rope with what pleased them, crying we should not approach the land, demanding immediately the exchange, taking nothing but knives, fishhooks and tools to cut." [Today this spot on the coast of Maine is called The Nubble.]

It is strange how the English and the French sailed the length of the East Coast Wilderness—staring at the waves running on its beaches and crashing on its rocks, catching glimpses of wonderful forests which change mysteriously from tall, sunny green trees to the low shore woodlands of pitch pines and scrub oaks, and then to the tall black spire forests of the north—without wanting to explore these mysteries.

This was because the Europeans who first arrived on the shores were looking for something which wasn't there. They thought in terms of their own castles, towns, and ports. The outside world to them consisted of civilizations such as the court of the Khan in Asia, and the picture in their minds of faraway lands resembled those of the eastern end of the Mediterranean. But America was all wilderness—dramatically different from Europe. It was filled with strange beasts, serpents, and birds and by wilderness people who were mostly naked. When these people wore clothing, it was not fine garments but grass and skins of wild beasts. So the English and French clung to the shore with only a few footholds for water and supplies. They were mariners and fishermen at heart, and the fishing was great offshore. This they understood.

They finally recognized that America was a new world as Amerigo Vespucci had said, but it was worthless and in the way. They had no idea of the distance from the Atlantic to the Pacific, no knowledge of the vast, sensational woodlands to the Mississippi Valley, and beyond that prairies and mountains and more mountains which could not be imagined.

The weather, too, was a surprise. One early report on Virginia said: "The sommer is hot as in Spaine . . . the colde is extreame sharpe, but no extreame long continueth." The weather of New England was an even greater puzzle. Its severe winters did not compare with England and they were hard to take. English colonists knew that their homeland was farther north and yet it had milder winters. They did not know about the Gulf Stream and how it makes England milder. People from England and France had not experienced northeast storms such as tear at the New England coast for three days, and they had known weeks of drought and hurricanes. This all added to the awe and fear of the American wilderness.

The only evidence they had about the width of the continent indicated it was very narrow. Balboa had struggled across only fifty miles at Panama, where he caught sight of the Pacific Ocean. Verrazano said that he had caught a glimpse of the Western Sea across a mile of beach. He was actually looking at a shallow body of water only thirty miles wide between the Outer Banks where Cape Hatteras lies and the coast of North Carolina.

For two hundred years after Columbus the great central wilderness of America with their animals and Indians were almost unknown and untouched. This was a strange period of history during which Europeans were crossing the seas in great numbers, wrecking their ships along the coast, fishing in the seas, establishing settlements on the edge of the continent. They hunted wild turkey and deer

and bear along the East Coast Wilderness. They made friends with some of the wilderness people and traded with them, but they stuck close to the shore where their ships were because of mysterious dangers that lurked in the inland depths of the forest.

They were on the alert at every hour of the night and day for the whirr of deadly arrows from shadows among the trees.

When an English colony settled at Jamestown, Virginia, they brought along cattle, sheep, swine, and horses but could find no pasture for their animals where they could be safe from both Indians and wolves. They were forced to live on islands and use the marsh grasses for pastures. They erected palisades on peninsulas or necks of land surrounded by the water on three sides. The wilderness denied them the mainland.

In this desperate situation the Outer Banks around Cape Hatteras offered the one safe place for the first English colony in America. This is a string of offshore islands two hundred miles long, mostly sand dunes, but with some forests and deer in those days and plenty of marsh-grass pasturage and good fishing. The report reaching Walter Raleigh in England by which he persuaded Queen Elizabeth to let him send colonists to the Outer Banks for safety shows how dangerous the situation was:

". . . A contiguous ledge of at least one hundred Ilands, and in the middest of those the incomparable Roanoke . . . the same distance from the Continent that the Ile of Wight is from Hampshire, all of hazardous accesse to Forrainers. [They were afraid of raids from Spaniards coming up from the West Indies.] And affording a secure convenience from surprizzal by the natives, will if possessed and protected by your power, be as an inoffensive Nursery to receive an infant Colony, till by an occasion of strength and number, we may poure our selves from thence upon the Mayneland, as our ancestors the Saxons from the Isle of Tanet into Brittaine."

Things did not turn out as predicted in the report to Raleigh. The East Coast Wilderness erased the Roanoke colony, and they disappeared as mysteriously as the Viking colony in Vinland five hundred years before. Three years after its settlement Roanoke was visited by an English ship bringing supplies, and there were only the earthworks of the fort, the houses caved in with vines growing over them, rusty weapons and implements scattered around under deep grass, the skeleton of one white person with an arrow through it, and no trace of anybody else. They had all vanished, including Virginia Dare, the first white girl born in America.

Today we can see the earthworks and moat of the fort at Roanoke, the blockhouses and watchtowers, the log cabins restored and looking much as they did three hundred and seventy-five years ago when those lonely people were defying the wilderness from their sanctuary on the Outer Banks.

Also, the Outer Banks have not changed their wilderness nature since that time. The sea is so shallow that at low tide the beach may be a mile wide. Horseshoe crabs two feet long still feed in that shallow water, and giant Atlantic turtles weighing two or three hundred pounds stagger across the beach to lay their eggs in warm, dry sand. North and south as far as the eye can see, flocks of gulls by the thousands are squawking and diving for food in the shallow water, and with them are sandpeeps wheeling in precise military formation. Colonies of these sandpipers are still running up the beach one inch ahead of the advancing edge of a wave and then suddenly turning, to follow close behind the retreating wave, rapidly pecking the wet sand, picking up their food at the rate of five swallows per second. Ghost-white sand crabs scurry across open places in the sand dunes and disappear in their burrows. Fiddler crabs beckon with a single oversized claw to their mates. When the shadow of a gull passes over the sand, they dive into their holes which are surrounded by little rings of mud.

Over on the bay side stretch many acres of marsh grass, just as when the Roanoke colonists pastured their cows and horses there. This is the winter home of the greater snow geese, and it is a lush feeding ground for flocks of migrating Canada geese also. Thou-

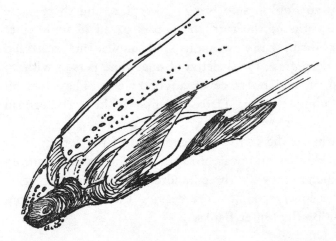

sands of ducks, herons, and egrets haunt the place. This wonderful area of the East Coast Wilderness is little changed since the time it was discovered because it has been inaccessible from the mainland until recently. This is the reason that the first settlers chose to live there, away from the wolves and savages.

To this day strange events take place among the shifting sands off Hatteras. Countless ships have been wrecked there, so that Diamond Shoals is known as a graveyard of the Atlantic. Frequently the swift currents dig up the body of a ship which has been long buried there, and the old hulk raises up from the water like a black phantom, seems to peer around for its ancient crew, and then silently sinks out of sight again. A hundred years ago the newfangled iron ship *Monitor* won a famous battle with the Confederate ship *Merrimac* in Chesapeake Bay, then put to sea and foundered off Hatteras. Her crew made the beach, but the *Monitor* was sucked under the sand and never seen again—until a few years ago when a plane spotted her on Diamond Shoal! A salvage party was speedily organized, but before they could get a chain around her she vanished again into her old grave.

In the 1920s the lookout on Hatteras light spotted a five-masted schooner under full sail on the outer shoals. She was upright, undamaged, and flew no flags of distress. Given a higher tide and a breeze from the right quarter, she should lift off and sail away. But when the high tide passed that day she was still there, with her keel deep in the shoal.

Although she called for no help, a Coast Guard boat put out through giant waves, and as the men drew near they hailed her. Nobody came to the rail. Nobody returned the call. They rowed around the schooner and noticed that she was the *Carroll A. Deering*, her home port Bath, Maine. Astonished that nobody came to the rail, after three days of the high winds they made fast and climbed aboard. As the men hit the deck they were greeted by the long, wailing meow of a cat standing in the door of the captain's cabin. That was the only living thing aboard. Everything was shipshape.

71

Pots with food stood on the galley stove, which was still warm. There was no sign of struggle or panic; the crew's belongings were in place. Nothing important was missing except two anchors and the lifeboats of the schooner.

Why had the captain and crew abandoned the *Carroll A. Deering?* How could they vanish? No lifeboat or equipment was ever cast ashore, and no man ever turned up to tell the story.

The mystery of the *Carroll A. Deering* takes its place beside the mystery of the Lost Colony!

Thus we see how this outpost of the East Coast Widerness still holds much of the wild, weird beauty that it had when the first white people saw it. It is both inviting and friendly, cruel and treacherous. Things happen that can never be explained.

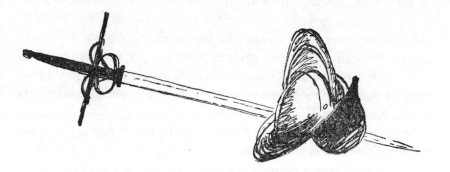

CHAPTER V

THE FIRST NEWS OF
WILDERNESS WONDERS

WHILE the English and French were sticking to their ships, exploring the long coast from Newfoundland to Florida, not concerned with what lay behind the frontier of the wilderness they were looking at, but only interested in finding a way to sail through, the Spanish were very excited about their New Spain down in Florida and around the Gulf of Mexico. Settlers were pouring across the sea, and every shipload brought an official reporter whose duty it was to write detailed reports about the wilderness of New Spain. Curiosity about what lay inland from the seacoast was stirred to fever pitch after Balboa penetrated the jungle, climbed the mountains, and saw the Pacific. Six years later something dazzling happened. Cortez reached Montezuma's city (where Mexico City is today) and saw the splendor of the Aztec civilization.

As luck would have it, but twenty-five years after Columbus, the Spanish discovered and plundered the only rich and civilized cities in the New World—those of the Mayans, the Aztecs, and the Incas. This whetted the appetite for more. Armies went forth to conquer in the medieval way. The big news was conquest. Where to find the rich nations and their cities? Nobody was interested in the wonders of the wilderness—except Gonzalo de Oviedo. He is the first person on record to be excited about the animals and plants of the New World.

At fourteen Gonzalo saw the blue and yellow parrots and the naked red men which Columbus paraded in the streets. He knew Amerigo and other supermen who were preparing trips into "outer space." The news of strange life in mysterious lands across the Ocean Sea was as thrilling in Madrid in that day as the thought of life on other planets is to us today. All reports came to the king and circulated first in the court; Gonzalo, who was a page, found himself in the middle of the excitement.

But Gonzalo had a different point of view from the others. He was not swept into all the talk about the conquest of new lands, news of gold and pearls, the capture of slaves, shiploads of horses, cannon and armor, swords, halberds, and arbalests. Perhaps the sight of those parrots stirred Gonzalo more than anything else. His imagination was playing with strange birds and animals, poisonous insects and serpents, fantastic plants to be discovered across the Ocean Sea.

Twenty years passed, and the boy Gonzalo is now a man whom we shall call Oviedo. The colonies in New Spain are well established, and ships are going back and forth all the time. Oviedo is

sailing on one of these as a public official with a fancy title—Royal Warden of the Mines of Mt. Castile in New Spain. We hear no more about the mines from Oviedo, but his duties let him travel far and wide in the New World. For some thirty years he went where no other white men had been, living with Indians, tramping in swamps and forests, burnt by the sun, beaten by hurricanes, almost drowned by floods. He hid in shadows watching animals and birds to which other people paid no attention. He watched rattlesnakes strike and kill and he tasted the meat of queer animals, deciding whether it was bitter and tough or delicious to eat.

It is an astonishing mystery how the man survived so many years in a wilderness where people died suddenly, stabbed by arrows or knives, poisoned by snakes or plants, or killed by disease and exposure. We know little about his narrow escapes or his personal life, but he had keen eyes and a marvelous memory, and he wrote endless notes about what he observed.

At length Oviedo returned to Madrid where he spent his old age writing a big book based on his thirty years in the American wilderness. He did not live to finish the book, and his work disappeared into the archives of ancient Spain. More than three hundred years passed before, in 1855, Oviedo's original unfinished book came to light from the archives and was published in four volumes with the title that Oviedo had given it—*General and Natural History of the Indies, Islands and Mainland of the Ocean Sea* by Captain Gonzalo de Oviedo. An English translation was published in Shakespeare's time, and you have to listen to the sound of some of the words to understand their meaning:

"In the fyrme lande [on the mainland] are manye toades so

bygge that the bones of sum of them, and especially the rybbes, are of suche greatnesse that they appere to bee the bones of cattes or of summe other beastes of the same byggenesse. . . . These toades synge after three or foure sortes. For summe of them synge pleasauntly; other, lyke owres of Spayne. Summe also whistle; and other summe make an other mayner of noyse. They are great, and fylthye and noyous by great multitude: yet they are not venemous.

"There are spyders of marveylous byggeness. [He is probably writing about the giant American tarantula with a two-inch body and a leg spread of five inches. Its great size and hairiness make it terrifying.] I have seen summe with body and legges bygger than a mannes hand extended every waye. I ones sawe one of suche byggenesse that onely her bodye was as bygge as a sparow.

"In the fyrme lande are vypers, that they are bytten of them dye in short space. Of these sume leape in the ayer to assayle men. One of theyme chaunced to byte an Indian mayde whiche served me in my house, to whome I caused the surgians to mynister theyre ordinarye cure, byt they coulde doo her no good so that shee dyed the thyrd day as the lyke hath chaunced to dyvers other. . . . There are lykewyse an other sorte. When this was slayne, I measured her to be more then XX foote longe, and sumwhat more than a mans fyst in byggness. She hadde three or foure deadely woundes with a swoorde, yet dyed she not nor stoonke the same daye. [In such a bewildering world it was easy to see miracles!] . . . There are also in the marysshes and desertes of the fyrme land many other kyndes of lyserts, dragons, and dyvers kyndes of serpentes. A kynde of adders so redde that in the nyght they appeare lyke burynyge cooles, and in the day seeme as redded as bludde.

"In the fyrme lande are certeyne byrdes so lyttle that the hole bodye is no bygger then the toppe of the byggest fynger of a mans hande: and yet is the bare bodye withowt the fethers not paste halfe so bygge. [He is speaking of hummingbirds.] This byrd, besyde her lyttlenes, is of such velocitie and swyftnes that who

seeth her fleing in the ayer can not se her flap or beate her winges after any sorte then do the humble bees or betels. When I consyder the fynesse of the clawes and feete of these byrdes I knowe not wherunto I may like them, then to the lyttle byrdes whiche the lymmers [illuminators] of bookes are accustomed to paynte on the margentes of churche bookes. . . . Their beake is verye longe for theyre bodyes: and as tyne and subtile as a sowying nedle. As touchying the byrdes, foules, and beastes of these Indies, bycause they are innumerable bothe lyttle and greate, I intende not to speake muche heare."

In the following comments Oviedo shows how he was sometimes overwhelmed and made speechless by what he saw. And then, perhaps after a good meal or a night's sleep, he seized his pen and wrote furiously. Listen to this:

"There are beastes in the fyrme lande very straunge and marveilous to the Chrystian men to beholde, and muche differynge from all other beastes which have byn seene in other partes of the worlde. . . . There is the beaste cauled Ante beare found near hyllockes where are great abundaunce of antes. . . . This enemie which nature hath gyven to these lyttle beastes resortethe to the hyllocke where the antes lye hid in theyre fortresse, he putteth his toonge to one of the ryftes [crack in the anthill] being as subtyle as the edge of a swoorde, and with continuall lycknynge it enlargeth the ryfte lyttle and lyttle that at length he easily in and owt at his pleasure, he thrusteth it into the hole as farre as he can reache, and so letteth it reste a good space untyl a great quantitie of the antes, whose nature reioyseth in heate and moysture, have laden hys toonge as many as he can conteyne in the holownesse thereof: at

77

which tyme he suddeynly draweth it into his mouth and eateth them, and returneth ageyne to the practice until he hath eaten as manye as hym lysteth. [This shows Oviedo's power for accurate observation. The animal, sometimes still called an 'ant bear,' is an anteater about the size of a small bear. It has a nozzle-shaped head over a foot long with a mouth that is a hole no larger than the blunt end of a lead pencil. Through this hole the tongue flashes out like a whiplash nine inches. This is round and smooth, moist with sticky saliva that traps countless numbers of termites which cling to it.]

"In the fyrme lande as in the Ilands there is a kind of serpente they caule *Iuannas*. They are terrible and fearefull to fyght, very delicate to bee eaten. It is not yet knowen whether they bee beastes of the lande or fyshes, because they lyve in the water and wander in the woddes. They are bigger then connies [the European cony rabbit], sum bygger than otters, with tayles lyke lisartes or eutes [a lizard of our Southwest from which the Ute Indians were named and through them the State of Utah]. Upon the ridge of their backes they have many long prickes, theyre throtes reachynge from theyr beardes to theyr breastes. They are dumme, and have no voyce to make any noyse. They are muche better to bee eaten then to beholde. Fewe that see them wyll have desyre to eate of them by reason of theyre horrible shape excepte suche as have byn accustomed to the beastes of these regyons which are more horrible and fearefull." Oviedo is describing the iguana. The black iguana is a brute, with thickset jowls, flashing dark eyes with blood-red corners, and a powerful tail that bristles with ugly spines. It is so quick it can catch young birds and mice. The prey is shaken to death and then swallowed whole.

Not only did birds and zoo kinds of animals catch the attention of Oviedo, but also he had a great deal to say about lice—"certeyne lyttle and troubleous beastes whiche maye seeme to bee engendered of nature to molest and vexe menne, to shewe them and gyve them to understand howe smaule and vyle a thynge may offende and disquiete them. . . . They can by no means avoyde theym for the space of certeyne days although they change theyr shertes two or three tymes in a day."

Ticks were leading their lives in the wilderness four hundred and twenty-five years ago, the same way as today in the woods and fields near our southeast coast. Oviedo makes us feel almost like scratching when we read his description of the ticks. "In many partes of the fyrme lande by the which as well the Christians as Indians doo travel, there are such marysshes in the way that they are fayne to go withowt breeches amonge the herbes and weedes, by reason whereof certeyne smaule beastes or woormes cleave fast to theyr legges. And cleave so fast they can be no means bee taken away except the place bee noynted with oyle. And after the partes where these lyttle tykes are fastened bee noynted awhyle with oyle they scrape the place with a knyfe. But the Indians which have no oyle smoke them and burne with fyer, and abyde great peynes in takynge them away."

Of all the hundreds of plants and animals which Oviedo discovered in America, nothing delighted him more than coconuts. He had seen date palms around the Mediterranean and he compared the coconut palms to date palms, but when it came to the fruit, that was entirely different. His smile of pleasure comes through his writing when he tells about drinking coconut milk. "These trees brynge furth a frute of greater circumference then the heade of a man. It is in forme lyke unto a walnutte or sum other rounde thynge sumwhat more longe than large, and very harde. Within cleaveth faste to the rynde a substaunce verye white, lyke unto almond. When this frute is chewed there remayne certeyne crummes. For althowgh that after the iewse or moysture bee gonne down the throte before the sayde crummes bee swalowed the reste whiche is eaten seem sumwhat sharpe and sower, yet doth not offende the taste so as to bee caste away. . . . In place of the stone there is a voyde full of a moste cleare and excellent water. The which water surely is the moste precious to bee droonke that maye be founde in the worlde. In the moment when it passeth the palate and begynneth to goo downe the throte it seemeth that from the sole of the foote to the crowne of the headde, there is no part of the boddye but that feelethe great comfort. It is doutless one of the most excellent thynges that may be tasted upon the earth, and suche as I am not able by wrytynge or toonge to express."

Around the same time that Oviedo was making notes about hummingbirds and coconuts, the wilderness was swallowing up a man named Cabeza de Vaca. He has left us another written account of what white men who first plunged deep into the American wildernesses found there.

Cabeza was not concerned with the discovery of strange and beautiful life. His only interest in plants, animals, and birds was in eating leaves, gnawing on roots and barks, picking flesh off the bones of a carcass. He stared death in the face a thousand times as he wandered, naked and lost, from northern Florida across the continent to the Gulf of California. He had secret qualities of heart and mind that enable a man to defeat death. He used his wits to meet every crisis and was a spellbinder among Indians who were always ready to murder a fearful stranger. He survived to tell the tale.

All this was the result of a series of accidents and surprises. Cabeza did not set out to conquer or explore anything. He was a humble and modest man who came to America as treasurer of an expedition of settlers, six hundred of them in five ships. A hurricane hit them near Cuba; two ships foundered, and the survivors landed on the west coast of Florida. They did not know where they were, so the ships started north along the coast, leaving ashore a party, which included Cabeza, sixty men in armor, and nine horses, to search inland.

So far nothing unusual had happened. They were used to losing people and ships in storms, and every Spanish expedition that went inland was based on the idea of conquering the Indians with horses and armor so as to get food, slaves, gold, and information about the country. But this party was small and based on its ships which had now sailed away. They were cut off with only a few days' rations of two pounds of biscuits, one-half pound of rice and a half pound of bacon each. They never again saw their ships.

This battalion, with horsemen out in front, followed by a column of foot soldiers with trumpets sounding and armor clanging, marched into the wilderness in battle array as though crossing the drawbridge of a castle moat. Cabeza, the educated gentleman, the civilian treasurer, went along with them, wearing no armor. He was not one to be easily alarmed. He looked at things with a steady eye and a level head. But one wonders what misgivings and questions filled him when he saw how quickly the beach vanished as the wilderness closed around them, the order of march wavered, and the men began to pick their way individually among the trees.

When Cabeza emerged eight years later, he told in his quiet, unexcited way what happened in that first weird month. They were lost in the first five minutes. They held to a northerly direction by the sun, but when they tried to recover the coast, they were stopped by bayous and bogged down in swamps. Wading across rivers "we were treading on oysters which cut our feet badly and made us much trouble." They saw no Indians and had no food except their original rations for fifteen days, "and besides this and the great fatigue many had galled shoulders from carrying armor on the back." Maddened by hunger, they tore off the fan leaves of palmetto trees, scraped away the tough skin, and gnawed at the thin layer of bitter pulp inside the leaf. They staggered on and on, leaving a trail of discarded helmets, breastplates, and leg armor to rust where it was left leaning against a tree or dropped among the reeds.

"Finally we came to a river which we passed with great difficulty by swimming and on rafts. It strained us to cross because of the very strong current. One of the mounted men, impatient of detention, entered the river. When the violence of the current cast him from his horse he grasped the reins of the bridle and both were drowned.

The horse afforded supper to many that night."

Just after they had crossed the river, two hundred Indians appeared. There was an hour of tense silence for them, not knowing whether they were about to be massacred or whether they were saved because the Indians would give them food. The Indians also were in doubt about what to do with these people. Perhaps the decision lay with a chief in a distant Indian village, or the Indians may have been thinking how nice it would be to have white-skinned slaves.

Finally the Indians gave the white men corn and they all set off together through northern Florida. Things were looking up: "They conducted us through a country difficult to travel and wonderful to look upon. In it are vast forests, the trees being astonishingly high. So many were fallen on the ground as to obstruct our way that we could not advance without much going about and a considerable increase of toil. . . . There are deer, rabbits, hares, bears, lions, and other wild beasts. [The lions that Cabeza saw or heard about were probably panthers, the big American cat which ranged widely in the American wilderness at that time.]

"Among them we saw an animal with a pocket on its belly in which it carries its young until they know how to seek food and if it happens that they should be out feeding and anyone come near, the mother will not run until she has gathered them in together."

This is the first record of a white man catching sight of the opossum, still a common animal from Florida to New England. Pouched animals were flourishing in the age of dinosaurs, and their descendants are Australian kangaroos and American opossums. Cabeza did not know that the opossum is one of the stupidest creatures in the American woods. It is bad tempered, unresponsive, and its only sound is a silly snarl. If it is caught in a flash of light when prowling in woods and swamps at night, it is so shocked that it falls down and looks dead instead of running away—it "plays 'possum."

After some days of travel they arrived at the Indian village, met the chief, and everybody seemed to be friends. They stayed there almost a month, resting, eating corn, beans, pumpkins, and fish. Then they took their departure, filled with hope that they could now gain the coast, where sooner or later their ships would find them. They were still a party of proud Spaniards with seven mounted men and fifty afoot. Although they had lost many pieces of armor, some still wore helmets and breastplates and carried cross-bows and halberds. When they took leave, the Indians stared at them without smiling and said not a word. There was an ominous silence.

"On the second day we came to a lake difficult of crossing, the water reaching to the paps, and in it were numerous logs. Reaching the middle, we were attacked by many Indians from behind trees. They drove their arrows with such effect that they wounded men and horses." With much struggling they reached the other side of this muddy lake. Men on horses dismounted and they counter-attacked on foot, while the Indians melted away among the trees.

After that they pushed on for eight days, desperately trying to reach the coast, repeatedly beset by Indians who would discharge vicious volleys of arrows and vanish.

"The journey was extremely arduous. There were not horses enough to carry the sick. It was piteous and painful to witness."

At long last they regained the coast and scanned the wide horizon, where there was not a ship in sight. "We saw on our arrival how small were the means for advancing farther. There was not any-where to go and if there had been, the people were unable to move forward. I cease here to relate more of this because anyone may suppose what would occur in a country so remote and malign, so destitute of all resource whereby either to live in it or to go out of it."

They were certain that "we could pass out of it only through death." But they set to work building boats.

"This appeared impossible to everyone; we knew not how to construct, nor were there tools nor iron nor forge nor tow nor

83

resin nor rigging, and above all, there was nothing to eat while building for those who should labor.

"Reflecting on all this one of the company said he could make some pipes out of wood which with deerskins might be made into bellows and we told him to set himself to work. We assented to the making of nails, saws, axes and other tools of which there was need from the stirrups, spurs, crossbows and other things of iron there were. On every third day a horse should be killed to be divided among those who labored in the work of the boats. . . . We proceeded with so great diligence that on the third day five boats were finished, each calked with the fiber of the palmetto. We pitched them with a resin made from the pine tree. From the husk of the palmetto and from the tails and manes of horses we made ropes and rigging. From our shirts, sails, and from the savins [red cedars] we made oars that appeared to us requisite. Such was the country that only by very great search could we find stone for ballast and anchors. We flayed the horses, taking the skin from their legs entire and tanning them to make bottles to carry water."

Cabeza does not say outright that it was he who inspired and led this terrible and noble crash program to survive. But we read between the lines that they were asking his advice at every turn.

They augmented the horse flesh when "some went gathering shellfish in the coves and creeks." But one day when this was happening, "Indians attacked and killed ten men in view of the camp without our being able to afford succor. We found their corpses traversed with arrows."

"When the horses had been consumed, only one remaining, on that day we embarked." They named that place the Bay of Horses.

They set sail on the stormy Gulf of Mexico (where stout ships would have had trouble surviving) in their crude, frail little boats, overloaded so that "not over a span of the gunnels remained above water, the boats were so crowded that we could not move; so much can necessity do which drove us to hazard our lives in this manner, running into a turbulent sea, not a single one who went having a knowledge of navigation."

As they struggled westward in their flimsy homemade boats, they passed the delta of the Mississippi River. Of course Cabeza did not know what it was. He noted the many low islands of the delta, and strong currents flowing among these carried them offshore and made a lot of trouble. He wrote, "We took fresh water from the sea, the stream entering it in a freshet." That was fourteen years before De Soto "discovered" the Mississippi River.

Of course the result of the dangerous voyage could only be tragic. They became separated and lost in gales, and after unknown time Cabeza's boat, in which most of them were dying of thirst and Cabeza was the only one left with a feeble energy to steer, was cast up on an island. He named it Malhado [Island of Misfortune]. It is a good guess that this was Galveston Island or the next island west.

Malhado became the starting point for Cabeza's amazing wanderings back and forth through Texas, New Mexico, and Arizona, where no white man had been before. During seven years he covered thousands of miles, barefoot and naked much of the time.

At first Indians made him a slave. "I was obliged to remain with the people belonging to the island. They put upon me hard work and harsh treatment. I had to get out roots from below the water and from among the cane, where they grew in the ground. From this employment I had my fingers so worn that did a straw but touch them they would bleed."

After a year of slavery he escaped with a small party and headed inland.

Cabeza and three companions, the first white men to discover the plains of Texas and the mountains and deserts of New Mexico and Arizona, had no desire to explore. They were simply lost in the wilderness and for seven years tried to find their way out. They paced off thousands of miles, not on horseback, but by painfully placing one bare foot in front of the other.

This long ordeal started with a few starved, shipwrecked men crawling up the beach on the Island of Misfortune: "We began to move on hands and knees, crawling into ravines. We were naked and the cold was very great. The weather was boisterous to cross rivers and bays by swimming. We were entirely without provisions."

Then a most surprising thing happened. Tall Indians with bows and arrows found them huddled together behind a sand dune. We can guess what astonishment stirred those Indians who had never seen white men before. If they raised their bows in alarm at first, they lowered them when they saw big beards and white skins. Aboriginal Indians did not have big beards. Nakedness and helplessness saved the lives of Cabeza and his friends. The Indians heard them make strange sounds and saw them wave their arms and act like people, not wild animals. At first the Indians were dumfounded and stared at those who had come out of the sea. Then, greatly excited, they ran off, and a couple of hours later a hundred Indians with bows and arrows and a throng of women and children returned to see the white beings.

In that interval Cabeza struggled to his feet and used his wits— by which he was to save his life countless times in the years to come. He returned to the wreck of their boat, half buried in the sand, and dug out some little bells and beads and metal trinkets which they had brought all the way from Spain. Also he found a roll of a valuable marten skin that they had taken from a tribal chief back in Florida.

Surrounded by Indians, Cabeza turned on all his charm: "I went out and called to them and endeavored the best I could to encourage them. We gave them beads and hawk bells and each of them gave me an arrow, which is a pledge of friendship." The next day the Indians returned with a large quantity of fish and roots they got from under the water. "They sent their women and children to look at us, who went back rich with bells and beads given them."

But when these Spaniards climbed trees on the Island of Misfortune, they saw nothing but bayous and vistas of reeds and dimly to the north a monotonous mainland. What lay inland was an utter blank. To them the sea was their only avenue of escape.

As soon as they were revived by the food and water which the Indians brought, they dug up their boat and tried to repair it. Indians stood on the beach and watched, probably thinking that the white beings would disappear over the horizon from which they had come. "At the distance of two crossbow shots in the sea we shipped a wave. The oars loosened in our hands. The next blow the sea struck us, capsized the boat." Again they crawled, half drowned, up the beach. When the Indians saw this, they were so scared they ran away, with Cabeza running after, calling to them. Then on that island off the coast of Texas occurred one of the strangest episodes in all the history of the wilderness.

"The Indians at sight of what had befallen us and our state of suffering, sat down among us and from the sorrow and pity they felt they all began to lament so that they might have been heard at a distance. It was strange to see these men, wild and untaught, howling like brutes over our misfortunes. It caused in me an increase of feeling."

Cabeza meant that these howling, weeping wild men made him realize that this was their final calamity. All hope of escaping from the terrible wilderness was gone. The strength of the white men was spent. They lay huddled together, their bare bodies glistening in the sun, in the center of the circle of howling and lamenting Indians.

The white men whispered hoarsely to each other. Eastward lay the dangerous water they had crossed in their flimsy boat, where their companions were drowned, and those horrible bayous, swamps, and jungles filled with wild men from which they had just escaped. They knew that southward beyond the horizon were colonies of their own people, but without a boat these were as out of reach as though they were on the moon. Northward and westward reached an unknown wilderness, filled with wild animals and savages where white men could go only if they were fully equipped with armor, horses, and weapons.

They were ready to give up and die when a peculiar idea occurred to Cabeza. Perhaps the Indians were howling because *white gods* were in trouble. They had appeared mysteriously out of the sea; they had brought presents; they had not threatened or killed—it could be that nakedness was a better weapon than armor and horses.

"I talked with the Christians, and said that if it appeared well to them I would beg the Indians to take us. They replied that we ought not to think of it, for if they should do so they would sacrifice us to their idols. But seeing no better course I disregarded what was said and besought the Indians to take us."

Then the Indians carried them back to their village, built a large fire to warm them up, gave them roots and fish to eat. "An hour after our arrival they began to dance and hold great rejoicing which lasted all night. For us there was no joy, festivity, nor sleep, awaiting the hour they should make us victims."

But in the morning something unexpected happened. Instead of killing them the Indians ordered them to heal their sick. Evidently there was no medicine man on hand. Cabeza says, "They wished to make us physicians without examination or inquiring for our diplomas. We knew not how to heal." But the Indians tried to show them what to do—how to cure by blowing upon the sick and touching them with the hands, and how to heal wounds by burning them in fire and then blowing on them, touching them. One Indian took them to one side, and with gestures he explained how stones of certain shapes and other things growing in the fields have virtue, and that passing a pebble along the stomach will take away pain. The Indian said that he could not work these cures but "certainly then we must possess these powers."

So Cabeza was forced to try his skill as a medicine man. They could be no worse off if it failed. They brought their sick to him. He pretended to go into a trance, using pebbles and herbs, breathing on sick Indians, touching their wounds with fire. Perhaps the Indians were most impressed when he earnestly muttered the Lord's prayer in Latin, blessed the sick, and made the sign of the cross. The cures worked; the Indians were delighted and "deprived themselves of food that they might give to us and presented us with skins and some trifles."

Their lives were saved, but they could never tell what an Indian would do next. After a few weeks of friendly treatment each white man was made a slave to an important member of the tribe. Some were taken to the mainland, but Cabeza slaved for the Indians on the island.

After more than a year of this tortured existence, Cabeza escaped to the mainland and joined Indians who were enemies of those on the island. They welcomed him because he had run away. His plan was to go westward and southward around the Gulf, so as to reach a Spanish settlement on the coast of Mexico. To do this, he knew that he must follow Indian trails through the great wilderness. But he had learned how to deal with Indians who had not seen white men before. He knew the kinds of shells they used for cutting and how they used colorful berries and seed pods for beads, red dyes from inner bark to paint their faces, certain straight shoots for arrows, and flint stones for arrowheads. He would collect these things and trade with the Indians, going from tribe to tribe on his way. Also, he could turn into a medicine man in an emergency and perform miracles of healing. So the first merchant in what was to be the United States was in business.

At first, with tribes along the coast, things went well. "I set to trafficking, and strove to make my employment profitable in the

ways I could best contrive. The Indians would beg me to go from one quarter to another for things of which they have need. This occupation suited me well and I was not a slave. The Indians gave me to eat out of regard to my commodities and I became well known." Cabeza remained in the area several years, as he did not want to abandon his Spanish friends who were still held slaves. He went from tribe to tribe to get news of the "other Christians," and during that time Cabeza himself became a slave again.

The four Spaniards who had crawled up on the beach met somehow in western Texas, where the tribes which held them slaves came together to feast on prickly pears.

Prickly pear is the most common cactus of the dry plains and deserts. We call it opuntia cactus or Indian fig. This odd plant has no ordinary stems or leaves. Its stems are green oval pads joined end to end, and its leaves are the fierce thorns that spring out of these peculiar stems. In the spring bright yellow flowers bloom from the tops of these, which soon turn into a purple-red "pear." This juicy fruit was the favorite food of the Indians, and at the right season they came from far and wide to enjoy it.

The Spaniards were overjoyed to find each other. They decided to escape from slavery together and flee westward, away from the tribes of the plains who would kill them if they were recaptured. They observed that the Indians shouted and danced all night, drunk with ecstasy, and this would give Cabeza and his friends a chance to get a head start before their absence was discovered. It was agreed they would take off just after sunset the very next evening.

But in the night when this plan was made the various tribes turned from making merry to furious fighting. "After striking with fists, beating with sticks, and bruising heads in great anger," each took his property, which included his slaves, and went his way. "In no way could we come together until another year."

But a year is not long in the eternity of a wilderness. When the prickly pear season returned, the Spaniards met again and made their escape. They were barefooted and barehanded, but by this time they had learned how to live in the wilderness as well as Indians. They counted on surviving with rain water, prickly pears, and acorns. They hurried on "in great dread lest the Indians should overtake us."

This was a desperate foot race. Cabeza knew they had played their last cards. They had no surprises left for Indians with whom they had lived as slaves for years. Nothing to trade, and their magic had lost its spell. They headed northward toward mountains they saw in the dim blue distance, perhaps a hundred miles away. Day and night they hurried on, barefooted, cutting their feet, stubbing their toes on sharp stones, their skin bloody from cactus needles and wicked thorns of desert bushes.

Three days later they had won the race. Smoke rising from scrub oaks and pines on the mountain led them to the huts of wild men "of a different nation and tongue."

In their death-defying dash Cabeza and his three friends crossed the great divide of their adventures. The ground over which they rushed was the vast grass-mesquite plain of western Texas, which

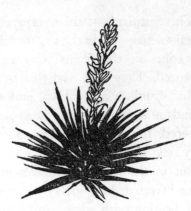

divided the cruel tribes of the Gulf Coast and mid-Texas from the western tribes who lived in the mesas and mountains.

The savages who had made them slaves were always hungry and poor, living for a few months off roots and fish and prickly pears on the eastern edge of the dry plain. Those in the mountains likewise enjoyed prickly pears (the delight of all Indians of our wild West), but they also had nourishing fare among pinyon pines, whose seeds are delicious. They had walnut trees and acorns. They had excellent bows and arrows with which to hunt rabbits, deer, and birds.

It was lucky for Cabeza and his three friends that in those days the Indians had no horses. For this reason the murderous tribes who had held them slaves through three terrible years could not catch up with the white men escaping on foot with but a few hours' head start. Also, without horses, very little news passed back and forth across the hundred-mile mesquite plain which separated the tribes of the Texas lowlands from those of the New Mexico and Arizona mountains.

The mountain Indians had heard a rumor about gods who had appeared on a faraway beach, out of the nothingness of sea and sky. They had white skins and could perform miracles of healing. The western Indians had not heard any later news—how in the course of time the miracles did not always work and that the strangers did not turn out to be gods, but that their white skin was a sign of a low form of humanity, only good as slaves for redskins. Thus the Spaniards were received with joy and thanksgiving.

From now on, instead of being starved and helpless and held as slaves by murderous wild men, Cabeza and his friends were free to travel as they wished, and wherever they went they were received with joy and showered with gifts. "They left us all the prickly pears they had without keeping one. They gave us flints of very high value. . . . They gave us of what they had to eat, the leaves of prickly pear and the green fruit roasted. They did this with kindness and good will and were happy to be without anything to eat that they might have food to give us. . . . When the people who had come departed, they left, the most satisfied beings in the world, having given us the best of all they had."

But one idea possessed the white men, to find their way out of the immense and bewildering wilderness and to return to Spanish settlements down in Mexico. They had been struggling for hopeless years, but now they were in good health and things were looking up. Yet they could not strike out on their own. They depended on the Indians both for food and for finding the way.

Sometimes they stayed only a day or two with a tribe, sometimes a few weeks. But they kept moving and they became timeless. The weeks stretched into months and the months into years as this wilderness wandering went on and on while they played the part of gods.

They were greeted in many different ways. "We saw two women with some boys walking in the forest who were frightened at the sight of us and fled, running into the woods to call the men. These arriving stopped behind trees to look at us. . . . The inhabitants were astonished at our appearance, showing much fear. After becoming somewhat accustomed to us, they reached out their hands to our faces and bodies and passed them in like manner over their own."

But as time went on and the news of the white gods spread over the Southwest, people came from far and near to see them. "They began their dances and festivities, sending to call others from a town nearby. . . . They gave us of what they had to eat and the deer they had killed that day. . . . They brought their children to us that we might touch their hands and gave us a great quantity of flour of mesquite. They presented us with beads, ochre and some little bags of pearl-mica. . . . Women brought us prickly pears, spiders, worms, and whatever else they could gather. . . . They gave us beans and squashes to eat, gourds to carry water in, blankets of cowhide, and other things."

The journey turned into a triumphal procession and the crowds became a great nuisance. "We received great inconvenience from the many persons following us. . . . We were accompanied by three thousand persons and we had to breathe upon and sanctify the food and drink for each, for even were they famishing they would eat nothing unless we gave it to them. . . .

"Had we attempted to escape we could not have succeeded, such was their haste in pursuit in order to touch us. We consumed three hours in going through with them that they might depart."

Cabeza tried hard to shake off the people, but he knew that the lives of himself and his companions were at stake and they could not stop for an instant acting like gods. Once they thought they really had escaped. "Soon after we had taken our leave some of the women from the same town followed behind us. But as there are no paths in the country we presently got lost and thus traveled four leagues [about ten miles] when stopping to drink we found the women in pursuit of us at the water who told us of the great exertion they had made to overtake us. [That was the day they crossed the Colorado River of Texas.] We passed over a river towards evening, the water reaching to the breast. It might be as wide as that river at Seville. Its current was very rapid."

Here were four Europeans deep in the heart of the mountains and deserts of our Southwest only thirty-five years after Columbus.

Everywhere they found wilderness people of many different tongues; and the whole empire of the western Indians was stirred by excitement.

Cabeza won out because he played the part of a god which the Indians could understand. "We always went naked like them and covered ourselves at night with deerskins. We dug our own food and brought our loads of wood and water." He felt real sympathy for those who were ill and he grew to admire the western Indians. "I believe these people see and hear better and have keener senses than any other in the world. They are great in hunger, thirst and cold, but they were made for the endurance more than other men."

And he understood how tricky the Indians were. When some were introducing him to another tribe, they said "we had power to heal the sick and to destroy and other lies even greater than these which none knew how to tell better than they when they find it convenient. They advised them to be careful not to offend us and to give us all they might possess. . . . These people are all very fond of romance and are great liars, particularly so where they have any interest."

The wilderness and its people had become such a real part of Cabeza's life that it must have seemed like a dream to him when, nearly eight years after the shipwreck on the west coast of Florida, he saw four of his countrymen. "I overtook four of them on horse-

95

back, who were astonished at the sight of me, so strangely habited as I was and in company with Indians. They stood staring at me a length of time, so confounded that they neither hailed me nor drew near to make an inquiry."

At that amazing moment Cabeza was still surrounded by Indians who were his faithful followers. The "strange habit" he wore consisted of being "naked and barefooted."

Thus he was rescued by his countrymen. His reports of the vast wilderness were carried across the Atlantic and became household tales throughout Spain.

Of all the haunted wildernesses which Cabeza was the first white man to see the strangest was along the Gulf Coast where swamps and low islands were filled with jungles of tall grasses. In freshwater areas these are canebrakes with bamboo grasses towering thirty and forty feet. Some of the fresh-water marshes are loaded with giant reeds which raise seed plumes fifteen feet in the air, appearing as a waving pink sea as far as the eye can reach.

Nature has never created more secure and secret hiding places for wild animals than in the depths of these cane and reed jungles. Here, through the muck and across drier shoulders of land, run the networks of trails of bears, bobcats, and peccaries forever undisturbed by man. Peccaries are the wild pigs of the American wilderness, the deadly enemies of the water moccasins and rattlesnakes

that haunt the canebrakes and the reed jungles.

When a peccary sees a snake, no matter how big, its hair stands on end and bristles in all directions. With a horrible snort it charges to within three feet of the snake and stops short. This fake attack causes the snake to strike, but the peccary has measured the distance perfectly, and it stops an inch out of reach. For a split second the snake is uncoiled. The peccary leaps in the air with back arched and its four sharp hoofs held close together. It cuts the snake to ribbons.

The giant reed jungles are fresh-water swamps. The Indian tribes did not come down to the coast to collect their roots, which are stringy and tough like any other roots, and where a hand grubbing in the muck would be struck by a deadly water moccasin. But there were vast cattail swamps along the Gulf Coast, sometimes invaded by sea water spilled into them by high winds or extra-high tides. Then the swamps would be salty for a time, and this would prevent the giant canes and reeds from growing there and would keep out the dangerous water moccasins.

Cabeza said that as a slave of the coast Indians he had to dig roots in the marshes until his hands bled. He was referring to the vast cattail swamps between the offshore islands and the mainland of the Gulf Coast.

The cattail is one of the most interesting and oldest plants of the wilderness. A cattail grows eight or ten feet in one season, sending up a straight stem with a brown cylinder near its top that looks like a big sausage on a spit. Around this long, slender leaves form circles and curves that never stop dancing. One big brown "sausage" is made with a half million flowers pressed closely together, and each flower produces a seed too small for the eye to see.

From one of these invisible seeds falling into the mud of the swamp a stem grows sidewise, not up like the stems of ordinary seeds. This stem is so filled with energy that in a few days it may be several feet long and putting out branches in all directions.

Where these branches touch, they join each other so that a net of stems is woven horizontally through the mud at the bottom of the swamp. A single cattail plant may spread its branches through three acres of swamp.

It was these under-mud stems which the Indian masters had forced the slave Cabeza to dig up. This was a tough and bloody job, and the Spaniard who thought of good food in terms of the fruits and spicy dishes of Spain never realized that the "roots," as he called them, were nourishing food.

Those under-mud cattail branches are not made of wood. They are filled with air and a pulpy substance that has as much nourishment as corn, rice, and potatoes. The stems are enclosed in a waterproof covering so that this food and air may be buried in the mud underneath water that is stale or salty and yet keep as fresh as though in cold storage. This big system for self-contained air and food enables the cattail to live if the swamp dries up and keeps it from suffocating in deep water if there is a flood. The buds on its stems buried in the bottom of the swamp can open, and, with the energy of food from below and the internal air supply, their shoots can grow up through eight feet or more of water to thrust their sausages up into the air and sunshine.

And those slender, curving leaves are hurricane-proof. Instead of a framework of lengthwise veins, the leaves have a series of crosswise girders, like the wing of an airplane. Such a leaf can be whipped in any direction without tearing. When a hurricane strikes a cattail swamp, the leaves fend the force of the blow by flowing in the wind, while the spikes bend over and bury themselves in the water. When the storm is spent, the spikes snap back to an erect position and the leaves gently rise, describing their circles and curves as though nothing had happened.

Cabeza was a shipwrecked treasurer and not a bird lover. So the first white man to discover the Gulf Coast does not tell us about the astonishing birds which live there. He was too busy with the wilderness people.

But the wilderness centering on the Mississippi delta, with its vast areas of canebrakes, giant reeds, and cattail swamps, its countless ponds, shallow bayous, and mud flats, is haunted by striding long-legged birds. Their populations would have been in the millions before the crack of a gun had ever broken the silence of those swamps.

Cabeza, splashing through the mud of a cattail swamp with dead stalks crackling as he pushed his way, must have been startled often by the weird whir of wings. It may have been a great blue heron. This superb bird stands four feet high and has a wingspread of six feet. From a standing position it jumps into the air and somehow, in two seconds, manages to get those great wings unfolded. They beat very slowly as it heads over the grass tops with its long, hoselike neck folded back in tight curves on its shoulders.

When a great bird is squared away on its course with slow, steady beating of wings, its flight is silent, but the rush of its take-off is a signal to countless other birds that are hiding nearby. They do not wait to know the cause of the alarm. If it happened to be a panther, bear, or raccoon, the delay of a second or two might be fatal. The sudden rush of whirring wings is heard across the swamps beginning near the trigger bird and fading into the dim distance as squads, regiments, and armies follow each other into the air. At first the myriads of beating wings appear to be mixed like snowflakes in a blizzard. Then the flocks gradually sort themselves out, settle back, and vanish into the marshy places from which they sprang.

Small flocks of pelicans and geese, flying in V formation behind a leader, set out to find a fresh feeding ground. The V formation allows each bird to travel through air that is undisturbed by whirlpools and eddies stirred up by the wingbeats of a bird in front.

One fantastically beautiful bird does not take wing every time the alarm bell sounds. Within the reed jungles are wide open spaces of mud flats. Here in the bright sun are clusters of round mounds, each about one foot high, appearing like villages of mud huts in the distance. They are flamingo nests. Some have the tall pink-and-white birds standing on them as still as graceful statues on pedestals. Thus it was in the days of the primeval wilderness.

The flamingo is the emperor of the living marshes. He fears nothing and takes no orders. He does not appear and disappear like the others, but he builds his house apart in full sight out in the

open. He wears the richest clothing of pink and white, sometimes flame-red, feathers. A flamingo's legs are more than twenty inches long, and his snakelike neck is even longer. He wades into deeper water than the others, stepping so gently that he scarcely makes a ripple. Then, standing perfectly still with head hanging down, two sharp eyes search the bottom. Suddenly the S curves of the neck unfold, a red tinged beak with a black tip punctures the water, and a little mollusk is sucked in. In some mysterious way the mollusk travels upward against gravity through the looping channel of the amazingly long neck.

The flamingo does not swoop and dive after prey; all his hunting is done while wading. He flies from mud mound straight to hunting ground at sunrise, returning at sunset. The bright white, pink, and red of his body blend with sky colors when the sun is close to the horizon. In flight his long legs are thrust straight out behind, while the neck points ahead, so that the marvelous body forms a swift horizontal line like a javelin shooting through the air.

Many other birds soar alone over the grass tops. One could be a roseate spoonbill with shell-pink feathers and blood-red marks on its shoulders. This comical-looking bird has a flat bill that widens at the tip, forming a wedge broader than its head. The bird uses this as a shovel to plow up the bottom of the swamp; then, holding its bill open just a crack, it is turned into a strainer, expelling a billful of mud and sand, retaining what is plump and good to eat.

When Cabeza crawled up the beach of the Island of Misfortune, there were thousands of whooping cranes in the area. They are the tallest birds of the American wilderness, and the Spaniards took

them for European storks, except that the pink and red colors on the head were surprising. These wonderful birds soar in small groups like squadrons of ships with white sails in the blue sky. There are trumpeters aboard those ships. Whooping cranes have long windpipes coiled like French horns inside their bodies, through which they blow and bugle as they go. As this is written, fewer than fifty whooping cranes live in the Gulf Coast wilderness. Any day now may bring the last time the beautiful bugling will resound over the tall grasses, and this most magnificent bird will vanish from the face of the earth.

With eight-foot wingspread, the whooping crane strokes the air slowly—one beat per second. The rate of wing strokes is in proportion to the size of a bird's body, the bigger the slower.

From the tallest to the smallest, hummingbirds' wings go so fast that they are a transparent blur like the blades of a whirling airplane propeller. Except for a small squeak, a hummingbird has no song or call except the sound which comes from the hum of its wings that gave this bird its name.

The hummingbird is the smallest bird in the world, with a body, in some species, the size of your thumb and its weight that of a penny, so light you can scarcely feel it. Yet this flying machine, as compact as a watch, has a range of 500 miles! It migrates farther than many big birds and can cross the Gulf of Mexico without stopping. Hummingbirds are not residents of the Gulf Coast wilderness but, passing that way, they visit the dunes and islands to load up with nectar from flowers—their high-octane fuel. These tiny birds can travel seventy miles an hour, and at that speed their tiny bodies are as invisible as a bullet going through the air.

East of the Gulf Coast reed jungle lies another grassy wilderness that has been impenetrable almost to our time—the mysterious Everglades. Its interior is a wide river of grass with blades that have sharp glass-like edges. Water seeps through this grass, slowly flowing from north to south. Thousands of oval islands called hammocks are scattered along this river of grass. Their ovals are arranged in the direction of the flow, and with the tall jungle trees that clump together on each hammock, they appear like ships sailing downstream.

The mouth of the Everglades is at the southwest tip of Florida. There the grass river and the hammocks disappear into a mangrove marsh with ten thousand islands. Here is such a maze of waterways that to this day there are channels and secret places among the mangroves where man has seldom been.

Shortly before the river of grass reaches the mangrove marshes, it flows among cypress trees which have long gray beards streaming from the branches. The water is glassy; the silence is so deep it feels like black velvet. Then a rumbling is heard. The place seems to be haunted by a huge male ghost. This is the boom of the big bull alligator looking for a mate—one of the last large-sized survivors of the "terrible lizards" of the Age of Reptiles have their refuge here in the depths of the Everglades.

An alligator at the edge of a pond watches for prey. Two eyes like big black knobs stick up above the water on the top of his snout. Back of this the scaly body, perhaps sixteen feet long, is

hidden under the glassy surface like a waterlogged log. The eye knobs are wide open and stare steadily at a place on the bank without blinking, without the slightest motion for a half hour or an hour—until live meat appears. An alligator must have fresh meat, but almost anything will do. It may be an otter, raccoon, wading bird, lizard, muskrat, snake, turtle, or, with good luck, a rabbit or skunk.

Or again the old reptile may prefer different fare. Slowly, very slowly, his eyes and tail sink out of sight. Then, like a shadowy submarine, he prowls after crabs and turtles, schools of little fish or big fish. He can never catch an otter under water. The otter is a great acrobat, the most graceful and skillful swimmer and diver of any land animal. He can easily keep out of the way of the alligator's yawning jaws under water.

How does an alligator keep from drowning when he opens his jaws so wide and shoots forward under water with a flip of his big tail? He wads his tongue and stops his windpipe with it and then uses his big mouth as a market basket for collecting food.

While the animals in the corners and caves and hide-outs of the Everglades wilderness are forever destroying each other—the bigger going after the smaller and the smaller after the littler— there is a dangerous plant in the ship-hammocks which is also following this way of life.

The strangling fig is closely related to the friendly food-giving figs of the Old World. But in the strange Everglades wilderness the fig tree turns into a killer.

At first glance it seems to offer no threat. It acts like a well-behaved vine growing on an oak or palm or any other good tree. In the shape of a vine, it mounts the tallest tree and puts out leaves at the top which mingle with the leaves of the tree. Then it mysteriously changes form. It begins to swell out on both sides over its whole length, and the wood of the fig vine proceeds to encircle the tree trunk from top to bottom. When the two sides meet, the host tree is completely encased. Its bark is useless and can no longer breathe. At this time many leafy branches spring out from the top of the wooden fig cylinder, throwing the leaves of the tree into deep shade, which strangles them by cutting off their sunlight. Soon the victim dies and decays away, while the victor stands there looking like a fine big tree with a heavy trunk —but the trunk is hollow.

Down in the tunnels of the mangroves, where little has changed during a million years, grows another dangerous tree, named machineel, which strikes terror into the hearts of those who meet it and know about it.

Machineel has many queer but pleasant relatives. Among the members of its family are the rubber tree, the castor oil and tapioca plant, the pretty poinsettia, a silver and mercury bush, queen's-delight, and snow-on-the-mountain. But with all its fine family, the machineel is a lonely, lurking demon in the mangrove maze.

If raindrops dripping from its leaves touch your skin, they raise big blisters. Its fruit when eaten deals sure and painful death.

It is rumored in the Everglades that once upon a time there was an Indian tribe in the Everglades wilderness who knew about the machineel tree. They persuaded their enemies to take shelter under its branches in a rainstorm. And gathering the leaves with great care not to touch them, they threw them into the springs where their enemies drank. The enemies did not live one day more after quenching their thirst from the springs touched by the machineel leaves.

Near the source of the Everglades' river of grass the saw grass grows deep on the banks of a channel. Here suddenly a shrill scream is heard, like that of a rusty hinge amplified a hundred times. Every creature within a mile is in earshot of this awful scream. But nothing happens. There is no panic. It is only blood-curdling to someone who thinks the Everglades is haunted. It is only a limpkin calling its mate.

The limpkin, a bird related to cranes, has the longest toes, the widest feet, which serve as snowshoes, or reed shoes to tread upon tall grasses. If the reeds are too slender, it grasps a bunch of them; then, by careful balancing and much swaying and bouncing with the motion of the grass, it walks airily upon the reeds.

But the limpkin does not do this just for fun. It is hunting giant snails. The snails, which live down in the mud, climb up the grasses to lay their little pink eggs in rows high up above the swamp, where they will surely be safe from the lizards down in the mud who love snail eggs.

Snails seem fat, heavy, and clumsy to be climbing high on frail, swaying grasses. But this giant snail of the Everglades is the acrobat of its kind. The only trouble is—here comes the limpkin striding across the tops of the grasses on its reed shoes. It does not eat the snail eggs but leaves those for the lizards; it plucks the fat snails off the tall grass blades as though it were picking apples. Then, with hooked tweezers on its beak, it pulls the snail out of its spiraling fortress, lets the shell plop into the mud, and gulps down something soft and delicious.

CHAPTER VI

THE GREEN WOODS WILDERNESS

THE Green Woods Wilderness of eastern America is the biggest, richest, most hospitable wilderness on the face of the earth. It is an ocean of green leaves extending from the Atlantic Coast to the Mississippi River, from the pine forests of Canada to the coastal plains and cypress swamps of Georgia and Florida.

The mass of this wilderness consists of trees with wide green leaves that turn to bright colors in the fall and then drop off their branches and shower down, covering the ground with a blanket of fertile leaf mold during the winter.

Leaf dropping promotes a tremendous amount of life. There is greater variety of plants in the Green Woods Wilderness than in any other forest of the world. The foliage never gets dark and tough and old, but it is born anew every year, keeping the life of this wilderness forever young. Even the forest floor is not in perpetual shadow, but it is sun-swept in the early spring, before the leaves are expanded.

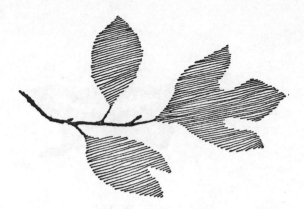

Every layer of this wilderness is fresh and new every year—above, tree canopies of young green leaves, and below these the new leaves and flowers of blueberries, blackberries, hazelnut, witch-hazel, and alder bushes. Down on the ground, in May, the floor of the forest is alive with wake-robin, bunchberry, enchanter's night-shade, wild ginger, columbine, wintergreen, and partridge berry. All this depth of fresh life appears when the forest is flooded with sunlight from top to bottom.

No one kind of tree has a monopoly in the Green Woods Wilderness. Oak, elm, maple, cherry, walnut, hickory, beech, tulip, poplar, sycamore grow together, mixing their leaves in the flood of nourishment that falls on the ground.

Every corner and cranny of this luxurious wilderness is packed with mushrooms, fruits, seeds, tender fresh leaves and buds, and young green shoots. The Green Woods Wilderness offers no end of hiding places and abundance of food to its vast populations of animals and birds.

Other forest wildernesses, as in our Northwest, have bigger trees and animals. Tropical wildernesses have tree orchids, parrots, and monkeys. The high plains of Africa have elephants, lions, tigers, and gorillas. But nowhere on the face of the earth is there a wilderness with such a multitude of animals of all sizes and alive with so many birds as the Green Woods Wilderness.

The trees, with different sizes and shapes, form various combinations in various locations. Oak, sugar maple, hickory, and walnut like a hillside where it is brighter and drier. Red maple and alder gather in low, wet places. Sycamore and willow line the banks of streams. White birch and poplar stand in the full sunlight at the front of the forest, facing an open place. Within the body of the wilderness there are blue lakes and rivers, open meadows and bogs, patches of hemlock in dark ravines, spruce and fir on mountain ridges, and acres of scrub pine on the sandy coastal plains.

In this pattern of hills, meadows, swamps, and lakeside woods, animals and birds choose living places where they feel most at home. The woodchuck has its burrow, often facing the warm south sun. The fox lives on the north slope. Rabbits venture out into the meadow to feed where bumblebees are buzzing in the clover. A brown thrasher is nesting in the bushes and a vireo in a blackberry tangle. The shrike likes a honey locust tree where it can impale its victim on the savage thorns. A pileated woodpecker has hacked out its home in the dead wood of the linden. A field sparrow has built itself a grassy nest in a hedgerow. Woodchucks and clover go together, and the fox has its burrow on the cool north side because it is handy to the young woodchucks and mice and rabbits. The owl has chosen its hollow tree so as to face the place

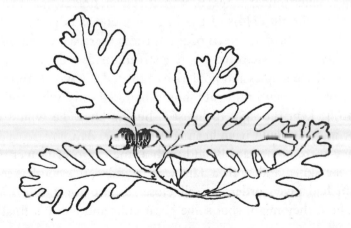

where the mice will run in the moonlight.

Two life forces bring every animal and bird to its place in the Green Woods Wilderness. One is the need of food, a particular choice of berries or seeds or grass or the flesh of another animal. Another is the need to hide—the mouse in its tunnels under the grass, the songbird in the high foliage, the owl in a hollow tree, the fox and woodchuck in their burrows, beaver and snake and frog under water. Everything has the same kind of needs, but each has a special place in this wilderness and its own way of filling its needs. The wonder of the Green Woods Wilderness is the myriad of opportunities for living places.

"Look, sir, at those objects on that rock!"

The words were spoken in French into the ear of Captain Champaigne. He was standing with his mate on the deck of their ship, scanning the rocky coast of Nova Scotia. It was October 1569, when the area around the Gulf of St. Lawrence was starting to be opened to French colonies. Cape Breton headland at the top of Isle Royale was the landmark and symbol of the New World to every French sailor that came that way.

This was one of those crystal-clear October days when the sky has turned permanently blue and the air is refreshingly cold. As they sailed under Cape Breton a few hours earlier, they had noticed the bright colors of the heavily wooded ridge back of the cape. Among the dark green of the spruces there were gold patches of birches, and at one place where a stream made a delta at the foot of the cliff the maples and poplars had turned the woods to red and gold. But a captain's thoughts should be filled only with rocks and sea. So he kept the sight to himself, but he knew he would never forget it. So it could have been that October day.

They were homeward bound with a fine cargo of beaver, mink, and bear skins, and with a fair west wind and smooth seas, the captain had given orders to sail close inshore for a few leagues. With luck they might spot some great auks and enjoy a final feast off the New World. But, instead of auks, Captain Champaigne and his crew found three men standing on the rock.

It was impossible. But so were red and gold trees and great auks. Captain Champaigne put off a boat and picked up the three English boys who were waving their arms from the rock. They said their names were David Ingram, Richard Browne, and Richard Twide. They were bearded, barefooted, and wore wild-animal skins. They were English sailors who could speak no French, but the captain, who had a smattering of English, thought they said that they had been put ashore on the Gulf of Mexico over a year ago and had walked from there to Nova Scotia. This was so nonsensical that the boys must be out of their minds.

It seemed that way also to people in England when the boys arrived back home and told their story. In those days nobody could imagine walking in the wilderness which stretched from Nova Scotia to Florida. Men might sail the length of the coast, but even that would take a special expedition.

David Ingram, the leader of the three, was a sailor of few words and few ideas. But he stuck to his story.

Ingram said that he and Browne and Twide had been crew men under John Hawkins when his three vessels sailed into the Gulf of Mexico to raid the Spaniards. They lost a battle in which one of Hawkins' ships was sunk and another driven aground. The survivors were crowded into the one remaining ship. Without enough food and water to get them all back to England, Hawkins was forced to put 114 men ashore in the Gulf of Mexico. The party was promptly shot up by Indians, so most of them decided to go southward and throw themselves on the mercy of the Spaniards. Afterward it was learned that the Spaniards sent these to Mexico City where they were tortured to death by the Inquisition.

Twenty-three others, including Ingram, decided to turn north. If they could reach the coast above the Spanish colonies, an English ship might pick them up. The three men on the rock near Cape Breton were the sole survivors of this band.

They had struggled forward for fifteen months. They had crossed Texas and the Mississippi River in Louisiana. They skirted the great inland swamps of Georgia and reached the coast. Then, because of bayous and rivers and marshes, they went inland again and followed Indian trails and animal trails, but always northward. At Chesapeake Bay and the big rivers they built rafts to get themselves across.

They lived and looked like Indians, except for their beards. Sometimes the Indians attacked them; sometimes they helped them by pointing out trails and let them share the carcass of a bear or deer. Ingram was not clear how many had been killed by Indians, how many had drowned when crossing rivers or died of hunger and injury. His account was confused and brief. But the fact was clear that David and the two Richards were rescued from the rock in Nova Scotia on a certain day in October 1569. This was confirmed by Captain Champaigne's logbook.

The other end of the story was confirmed by John Hawkins.

His ship's papers showed that Ingram, Browne, and Twide were members of his crews that sailed into the Gulf of Mexico to raid the Spaniards in 1568. Also, that those three were among the 114 men that Hawkins was forced to put ashore some thirty miles north of Tampico in July 1568.

This log tells us that Ingram and his two friends were on their way through the wilderness for 450 days, and they averaged over five miles per day. They probably often spent days resting, stopping with Indians, building rafts, nursing cut feet, picking berries, trapping an animal, or figuring out how to get around an impenetrable tangle. To offset such delays, there must have been days when they made good mileage. For example, it would be possible to cover twenty or thirty miles a day rafting or canoeing, crossing the wide, dry bogs of Georgia and South Carolina, plodding along northbound beaches which they could have picked up sometimes between the Carolinas and Massachusetts, walking through pine barrens as in New Jersey where there is little underbrush, and trotting along Indian and animal trails.

We do not know the details of this "impossible" journey. At first nobody believed Ingram. He was thought to be a survivor of a shipwreck on the northern coast who was out of his head. When the records confirmed the beginning and the end of the tale, Ingram's story created quite a stir. He was quizzed by Queen Elizabeth's Chief of Secret Service. Then he was really confused with excitement. His story became all mixed up. He even told about seeing elephants in the New World, while actually he had seen them on an earlier expedition to Africa.

Ingram emerges from all this as an ignorant, happy-go-lucky sailor who was tough, tireless, and fearless. His adventures with Hawkins had hardened him to death and danger. When lost in the Green Woods Wilderness, he did not try to imagine how big that wilderness was. He did not worry about its dangers. Without imagination he did not suffer too much; he became timeless and lived only from day to day. He was possessed by one thought—

to get away from the Spaniards, to go northeastward to the coast where English ships fishing around Newfoundland might pick him up.

He was sailor enough to hold to a course with the help of the sun and stars. Because he kept in touch with the coast, either by looking at the sea once in a while or by following the trails of the coastal tribes, Ingram avoided impassable ravines and steep mountainsides. The mountain ranges which are the backbone of the eastern hardwood wilderness, running from southern Georgia to Mt. Katahdin in Maine, lie fifty to a hundred miles inland from the Atlantic coast.

Ingram, Browne, and Twide were the first white men ever to see the depths of the Green Woods Wilderness. And no man has ever since been known to walk the length of that vast woodland wilderness through which they struggled. They did it some twenty years before the lost English colony set foot on Roanoke Island, North Carolina; some forty years before Englishmen landed at Jamestown, Virginia; and fifty-two years before the Pilgrims stepped ashore at Plymouth, Massachusetts.

Those first English settlements clung to the seacoast. For a century no white man ventured into the Green Woods Wilderness. It was penetrated only for a few miles by canoes. So great was the awe and mystery of the Green Woods Wilderness that John Bartram, 170 years after Ingram, showed great daring exploring as far as the Blue Ridge Mountains of Virginia and circling back to the Potomac River in Maryland. A report of this 1738 trip of Bartram's says, "He could find no one to share the hardships of his explorations. Traveling alone, therefore, he ventured into unsettled regions, crossing rivers, climbing mountains and precipices, often following the paths made by the beasts of the forest. . . ."

When Ingram passed that way the primeval wilderness was in its prime.

Taking a northern course in Georgia, Ingram would have rounded the great Okefinokee Swamp. At noonday a great stillness descends on the swamp. It is like a painting, with glassy water and acres of water lilies on it and a few golden clubs sticking up here and there through the glass. Long gray beards of Spanish moss hang motionless from the limbs of cypress, swamp bay, and black gum. Tiny events like a plop where a frog jumps in, and ripples on a glassy surface where a water spider skates, emphasize the stillness.

But during the hour after sunrise every part of Okefinokee resounds and quivers with life. The squealing cries of wood ducks fill the air, punctuated by the occasional squawks of herons and egrets. A vulture soars overhead, and a flock of white ibis glides by at treetop level. Among the trees there sounds a tattoo of woodpeckers and a Carolina wren is singing, while in the distance the guttural notes of the Florida crane can be heard.

A barred owl is hooting in chorus with the deep notes of an old bull alligator. The almost horizontal sun's rays touch the edge of a floating island made of little mats of vegetation acting like a baton that summons up a chorus of frogs.

Snakebirds are lined up on a dry, moss-draped limb hanging

over the water. Their tails are expanded like open fans and they hold their wings out, expanding the feathers to catch every breeze. These beautiful birds have extremely long, slender necks and heads with small faces. They seem to be looking at their images in the mirror of the water. But if they hear a footstep or a twig snap, they drop off the limb as though shot dead and vanish under water like a stone. A minute later, some distance away, a little head and neck suddenly pop up, looking exactly like a snake swimming around.

Great numbers of Carolina parakeets peppered the green woods among the big timbers of sycamore and cypress. Their favorite fruit was the tough, prickly buttonballs of the sycamore, the oldest patriarch of the Green Woods Wilderness.

Many of these beautiful birds were still to be seen in the Green Woods Wilderness as late as the nineteenth century, when Carolina parakeet became unpopular because swarms of them would alight on an apple tree and twist off all the fruit, one by one, strewing it in every direction around the tree. This seemed to be a game the parakeets were playing, because they never descended to pick up the fruit. There was no sense to it. They also twisted off green

oranges and peaches before they were ripe. On the other hand, the parakeets brought big prices in city markets because they looked so pretty sitting in cages. So, for two reasons, the parrots were doomed and the last wild Carolina parakeet was collected in 1901.

There is no doubt that Ingram saw wild turkeys. The woods were full of them. These strapping big American birds eat the seeds of grasses, so they spent most of their time gobbling in the open grassy places of the forest. They loved to have tall trees around to hide the grassy spots, but they could never fly among the trees with their big wings. They hurled themselves over the treetops and descended on the far meadows. They were nervous, never stood still, kept striding around and flapping their wings and gobbling. Turkeys abounded in the whole length of the Green Woods Wilderness from Florida to Maine. Today one small flock still lives in a fragment of the old primeval forest on Bull's Island, three miles off the coast of South Carolina.

Within fifty miles of the coast of North Carolina there are peculiar level patches of ground where the soft mud of a bog is covered by a tough, dry crust, a sort of matting of short grasses and mosses. Rain and flood waters sink through this crust quickly, leaving the bog always hard and dry and easy to walk on.

Venus's flytrap grows on the crust of these bogs and nowhere else in the world. The plant acts like a steel trap! Its two leaves resemble two hands held together with palms up. Rows of long

117

spines around the outer edges are like fingers. The palms are rosy colored and glistening, attracting prey with the color of good food and the sparkle of nectar. Three little hairs, widely separated on the surface of the rosy palms, are triggers. Anything crawling or walking on these outspread hands has only to stumble over two of these triggers to make the two palms close like a book.

But the infernal machine pauses in its closing, leaving a fraction of an inch space between the faces of its blades. Then the two rows of spines promptly swing over and interlock, forming prison bars with only small openings between. In this way things that are too tiny to bother with, like a mosquito, are given a chance to escape. They climb out through the holes between the bars and flee in a panic. Things that are big and delicious are trapped and can only await their fate.

This comes in a few moments, when the sides of the trap start moving again, press tightly together, and crush the prey. Digestive juices do their part, and Venus flytrap proceeds to enjoy its dinner at leisure. If the prey is a good-sized caterpillar, or a small frog, it may be a few days before the plant is ready for another feast when the trap will open again to welcome the next victim.

There is no record of the discovery of this strange plant catcher of little animals either by Indians or early explorers. The first mention of it was when Governor Dobbs of North Carolina wrote a letter to a friend in England in 1760: "The greatest wonder of the wilderness is an unknown plant like an iron spring fox trap; upon anything touching them, they instantly close. . . ." The Queen's botanist was dispatched to look into this, and, three years after the Dobbs letter, he found many Venus's flytraps slamming shut on many little creatures in North Carolina dry bogs.

The Green Woods Wilderness created white-tailed deer and then handed over the title to them. You can be sure that this is one animal which Ingram didn't overlook. He must have seen hundreds of them. They peered at him out of the shadows with big, soft eyes; they broke cover with a sudden rush and bounced along the trail ahead of him; in groups of twos and threes they were browsing on the bushes in a forest opening. There were millions and millions of white-tailed deer everywhere in that ocean of green.

The white-tailed deer is slender and lissom; it pours like fluid among tree trunks and bushes, over fallen logs and across brooks. Only an occasional breaking stick tells where a deer is going. For the most part it is silent and frictionless.

The whitetail does not really travel through the woods unless it is chased by a panther. Then it can run twenty miles without stopping, pouring up and down hill, bounding over boulders, dodging trees its body never seems to touch anything. But it falls dead at the end of a twenty-mile dash—and this the panther seems to know.

The Green Woods offers whitetails a wealth of food. The

animal, four feet high, has a graceful, fairly long neck with which it can reach up or down a few feet. Within this range it can browse on low twigs and leaves, and all shrubs are easily within its reach. It can eat almost anything that is the substance of the forest, such as fruits and acorns, goldenrod and fern, mushrooms and pond lilies. But white cedar and birch trees are the deer's favorite food, because the whitetail can browse on these with its head held high, while the big eyes on each side of its head can scan a complete circle without moving its body.

The white-tail is normally the most contented animal in the Green Woods. No one sees the deer without cheering up. There is nothing cruel about it. It is never out of place. It is the true creature of the Green Woods Wilderness.

Nevertheless it is the nature of a wilderness to be not only hospitable and generous but also cruel, with many hidden dangers and deadly surprises. White-tails traveling smoothly through the woods, pouring over fallen logs, may suddenly be speared by bayonet-like projections. Their bodies have been found with branches a foot long and half an inch thick driven through them.

A tree struck by lightning may topple so as to leave an arch of dangerous splits and splinters. A deer was once found dead of starvation, with its head caught in a split at the top of such an arch. It had stooped to eat ferns under the fallen tree, and then, surprised by a crackling twig, it whipped up its head so vigorously that its neck was wedged in the split of the tree. Or perhaps a rabbit in a panic is going full tilt when it collides with the slender legs of a deer also at full tilt. The white-tail is tripped and breaks its neck against a tree.

When the antlers of a white-tail buck are full-grown in October, he seems to be wearing a sort of bush with heavy branches on his head. He carries this proudly, as though it were a royal standard. The antlers tell the world that this animal is a white-tailed buck looking for a mate and ready to fight any other buck which gets in his way.

Another buck with antlers just as proud meets him in an opening in the woods. After prancing around awhile, the two bucks come to grips—not with a charge and a plunge and a crash of antlers, but by putting their heads down and pushing with their antlers against each other. They push and push with all their strength without separating, grunting, digging up the ground with their hoofs. But this pushing match of the white-tail bucks is not too terrible. When they are all tired out, one buck quits the premises and leaves the other buck in full possession of the field.

This peculiar duel, however, may lead to a weird accident. When the bucks are ready to separate, they may find their antlers hopelessly locked together. They can pull, wrench, and rear, and tear up the whole place, but they cannot separate. At last they fall down dead of starvation.

Ingram and the other three lost sailors must have stared sometimes at the Virginia opossum with a face like a fox, the tail of a monkey, ears like a bat, and claws like a human hand with a grasping thumb, snarling in an ugly temper from a high limb. The nearest relative of the Virginia opossum is the Australian kangaroo, and when the Green Woods Wilderness was first discovered, no animal like this, which carries its young in its pouch, had ever been seen before.

If the first explorers in the Green Tree Wilderness felt that they had friends among the wild animals, one of them would have been the raccoon, who looks like a funny little highwayman wearing a black mask. He would come into the circle of light of a campfire, ready to pick up apple cores or bones cast away with meat still on them. Like a hungry man in the woods, he is ready to eat anything. Poised in the light of a full moon on the bank of a river or lake, he reaches out with long, sensitive fingers to snatch crayfish, frogs, salamanders. Up in the woods he pounces on eggs, birds, insects, mice, and everything that creeps. If there is water nearby, the raccoon waddles over to it, and holding his handful of food tenderly, he swishes it back and forth. This makes the highwayman

amusing. He is not only washing off the mud but also he is turning the food to find the tenderest part, and softening it, as a man softens a doughnut by dunking it in coffee.

In the depths of the Green Tree Wilderness of untouched glory and primeval splendor there was another truly American animal found nowhere else in the world. It still lives all over North America and it is famous for its fine fur and its smell, which announces its presence a half mile away. The American skunk has a European cousin called civet-martin or polecat. This is a different animal, but it has the same odor.

The skunk has a tremendous appetite for pests around farmhouses, such as grasshoppers, yellow jackets, rats, mice, and snakes. The populations of these pests increase where man builds his farms, and this tempts the skunk to come out of the woodland and live on the farm in stone walls and under the floor boards of barns. Thus this fur-bearing animal of the primeval wilderness has increased in population since the days of the early explorers.

The bad odor of the skunk does not mean that he is a bad animal. He is merely well equipped for gas warfare. He is a good-natured exterminator of pests. Most of the time he ambles around ferreting out yellow jackets, mice, and snakes and making life miserable for grasshoppers. If another animal, including a person, gets in his way, he stands his ground, facing the enemy. Then he stamps the ground with stiff front legs, clicks his teeth, gives a little hiss. If this is not enough warning, the skunk suddenly twists his body into a U, so that both his face and his rear end are toward the target, lifts his tail high with hairs standing out at right angles, forming a great plume, and releases two jets of smelly vapor.

The skunk does not use his tail as a hose. He is simply lifting it up out of the way so that the oily odor will not touch his own fur. A skunk does not spill his fluid on himself, and his body is not the least bit smelly.

Many wildernesses have rainstorms, snowstorms, and thunderstorms. But only the Green Woods Wilderness ever had a birdstorm. Only the Green Woods Wilderness was big enough to contain a flock of pigeons 240 miles long, packed with more than a billion birds in close formation flying at sixty miles an hour. Only this vast green woods could produce enough acorns, nuts, and seeds to pack this cloud of birds with the energy of ten million bushels of solid food per day.

The cloud of pigeons came up out of the southern forest with the sunrise and headed north in March like an immense pennant of smoke. Again, in October, it came up at sunrise out of the gold and yellow northern woods and streamed southward.

Unlike most birds, the passenger pigeon could not lead an individual life. This beautiful pigeon could live only in the midst of a great crowd. It had to feel the heave and the breeze of a compact mass, not merely the gentle sense of a few companions in a small flock.

The dark cloud of the bird storm, which blotted out the sun, was like a single organism. The giant flock was, in a sense, the biggest organism that a giant wilderness has ever produced. Inside this cloud the pigeons flew in perfect formation, wing to wing. At sunset they descended en masse, pressing even closer together, covering the woods with a blanket of birds four miles in length. There was hardly a twig or a branch which they did not cover. They even piled themselves up on each other's backs to a depth of three feet at times. So great was their weight that limbs and branches broke down, and trees not firmly rooted toppled over.

Passenger pigeons did not fly high like ducks and geese in migration. They swept low over the treetops, and the rush of their wings was like that of a great wind. Their cloud turned into a river of pigeons undulating, rising and falling, as they seemed joyfully to ride the roller coaster of the air. Where the river dipped, trees would bend and quiver and leaves flutter from the sudden breeze of myriad wings. Wisps of birds would project like fingers from the sides of the cloud, probing the woods along the course. Sometimes a flock of a few thousand pigeons would separate and dive at white-tails feeding in a clearing. This was a sign of a forest of oak laden with acorns. Or the probing fingers might find a thicket of blueberry bushes loaded with fruit in the sand barrens —then pigeons clapped their wings with thunderous applause.

We do not know whether Ingram, Browne, and Twide saw the weird bird storm darken the sky. During the 450 days they trod among the mysteries of the Green Woods Wilderness, this event must have happened three times. But they were not making notes. A storm cloud that darkens the sun and brings a rush of wind would not seem unusual to sailors, even when simulated by pigeons. Everything else in the American wilderness would be more astonishing to them—parakeet, wild turkey, naked red men, white-tailed deer bouncing around.

When Ingram was quizzed later in London, if he mentioned the bird storm of the pigeons it may have seemed purely imaginary or unimportant to the Queen's Chief of the Secret Service. There was no record of them until people penetrated the wilderness many years after Ingram passed that way.

William Wood, an early settler in Massachusetts, wrote in 1635: "Birds come into the country to go north in the beginning of our spring. I have seen them fly as if the airy regiment had been pigeons, seeing neither beginning nor ending, length or breadth of these millions of millions. The shouting of people, the rattling of guns,

the pelting of small shot, could not drive them out of their course, but so they continued for five hours together."

A man writing in the *Chautauqua Magazine* in 1895 spoke of seeing the pigeons when he was a boy: "I have seen their unbroken columns, like an army of trained soldiers pushing to the front, while detached bodies of birds appear in different parts of the heavens, pressing forward in haste like raw recruits rushing to battle. . . . I have seen [when they were descending to roost for the night] the living mass pour headlong down hundreds of feet, sounding as though a whirlwind were abroad in the land."

A writer in 1832 tells what happened when the bird storm passed over the city of Toronto: "For three days the town resounded with one continuous roll of firing, as if a skirmish were going on in the streets—every gun, pistol, musket, blunderbuss, and fire-arm of whatever description was put in requisition. Among those who took part in the fray were honorable members of the executive and legislative councils, crown lawyers, respectable, staid citizens, and last of all the sheriff of the county. At last it was found that pigeons flying within easy shot were a temptation too strong for human virtué to withstand."

A. B. Welford of Woodstock, Ontario, an eyewitness, tells about the last great flight of the passenger pigeons, in 1870: "I was up that morning very early, and so were the birds. I took up a position on a rise of ground. They came in such numbers that thousands would pass between the discharge of my double-barrelled gun and its reloading—a longer process then in the days of muzzle loading than now. It was possible to get from fifteen to twenty-five with a right and left barrel. At about 10:00 A.M., I ran out of powder and shot, having then 400 birds to my credit. I hurried home one and a half miles to get a horse and wagon and returned with grain bags, filling them with pigeons and making tracks for home again. While I was filling the sacks, the birds were still streaming over, so that I hid myself behind a fence, and taking a long, slender cedar rail I knocked down many more. This, however, did not appeal so much as shooting. After dropping my birds at home, I drove into town three and a half miles for more powder and shot. During the drive there and back, millions of pigeons filled the air and cast a great shadow. The roar of their wings resembled low, rumbling thunder, and shooting could be heard for miles, resounding from wood to wood like a battle."

So dense were the ranks of the pigeons and so low did they fly at times that anything thrown at them would bring down a pigeon. A boy carrying a pair of sheep shears threw the shears into the air and down came a pigeon. Brickbats, clubs, and stones thrown into a low-flying flock brought birds tumbling out of the air.

Another observer writes, "We had a big watchdog. When pigeons came, he was always the first to reach the hill. Then, whining with excitement and jumping around in a frenzy, I have seen him spring into the air and grab a bird on the wing."

The last passenger pigeon alive on earth died at the Cincinnati Zoo at 1:00 P.M., September 1, 1914.

CHAPTER VII

THE NORTH PINE
WILDERNESS

FOR a hundred years after Ingram's miraculous escape in 1569, the Green Woods Wilderness was considered impassable, with little to offer settlers, and full of savages, which made it all the more dangerous. It was a sort of vacuum of green leaves, with no shape or dimension.

To Ingram, to the Indians, to the English colonists who settled at Jamestown, Virginia, and Plymouth, Massachusetts, the Green Woods Wilderness went on and on, and so forever would. What lay inland to the west was unknown and out of reach, for at that time the only way to explore far into the Green Woods Wilderness was by boat. Every colonist arriving from Europe, every trader, clung to the coast and waterways.

The chief obstacle to exploring westward was the big backbone of the Green Woods Wilderness, the Allegheny Mountains. Waterways did not run westward from the coast. The two big ones, the Chesapeake Bay system and the Hudson, point north. And so the richest wilderness in the world, the primeval green tree forest of eastern United States, remained almost unknown and untouched until the eighteen hundreds.

The first pioneers who followed Indian trails and mountain streams westward over the mountains into the Ohio River Valley are unknown. They were adventurers who vanished into a big wilderness. The first definite records of pioneers traveling due west from Virginia all the way through the mountain fastness of the Blue Ridge, Cumberland, and Great Smoky ranges do not appear until the first half of the eighteenth century. Then English traders led their pack horses through the mountains, bringing cloth and blankets, hatchets and beads, rum and gunpowder, which showed the savages how civilized the white man is.

When these traders, after laboriously traversing the heavy wilderness of the Alleghenies, descended the west slopes of the mountains, they encountered Frenchmen who had been trading with the Indians for years in the Ohio River Valley and around the Great Lakes. The Frenchmen had slipped into the mid-continent, not by hewing a trail straight west through the rugged Alleghenies, but by sliding in with canoes by way of the St. Lawrence River.

While English colonists were pinned down on the rocky shore of New England and the marshy coast of Virginia, the French made an enormous end run around the north into the heart of America. It was enormous in time—150 years passed between the discovery

of the mouth of the St. Lawrence River and planting the French flag at the mouth of the Mississippi. It was enormous in distance, reaching two thousand miles westward into the wilderness around Lake Superior, there discovering the Mississippi and riding its un-obstructed current twenty-five hundred miles south to the Gulf of Mexico. It was enormous in the imagination and daring of the captains of the French team.

The magnitude of this maneuver, by which the French encircled the Green Woods Wilderness on the north and west, is seen in the fact that the three principal captains of it lived in different genera-tions. Cartier discovered the St. Lawrence River in 1535 and sailed up it a thousand miles to plant the French flag on Mount Royal (Montreal). Champlain, born fifteen years after Cartier died, estab-lished the fortress at Quebec in 1608, commanding the St. Lawrence gateway into the heart of North America. Champlain discovered the Great Lakes in 1615. La Salle, born eight years after Champlain died, completed the enormous end run by reaching the mouth of the Mississippi in 1682.

These three great explorers, one pushing forward where another had stopped, traveled clear through the far and deep interior of the continent. Strange as it seems, they were all trying to find a water route through America to Asia, like Columbus and Cabot in an earlier century. They were prepared to grapple with the wilderness until they found the waterway. But they did not cross the Atlantic for a sight-seeing tour of some of the world's most exciting forests filled with amazing animal and bird life, and of the beautiful Great Lakes region, and of the forests and prairie to be seen along the Mississippi—at least not at first and not in the eyes of the French monarch who promoted the expeditions.

But as we read their accounts and see through their eyes what they saw day by day we sense a changed feeling toward the New World. They had their full share of pioneer suffering from hunger and disease and bloodthirsty Indians, but gradually the wilderness turned into a great adventure. White birches against dark spruce trees look beautiful; rivers and lakes are silvery; waterfalls and rapids are exciting. Moreover, the eyes of the French explorers opened at the numbers of fish in the water, of animals in the woods, and of birds in the air.

The French were the first Europeans to surmount the historic illusion that the American wilderness was a stumbling block and a frustration on the way to some other place. In a sense they were the first white people to discover North America. To their surprise they discovered that its wealth was not the gold, pearls, and spices of the

Orient but a wealth of fur—the fur of beaver, fox, deer, bear, muskrat, marten, mink, and otter. They realized that the Great Lakes were not such a great disappointment when they did not turn out to be the Pacific Ocean which explorers sought. The wonderful lakes were alive with an abundance of fish, and on their shores stood forests of the tallest, straightest oaks, maples, hickories, and white cedars in the world. When, burning with curiosity, they probed deeper and deeper into the continent, they found west of Lake Michigan what are known today as the "bur oak openings" between groves of tall trees. There where the soil was deep and rich, and with the long summer days of that latitude, they discovered that these openings could produce marvelous crops. The great fort which Champlain built at Quebec in 1608 became the main portal to these inland wildernesses of the New World.

Perhaps the French were best fitted by imagination and temperament to explore the wilderness for itself, to study woodcraft, to travel in birchbark canoes, to read the signs, sounds, and odors of the wilderness, to make friends with the Indians, honoring their chiefs, trapping, hunting, and camping with them.

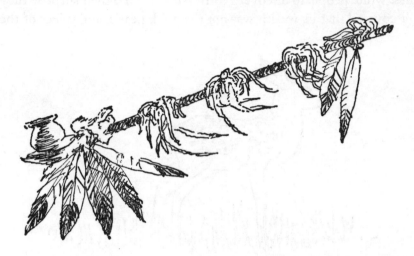

But also the French had good luck. They made their end run because they discovered the St. Lawrence River. After sailing a thousand miles upstream, they were stopped by rapids, but then, with a portage around the rapids, lo and behold, the river was again navigable. A few more portages, and the Great Lakes opened up before their eyes. These broad waters carried them a thousand miles farther west. Then more rivers and a short carrying of canoes (near Portage, Wisconsin) and they crossed a low divide into the Mississippi Valley.

Only about forty years after Columbus two little ships commanded by Jacques Cartier sighted a headland on the east coast of Newfoundland. They had crossed the Atlantic in twenty days, enjoying fair weather all the way. Now they had more good luck by coming upon an island loaded with thousands of great auks. "In less than halfe an houre we filled two boats full of them, so that besides them we did eat fresh, each ship did powder and salt five barrels full of them."

At this time of year icebergs and sea ice coming down the Labrador current clutter the coast of Newfoundland, so Cartier's expedition had to wait ten days for an opening. After that, more fine weather, and they sailed around Newfoundland into the Gulf of St. Lawrence. That, on a fine summer's day, is one of the most beautiful bodies of water in the world. It is an arm of the sea with tantalizing headlands showing above the horizon in every direction.

Cartier, now on the west shore of Newfoundland, entered the Bay of Isles, where a hundred tiny islands, each with a grove of dense tall spruce, imitate a fleet of ships under sail.

Continuing around the gulf, they passed under the towering headland of Cape Breton, tinted with bright spring greens of birch and poplar. Then they came upon an opening, only a few hundred yards wide, which they entered with their pinnaces and found themselves in the Bras d'Or (Arm of Gold). They passed the yellow cliffs, crowned by dark spruce forest, on Anticosti Island. They admired the red cliffs of the Gaspé Peninsula.

Thus they probed the shores of this strange body, looking for a waterway westward. Their landmarks were headlands on distant horizons. They found bays instead of rivers, and big land that looked like mainland turned into islands. They saw walruses, "fishes shaped like horses which all the day long lie in the water. . . . They are beasts as great as oxen which have two great teeth in their mouths like unto elephants."

They were greatly excited by bears and wolves when they made landings. They delighted in the wild grapes and the Canadian plums.

Having spent the summer in this way, Cartier headed his two ships homeward, having just missed discovering the mouth of the

St. Lawrence. But the weather was so good all that summer, and they were so fascinated by what they saw, that they brought glowing reports of the New World back to France. Thus ended the first sight-seeing tour of the American wilderness.

The next spring found Cartier back in the Gulf of St. Lawrence. This time he promptly found the big river. He had not recognized it because it did not break through the coast line with a mouth as rivers usually do. The Gulf of St. Lawrence narrows at its southwest end while yet as wide as an arm of the sea. One would keep going for several hundred miles without realizing this was a river. Very gradually the high shores standing on the horizons on each side close in.

They sailed up the St. Lawrence as far as the Saguenay River, and all was wonder. The Saguenay has great depth, issues from between tall mountains, and it is filled with big fish. Indian canoes danced in the foam. The red men told Cartier that the Saguenay River led to Saguenay, land of wealth, but that straight up the main river was the "land of Canada." This is the first time white men heard the name. In the Indian language it means a settlement of lodges or a town. Such tales whetted Cartier's appetite. With Indian guides and with fair wind, his little sailboats kept on up the main river until they found the "land of Canada."

As the Indians said, it was a big town—fifty lodges, each 150 feet long, and a stockade thirty feet high. This metropolis in the heart of the wilderness had a rock mountain just behind it, a great lookout. Cartier picked twenty of his men and ordered the Indians to escort him to the top. There he planted the French king's flag and called it Mount Royal (Montreal).

A white man had traversed the North Pine Wilderness for the first time. He had come through with good ships, good company, and pleasure in the wonderful surprises that unfolded day by day. From the top of Mount Royal he looked out on the endless sea of spruce and pine stretching westward. He saw the winding Ottawa River bringing vast volumes of water from the northwest, and lakes, and islands.

He turned back, happy and satisfied—but he was too late. On the way down the St. Lawrence they were overtaken by winter—which smothers the North Pine Wilderness under deep snow and silences it with below-zero temperatures. Their ships were frozen in. They landed and built a stockade, mounting cannon which they had brought along. Indian friendship changed to treachery. The Frenchmen froze and starved to death. By February only ten out of 110 were fit for service. Yet still they manned the ramparts and held off the Indians.

Cartier proved to be as dauntless a soldier as he had been an enthusiastic explorer. Then, suddenly, in April spring came just in time. The snow melted and the brooks splashed. Bears crawled out from under the roots of fallen trees where they had been hibernating. Beavers appeared from their houses in the ponds. Rabbits scampered past the stockade. Moose could be heard crackling branches as they stumbled through the forest. It was the time of the annual deliverance of the North Pine Wilderness.

The river opened, and the survivors of Cartier's expedition sailed back to France, reaching there in July, 1536. After that the North Pine Wilderness kept its secrets unknown and unseen to white men for seventy years.

We can only guess what the Indians along the St. Lawrence wondered about the apparition of white men who sailed in from nowhere and then sailed off and vanished into nowhere. They must have thought of it as a dream, meeting them at the mouth of the Saguenay, escorting them to their lodges in Canada, climbing with them to the top of the lookout mountain, watching them hide in their stockade where they produced terrible thunder. And then they were gone, never to be seen again.

All this must have turned into an Indian legend for those tribes. But we shall never know the answers, just as the Indians never knew the answers. Several generations later the great-grandchildren of those Indians guided Champlain to the shore of Lake Huron.

The North Pine Wilderness is mostly spruce trees, very straight, standing side by side, equally spaced. Lower branches, smothered by dark shadows, have lost their needles and have broken off, so that the trunks are like pillars supporting a roof of interlocking needles on higher branches. The floor of this forest is a cushion of fallen needles, soft and springy to walk on. Here are scattered clumps of mushrooms and ferns and many fallen tree trunks covered with moss and lichens. The light is dim and the shadows are black.

These trees do not change much from summer to winter. They stand there just the same, holding up their dark green roof. Then

snow piles up on this roof. Sometimes the fluffy white becomes a foot deep on the outstretched branches causing the branches to bend down under the burden and a pile of snow slides to the floor of the forest. When a blizzard plays above the roof, snowflakes sift down through the branches and pour down through openings between the trees, so that in an ordinary winter in the North Pine Wilderness the floor may be buried under four feet of snow.

The North Pine Wilderness seems to have no boundary. It goes on and on, with the same trees standing side by side across a thousand square miles of valleys and hillsides and around lakes which are surrounded so densely by trees that they seem to have no shores. Only silver flashes from the largest lakes and rivers interrupt the dark green mantle that covers the earth from horizon to horizon. But the openings are everywhere, nevertheless, especially in lowlands, where shallow lakes and bogs are filled with lily pads and water weeds. These are the haunts of the wonderful fur bearing animals of the North Pine Wilderness.

The spruce trees which stand shoulder to shoulder give isolation and security to its marvelous animals. Squirrel, weasel, and marten travel swiftly through the branches. Down on the ground the black bear makes its den and hibernates under the upturned roots of a fallen tree. Squirrels bite off cones, let them drop to the ground, then scamper down and collect the seeds, which they hide under the needles on the floor for their winter's food supply. Groves of canoe birches and trembling aspens are exposed to the sun but not to the outer world. Beavers can live among the poplars by a pond

side or along a stream and build dams unknown and undisturbed—
except by wilderness enemies which they well know how to deal
with.

Deer and bear, wolf and fox, everything that runs and travels
through the North Pine Wilderness, can go their ways and enjoy
their fellows without getting in each other's way. Their trails between the trees run in every direction, connecting all the living
places of the forest far and wide. These trails are completely hidden,
running through the tunnels of the dark forest, and there is always
a black shadow to disappear into one jump away.

The giant of the North Pine Wilderness does not have to disappear. No animal dares to attack the bull moose, who stands six
feet at the shoulders and weighs half a ton. When this masculine
animal is at full power, he wears a crown of antlers, weighing sixty
pounds, that looks like colossal hands outspread with palms and
fingers made of solid bone.

The moose does not use the tunnel trails along which other
animals speed under and over fallen trunks, between trees, around
boulders, skirting ponds. The moose strides straight ahead on his
course through the woods, along a moose road bulldozed by his

big body. The forelegs of a moose seem much too long for humped back and short neck. But they act like powerful stilts with which he can step over tangled masses of fallen timber that would stop an animal with shorter legs.

Compared to his lovely, graceful relative, the white-tailed deer, the moose looks clumsy and homemade. He has a banjo muzzle; his upper lip is overlarge and droops; he is humpbacked, and a bag of loose skin, called a bell, dangles under his chin.

The moose is indeed homemade. He is the primitive creation of a monster wilderness. A moose cannot be tamed. He lives as the North Pine Wilderness lives. A moose that is put in a zoo grows thin and sad and hangs on to life only a year or so. Nobody knows the age of this superb primeval animal in the wild.

Usually moose inhabit the lowlands where black woods alternate with a swamp and thickets of birch and willow. When snow is deep in the forest, the moose stakes out an area over which he keeps trails open by constant travel. This area is known as a moose yard, and it always contains thickets of willows, striped maple, witch hazel, and other tall shrubs that stand above deep snow. There the moose's extra-long forelegs are useful for reaching the tenderest twigs at the tops of the bushes, the favorite food of a moose.

The grand old animal is not as awkward as he looks. A moose has been clocked traveling thirty-five miles per hour. He does not leap forward but gathers momentum gradually like a heavy railroad engine. He is a good swimmer, and there is nothing more graceful in the wilderness than the mirror of a pond in the silent depths with the long straight ripples of a big V from a moose nose advancing across the surface.

He may look sad and silent most of the time, but in October and November, when his antlers are full-grown and they are shining bone with all the fuzz rubbed off, he holds high his head and breaks the deep silence of the wilderness with a roaring and bawling that resounds for miles around. The emperor of the North Pine Wilderness is making himself heard.

Soon after that a strange thing happens. Early in the winter the antlers fall off, and all that is left on top of the bull moose's head are two little hairy knobs. Then the bull moose is silent. He goes off by himself to live in his moose yard until the snow melts and he can swim in the ponds and eat water lilies. Next summer his antlers will grow again, and as they build up, his confidence builds up, until the wilderness vibrates again with the roaring and bawling of the bull moose.

It is the art of the North Pine Wilderness to summon up many different kinds of fur bearing animals. They are created in all sorts of sizes and shapes, so that each fits into its own particular place in the wilderness.

Moose is big and heavy and slow on the take-off, because he does not have to catch anything and he does not have to run away from anything. His food consists of twigs peppered with buds, and bark and berries and fruit of all sorts—and he swallows a water lily and its leaves with one gulp. Things like these can be eaten at leisure, standing on stilts among trees or up to the belly in a bog.

A moose has no enemies as long as he stands high and strong on

his front legs. The other wild animals hold him in respect, and none dares consider him for dinner. But when a moose becomes old and feeble, shaky on his legs, the meat eaters suddenly begin to take notice. Let him then sit down on his haunches to rest in the moonlight; the great horned owl drops down with a flutter of feathers and huge outspread talons, ready to tear out the moose's eyes. After that a parade of scavengers, starting with the lynx, sneak up one by one, the smaller one waiting for the next larger one to finish, and chew, tear, pull their portions, leaving a few bones that soon vanish.

Nearby a young moose has been born, replacing the one which has sunk out of sight. This is the way of the North Pine Wilderness, where spruce trees standing side by side with thickets and birch and poplar groves, ponds and brooks, are in balance with the seasons and with the fur bearing animals.

Suddenly there is a scratching and scampering of little feet in the tree branches. This is a local sound, a mere whisper compared to the roar of the bull moose. In the immensity of the North Pine Wilderness this sound of little claws scratching bark seems trifling. But it is not a trifling matter to the red squirrel, who is so terror-stricken that he cannot even squeak. He must pour the full energy of each heartbeat into a race with death through the treetops.

The red squirrel is the cutest little thief of the North Pine Wilderness. He stakes out his property which is about six hundred feet across. In this estate he knows every knothole, hollow, and mouse hide-out, the direction of every fallen trunk, and where lizards, ants, and thousand-legged bugs are living. He knows every branch and twig to the top of every tree, the directions they go, and the best jumping places from one tree to another. He has planned his highways through the treetops and travels over the same routes regularly. He can leap across a space of eight feet, a tremendous distance for such a little animal. To do this he has to have a straight runway along a firm limb, and the point where he lands must be two or three feet lower than the take-off.

The red squirrel defends everything within his property, with much scolding, squealing, chattering, and baring of sharp teeth. Since he considers that everything there belongs to him, he spends much time robbing the nests of others, carrying off the seed piles of mice and the garnered treasures of chipmunks and kidnaping newly hatched birds from the nests of bluejays and woodpeckers.

Sooner or later the wilderness sends a policeman to take care of the red squirrel and restore the balance of life in the territory. This will be the pine marten or sable, which wears the most valuable fur coat in the North Woods. This animal looks like a giant golden-brown squirrel with a bushy tail and a round-eyed squirrel expression. The pine marten is very alert and travels gracefully through the treetops like a brown flash. The wildest leap from tree to tree will not save the red squirrel, because the pine marten can leap faster and farther.

The pine marten hates everything, including members of his own

family. And almost everything in the neighborhood may sometime get on the menu of this marvelous treetop runner, which includes rabbits, chipmunks, woodchucks, wood rats, mice, grouse, ducks, frogs, snakes, insects, fruits, and nuts—but red squirrel is first choice. It is as though the pine marten was specially created to streak through the forest after the red squirrel.

When a red squirrel catches sight of two eyes glowing red, slowly coming up the trunk of a tree toward him, he takes off in a panic. He knows instinctively that this is a race with death. He is lost unless he can get between rocks or inside a hollow tree where the entrance is too small for a pine marten to squeeze through. Or unless a fisher joins the race!

Fisher is the peaceful name for the terror of the North Pine Wilderness. The animal never goes fishing, but every furry thing on four legs is its meat. It is the size of a fox and it bounds over the ground like a big weasel, covering four feet at a jump. The fisher is afraid of nothing. When mad, it is a furious whirlwind. Its eyes blaze with a green light. It hisses, snarls, and screams. It arches its back and plunges into battle. The fisher can kill a deer by biting its jugular veins. It will take on a bear which is too slow and clumsy to handle a spitfire. Only a cougar, a wolverine, or a pack of wolves can repel a fisher.

The porcupine waddles around behind his battery of threatening spears, feeling as safe and carefree as any animal in the forest. Soft-nosed fur bearers who sniff at him run away with a nose full of

needles. When a fisher comes along, the porcupine goes through his usual routine. He tucks his head under a root or log, raises his quills so that they stick out in all directions from the small of his back, and lashes with his tail. The porcupine does not hurl quills, as some people think, but they stab deeply and painfully at the merest touch.

A fisher knows how to handle this situation. While he keeps his face an inch clear of the needle points, a paw flashes out, and the porcupine is whirled over on his back, exposing a soft belly where there are no quills. With a lightning stroke the fisher rips open the belly and feasts on the delicious insides of the porcupine.

This is the nature of the animal which joined in the treetop race where the pine marten was outrunning and outjumping the red squirrel through the treetops. The red squirrel is just a little way out in front. In his panic he has lost track of his usual routes of travel. He is taking desperate chances and making longer leaps between trees than he has ever made before. Trying to shake off the pursuer, he has gone higher and higher, and now he is dashing out on a high limb, from which there is no jump but only a dizzy fall of fifty feet straight down.

At this moment the fisher, hurling his body like lightning, closes the gap with the brown flash. Sharp teeth suddenly crunch into the neck of the pine marten. His body lands with a gentle thud on the needles below. The fisher turns and races down the trunk of the tree headfirst—a less violent animal would back down in respect to the law of gravity.

The red squirrel did not stop to consider the turn of events. He kept right on to the end of the high limb, leaped far out, and came to the ground fifty feet below. Then he picked himself up and ran off, chattering and mad. A red squirrel has a way of flattening his body and tail against the air to break his fall with a parachute effect as the squirrel comes down.

The last time we see this red squirrel, the smartest animal in the North Pine Wilderness, he may be sitting on a floating bit of wood with his tail curled up over his back as, with a fair wind, he sails across the pond. An Indian uses the same idea when he puts a spruce bush in the bow of his canoe and lets the wind do his work for him.

On a beautiful early summer day, June 17, 1673, a birchbark canoe paddled by two French explorers floated gently out of the mouth of the Wisconsin River into the Mississippi. This is the first record of white men reaching the western boundary of the Green Woods Wilderness at the bank of the Mississippi.

One of the men in the canoe was Louis Jolliet, who was born in Canada and was respected in the Great Lakes region as a woodsman and as knowing the languages of the Indians. It is said of him in the *Jesuit Relations* that "he has the courage to dread nothing, where everything is to be feared." The other was Jacques Marquette, a Jesuit Father who saw with great delight the wonders of the American wilderness through which they glided in their canoe.

Jolliet and Marquette were the most happy and buoyant of all the first explorers of the American wilderness. Why not? They had set forth in June, not stumbling under heavy packs, torn and baffled by dense, trackless wilderness, but riding easily in a white birchbark canoe. They followed the broad blue Great Lakes highway that carried them smoothly a thousand miles farther into the wilderness. They enjoyed blue water and blue skies, and along the shores where they made their camps tall oak, maple, cherry, and nut trees were fresh light green. Here, instead of the damp, black shadows of the spruce forest, there were sunny, green, grassy places, and brooks and springs of fresh water, and clumps of huckleberry and buffalo berry bushes. The waters abounded in fish and the woods with birds and animals, so that no man could go hungry in this land of plenty.

Marquette wrote: "We joyfully plied our paddles on Lake Huron and on that of the Illinois [Lake Michigan] and on the Bay des Puants [Green Bay]. . . . Wild oat grows in the small rivers. The grain is twice as long as that of our oats and the meal therefrom is abundant. . . . We left this bay to enter a river that is very beautiful and flows gently; it is full of bustards, ducks, teal, and other birds attracted thither by the wild oats. . . . I took time to look for a medicinal plant which a savage who knows its secret showed how its root is employed to counteract snake bites, God having been pleased to give this antidote against a poison which is very common in these countries. I put some in my canoe in order to examine it at leisure while we continued to advance."

They were traveling up the Fox River, which led them southwestward into a maze of lakes and swamps in the Lake Winnebago area. This was the critical time of their trip. They were lost in the wilderness west of the Great Lakes. No white man had seen what lay beyond this point. As long as there was any water they pushed and pulled and paddled their canoe southwestward. "The road is so full of wild oats that it is difficult to find the channel."

Where the water finally ended at a spring gushing out of the ground, they could not know how close they were to the most historic discovery of the interior American wilderness. They stood at the low divide between the St. Lawrence Valley (which includes the Great Lakes) and the Mississippi Valley. There had been rumors of a big river toward the west, but there was no sign of it here as they sat on a rock in the woods at the head of a dead-end stream and wondered what to do next.

Marquette does not tell the details of what happened next, but we know that somehow two Indians turned up and told them that

another river flowing toward the southwest was only a mile and a quarter away. "We greatly needed the two guides who conducted us to a portage of 2,700 paces and helped us to transport our canoes to enter that river they called MesKousing. [This is the first mention of the word Wisconsin, as it was spoken by the two Indians who helped Jolliet and Marquette across the portage.] After which they returned home, leaving us alone in this unknown country. Thus we left the waters flowing to Quebec [Quebec was some two thousand miles behind them, but it was still home base] to float on those that would thenceforward take us through strange lands."

The two men in the canoe were excited. This is one of the few times when explorers in the wilderness seemed to understand the importance of what they were discovering. They felt this way because the Wisconsin River was flowing westward, away from the Great Lakes and the Atlantic Ocean. Naturally they supposed that they had crossed the Great Divide of the continent. "The Mes-Kousing is very wide. A sandy bottom forms shoals. It is full of islands covered with vines. On the banks one sees fertile land with woods, prairies, and hills. There are oak, walnut, and basswood trees and another with branches armed with long thorns [honey locust]. We saw no feathered game or fish, but many deer and a large number of cattle." The cattle were American buffaloes, which at that time spilled over from the western prairies to graze in the openings in this northwest corner of the Green Woods Wilderness.

Perhaps the most important part of this adventure of the white canoe was not the discovery of the marvels of the interior wilderness but the opening of the eyes of the explorers to the beauty and abundance of life of the New World itself. Jolliet and Marquette thought that this was an exciting and interesting place to find themselves and with limitless wealth of plants and animals around them. At last explorers were turning away from the great misunderstanding that the New World wilderness was a dangerous and terrifying obstacle on the road to oriental riches. For 160 years after Columbus, Europeans continued to assault the American wilderness, trying to leave it behind them and come out on the other side.

To us it is difficult to believe that the prairies, the Great Plains, and the Rockies were almost unknown until the early nineteenth century. Even this expedition of Jolliet and Marquette had the official purpose of discovering China. The father of the mission to which Marquette belonged tells us why they were sent exploring beyond the Great Lakes: "Monsieur the Count de Frontenac, our Governor, sent them to seek a passage from here to the Sea of China by the river that discharges into the California Sea; or to verify what has for some time been said concerning the Kingdom of Quivira in which numerous gold mines are reported to exist." The French heard about Quivira from the Spaniards. This was the imaginary rich city that Cabeza heard rumors about from his Indian friends and which Coronado crossed thousands of miles of desert to find (see Chapter X). After Jolliet and Marquette had been on their way a few weeks they found themselves enjoying sights and discovering things which made them forget the Sea of China and Quivira.

Forty years before that birchbark canoe was paddled through Green Bay, an incident occurred in that area which shows how the false beliefs of Columbus still dazzled the French explorers.

A young man named Nicolet, skilled in woodcraft, had lived for two years alone with the Indians, "undergoing such fatigues as none but eye witnesses can conceive; he often passed seven or eight days without food and once seven weeks with no other nourishment than a little bark from the trees." In this way Nicolet was being trained

to go alone on a daring expedition during which he discovered Lake Michigan.

Nicolet was one man against the wilderness, and he penetrated far beyond where any white man had been before. He carried a certain package with him everywhere he went on north woods trails, around falls and rapids, and on hundreds of miles of canoeing and tramping. The package contained a damask robe. Damask is a rich silk woven with elaborate patterns and bright colors. It was the kind of robe which an oriental potentate would wear. The French governor, Champlain, gave this to Nicolet, ordering him to carry it with him through the wilderness because his mission was to find the People of the Sea who were dwellers in Asia or on the shores of the Western Ocean (the Pacific).

Nicolet probably told Champlain that he could count on him to carry out this mission. When, after months of travel, he arrived among the Winnebago Indians on the west shore of Lake Michigan, instead of wearing buckskins like an Indian he put on "the grand robe of China damask, all strewn with flowers and birds of many colors."

It appears that he decided to make good use of that package, even though he must have realized that he had not reached Asia. We know that both Champlain and Nicolet were disappointed at his finding savages instead of Moguls, fresh-water lakes instead of the Western Ocean.

Nevertheless the damask robe was a great success. He strode among the Indians wearing the glittering silk with its bright-colored patterns of birds and flowers of the Orient and bearing a pistol in each hand. They gave him a bodyguard of several young warriors and they called him "the wonderful man." The report continues: "They met him; they escorted him; they carried all his baggage. No sooner did they perceive than the women and children fled at the sight of a man who carried thunder in both hands—for thus they called the two pistols that he held. The news of his coming quickly spread to the places round about and there assembled four thousand

men. Each of the chief men made feast for him and at one of these banquets they served at least six score beavers."

The beaver is the unique animal of all the American forests. Because of its amazing skills it helped to make the wilderness; and because of its rich fur it made more history than any other wild animal of this amazing continent.

Each animal fits into its place in the wilderness. There are many different places: up in the tree branches; inside tree trunks; under bark; beneath roots of fallen trees; under stones, pine needles, and leaves; in marshes, ponds, and streams; under overhanging banks; in clumps of bushes and the tall grasses of meadows; and in hundreds of other living places—there is some kind of animal, bird, snake, frog, insect, lizard, snail, or spider which is just the right size and has just the right body tools and instincts to live in that place.

Only the beaver does not accept the living place which is presented to him. He completely rebuilds his neck of the woods. He does not merely throw together a nest like a bird or fashion a den like a bear, or run a tunnel like a woodchuck. He actually builds a house with a basement, a first floor, living room, a roof, a food-storage place, a secret back door and hallway through which he can come and go without being seen. He landscapes a few acres, with a dam so that he has his private lake and with a network of canals for transporting timber which he cuts down.

That a wild animal in the wilderness could do all these things sounds fantastic, like another wilderness legend. For the same kind of work a man would use engineers and architects, bulldozers, steam shovels, and axes—and quickly make the place unlivable for wilderness life. On the other hand, beavers and their works are a feature of the primeval wilderness. Their ponds store up water which helps plants and animals in the area in time of drought. Fishes and frogs and otters come there to live. Long-legged herons wade in them. They are stopping places for migrating ducks. Bear fish in the ponds and white-tailed deer drink in them. Muskrat, mink, and big moose come to live around the beaver pond.

The only raw materials which this builder requires are running water and a grove of trees. Trembling aspen is first choice, but willow, birch, cherry, alder, red maple, and beech will also do. The stream may be a small brook or a good-size creek, but it must not be swift with rapids or wedged between banks. The dam may be twenty feet across or three hundred. The longest beaver dam on record was two fifths of a mile.

Before he starts to build, the beaver somehow takes in the lay of the land with his blinking, beady eyes. Without surveying instruments he estimates how high the dam must be in order to give the pond a certain width and depth. He likes a big pond for a big family with plenty of room to exercise in, and he likes a deep pond that will never drop below three feet in a drought and which in the hardest winter will never freeze down to his underwater doorway and imprison his family in their house.

Moreover, a great quantity of green twigs for a winter food supply will be stored at the bottom of the pond near the house. If the pond is not deep enough, this food would be frozen in and the beavers would have no winter rations. To insure against this calamity, the height of the dam for a certain depth of the future pond must be calculated before dam building begins. This wild animal, who wobbles along clumsily with his head near the ground,

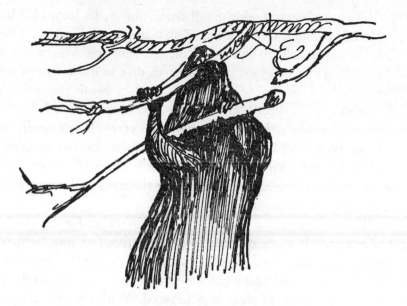

can size up the situation instantly in the heart of the woods where contours of the ground are hidden by trees and brush.

Deep in beaver land before white men ever saw it, Indians heard the crack and crash of tall falling trees. This was a familiar and pleasant sound. It meant beaver skins, beaver meat, and beaver teeth for making chisels.

A beaver can cut down a tree five inches thick in three minutes. When he sits up at the foot of a tree, his big behind gives him a firm base which he anchors by spreading his hind feet and digging the claws into the ground. The big flat tail is laid on the ground behind, where it serves as a prop. The beaver reaches up and hugs the trunk, digging in the claws of his forefeet. He opens his mouth wide and stabs into the tree with his upper teeth which sink in and hold like the sharp points of linesmen's irons. Then he slowly closes his mouth —those fat cheeks have powerful muscles. The lower teeth with sharp chisel edges are very long and curve up. They slice up through the wood toward the upper teeth, and in this way the beaver bites out a big chip, as deep and clean as an ax could do it.

When the beaver feels the tall trunk quiver, he jumps back and waits a few seconds. If it doesn't fall, it needs another bite. Then it crackles on the stump and sways crazily while the beaver watches. At the final crash all beavers in the area dive into the nearest water and vanish. After a few seconds little noses break the water and beady eyes scan the woods to make sure that no dreaded enemy, hearing the crash, has come running over. Timber wolf, bear, weasel, lynx, and bobcat enjoy beaver meat, not to mention an Indian. After a respectful three or four minutes the beavers come out of the pond, gallop back up among the trees, and continue their forestry operations.

The beaver uses tree trunks and larger branches for dam building and repair. They are cut into logs about five feet long which are nudged, pushed, pulled, and floated to the dam. He also spends much time building canals, sometimes five hundred feet long, to float the logs to places where they will be used. With tree trunks as the foundation of the dam the beaver piles on stones, twigs, mud, wet leaves and perhaps throws on the discarded antler of a moose.

After working all summer felling trees, building and repairing dams, the beaver is ready to build his lodge in the pond. This may be fifteen feet across and five feet high. It has one big living room for the beaver family with a floor above the water level and a trap door in the floor into a tunnel of branches in the basement. The frame of the house consists of heavy poles and thick sticks. Its dome is a tangle of claw-proof branches, plastered with mud. Beavers never stop growing, so an old beaver needs a bigger house.

The lynx is on the prowl and very hungry in winter. He may catch beaver scent filtering through the dome of the beaver's house. Lynx eyes glow like two coals in the dusk of the winter woods. His fierce screech breaks the silence as he whirls across the snow and leaps onto the beaver house, but this bloodthirsty prowler's claws are caught and tangled as they tear into the twigs and his teeth scratch on mud frozen as hard as iron. The beaver and his family sit in their home enjoying a dinner of soft green wood which they

have hauled up from the water below, paying no attention to the screeching lynx who is tearing at their roof. Finally the lynx, still maddened by the odor of the beavers, sneaks away hissing and disappears as a gray shadow into the forest.

In March, when nights are freezing and daylight sunshine is warm, water flows from under the deep snow and slides over the ice of brooks and ponds. Snowbanks shrink; spots of wet red leaves appear under trees; icicles on stony cliffs drip fast and ice tinkles from little ledges. Fuzzy tassels dangle from the tips of aspen twigs. Willow bushes are covered with white puffs, and the tops of the red maples are suddenly tinted with bright red against the blue sky. A beaver slides down his tunnel and swims upward toward a white patch of water, sticks his little head out, and takes a good look. Then beavers who had been sitting in their house in darkness through the winter months become excited with energy. They ram jagged holes through the rotting ice along the shores of their pond. They pick out an aspen where the snow has melted away from the base and fell it with furious joy!

A snowshoe rabbit, which had spent most of the winter hiding in deep snowdrifts and trembled with terror when the lynx passed that way, jerks with surprise. Everything is changing—his long white hairs are falling off and he is turning mottled brown. At the same time his deep, fluffy snowdrift is disappearing into thin air.

The whole world is changing. High overhead a flock of Canada geese cleave the sky with their big wedge. They are honking, gabbling, calling to one another as they press northward, looking for an open river where they can drop down, rest, and feed. Down where the snowshoe rabbit is turning his head this way and that, wondering what to do next, the woodcock and jacksnipe are bouncing up and down, making a trembling, whistling sound with the air rushing through their feathers. Through those odd sounds the slow beat of a drum can be heard—*thrump! thrump! thrump!* The beat sound grows faster, quickens to a sustained roll, then sudden silence. Again the drumbeat and the roll and silence. It is the ruffed grouse celebrating spring. Like the odd sounds of woodcock and jacksnipe this is not made by vocal cords. The ruffed grouse drumbeat is made by lightning vertical strokes of its wings. It is the same kind of sound as thunder or as a jet plane breaking the sound barrier.

These sounds are music to the snowshoe rabbit's ears. He has been waiting for spring as eagerly as the others in the wilderness. His familiar snowdrift which had loomed so large is now only wet humps and bumps and stained by brown rabbit pellets. Silently a little cloud casts a shadow on the snowshoe rabbit. There is no more time to be surprised or to think or enjoy. He is suddenly paralyzed, and the wilderness disappears in blackness. His leap and squeak of terror are cut short as sharp talons pierce his flesh. His head droops limply as he is jerked up into the air and the snowy owl carries off its prey. The wilderness has awakened in the spring.

CHAPTER VIII

THE FAR GRASS WILDERNESS

WHEN Jolliet and Marquette paddled into the Mississippi River in 1673, the push westward seemed to have reached a final goal. The French explorers who had made their end run so deep into the continent were now carried southward by the Father of Rivers. Nine years later La Salle completed the circuit by paddling his canoe out of the mouth of the Mississippi into the Gulf of Mexico. It seems unbelievable to us who know so well the wonders of America's Far West that they were locked in mystery, unseen and unknown, for a hundred years after the French reached the Mississippi.

Of course people could see plenty of land toward the west. All of a sudden they could see very far. It was startling to look across the grass to the horizon, after having struggled for thousands of miles across lakes with shores hedged by tall trees and along rivers and trails blinded by timber. Those explorers had come to know the deep forest and how to live on its abundance of food and shelter like the Indians. They enjoyed its surprises and its people. No wonder that after reaching the Mississippi they stopped to explore new trails on the *east* side of the river. Their pleasure in that woodland is expressed by Antoine Cadillac who led fifty soldiers and fifty settlers to found Detroit in 1701. Cadillac said:

"They are the finest lands I've ever seen, broken by an infinitude of large and beautiful rivers which replenish all the lakes. They are covered with virgin forests of elm, walnut, chestnut, oak, cherry, and hazel trees. There are long avenues of apple and plum. And an infinite number of animals—deer, elk, moose, beavers, and abundance of small game, bustards, geese, ducks, teal, pigeons, partridges, quail, Indian pheasants and others." Cadillac saw no bustards. This is a European bird so heavy, perhaps thirty pounds, that it has much trouble getting off the ground. In France they hunted bustards on horseback. Cadillac probably saw the great sand-hill crane which nested in Michigan in his day. This giant bird also has trouble getting off the ground. It would stalk across a grassy place in the warm evening light, give a loud croak which could be heard a long way and startle a man. While croaking, it would spread its big wings, fan the air with whooshing strokes, rise a couple of feet from the ground and settle back into the grass.

Men dazzled by a wilderness like this would catch sight of nothing west of the Mississippi to excite their curiosity. Of course there was then no hint of the terrific glaciers and forests, grizzly bears and waterfalls of the Rocky Mountains, a thousand miles out of sight beyond the Far Grass Wilderness.

The outlook that stopped explorers at the Mississippi for three generations is described by a young Englishman named Ruxton who crossed the prairie in 1847: "No scenery in nature is more dreary and monotonous than the aspect of the grand prairies through which we have been passing. Nothing meets the eye but a vast, undulating, expansive arid waste; the buffalo grass never grows higher than two or three inches and is seldom green—the prairie never looks green and turflike. Not a tree or shrub is to be seen except on the creeks where a narrow strip of unpicturesque cotton-woods occasionally relieves the eyes. The sky, too, is generally overcast and storms sweep incessantly over the bare plains, boisterous winds prevailing at all times, carrying a chilling sleet or clouds of driving snow." Ruxton was certainly bored and uncomfortable about the prairie.

The Far Grass Wilderness kept its secrets through the eighteenth century while the rest of the continent was being framed by discovery. The Spanish were well established in New Mexico and Arizona. Spanish missions dotted the California coast as far north as San Francisco. Drake had long since rounded South America and explored the Pacific coast as far north as Oregon. In 1741 Bering saw the mainland of Alaska and his people built a well-timbered house there. The Spaniards for many years had been ship-building on the Pacific coast and going there by way of the Philippines. The English were also coming across the Pacific and turning from explorers into traders on the west coast. The north side of the great frame ran across Canada, where the explorers were French and English trappers. They did not cross the "vast naked prairie" but were led westward by the beaver through the streams and lakes of the North Pine Wilderness.

Because they were canoe men the French did not penetrate far beyond Lake Superior for a long time. They built waterside log forts to which Indians brought furs, some of them from mysterious depths of wilderness farther west. The Indians told glowing stories of the countries where these furs came from, and they drew crude maps on birch bark or traced them with a finger in the sand while bearded Frenchmen in their deerskins crowded around, speculating and arguing about what the land west of Superior was like.

At last one daredevil, named La Vérendrye, decided to leave his canoe at the lakeside and take off on foot into the unknown. He established an outpost fort several hundred miles west of Lake Superior to impress the Indians and get first choice of the furs which they brought from wilderness where no white man had ever trod. The fort did business for a few years but its doom was sealed—it was too far out, too far west. The day came when the twenty Frenchmen at the post were massacred, after which the logs of the fort decayed and the wilderness swallowed it up. But before that happened a bold, personal first discovery was made.

La Vérendrye was not feeling well so he sent his two sons to explore *south*west. This was a contrary direction. The forest and beavers were northwest, and all rumors had it that southward the land was desolate and worthless. But another rumor had reached the Vérendryes that did not relate to beavers; it had traveled all the way across the prairie—some Indians very far away in the setting sun had horses. This was sensational—the wild horses of America had disappeared with the Ice Age; if Indians had horses they must have got them from Spaniards around the Gulf of California, an arm of the Pacific Ocean. When this rumor reached one of the La Vérendrye boys, who was called the Chevalier, it swept from his mind all thoughts of beavers, and he was lured by the old vision of reaching the Western Sea (the Pacific).

The Chevalier, on foot with a small, fast-moving party of French-men and Indians, laid a course west-southwest. They pressed across the northern prairie and the high plains, staring at the empty hori-zons, each day yearning for a glimpse of the horse Indians. They traversed the Dakotas and, as nearly as their reports can be in-terpreted, they reached a point where today southeast Montana, northeast Wyoming, and South Dakota meet. Like clouds on the horizon they caught sight of tremendous mountains in the distance, probably the Big Horn Range of the Rockies.

Then, instead of throwing a hat in the air, shaking hands, and firing off a musket in celebration of the discovery of the other side of the Far Grass Wilderness, they turned around and went back to the lakes and beavers. Mountains were not the Western Sea! The first white men to see the Rockies felt frustrated, deeply disappointed; their mission was a failure. And thus the old pattern was repeated. Men who had extended themselves to the brink of starvation and death while discovering another wonder of the American wilderness, did not know what they had found and felt only defeat.

In 1913 two school friends, Harriet and George, fifteen years old, were crossing a field near Pierre, South Dakota. Harriet stumbled over a piece of metal sticking up where the field had been plowed. She gave it a kick; it was loose. They picked it up and saw words carved on it with a sharp knife. It turned out to be a copper marker with which Vérendrye had claimed that land for King Louis XV of France one hundred seventy years before. On one side Latin words said that this was the property of the French Crown. French words on the other side said, "Placed here by Chevalier La Vérendrye the 30th of March 1743."

Sixty years after Chevalier La Vérendrye the big country between the Mississippi and the Pacific coast was still an unexplored blank on the map. But fantastic rumors about the Far West were reaching the Mississippi frontier.

Beyond the sunset lived Indians the size of giants. There were deadly serpents which, forming big hoops by taking their tails in their mouths, could roll downhill, catch their victims, and strike

them dead. One thousand miles up the Missouri River rose a mountain of pure salt, 180 miles long, forty-five miles wide, without a tree or blade of grass on its dazzling white surface. Streams of pure salt water gushed out of caves in this mountain. There were prairies with a peculiar fertility where no trees would grow, but the grasses were so rich, millions and millions of giant animals grazed on them. In one area there were castles with towers and spires and red walls built by the giant Indians.

Such tall tales (with much truth in them that people laughed off) were brought back by individual trappers who were pushing up rivers into the West. They had picked them up from Indians and from other French trappers they had met. By 1800 everybody in the young United States was excited by strong stories coming across the Mississippi from unknown lands out West where vague areas were claimed by Spain and France.

When President Jefferson signed the Louisiana Purchase in 1803, suddenly the size of the United States was doubled. The country's territory now stretched to the crest of the Rockies, from Louisiana to Montana. But Americans did not know what they had purchased. They had not surveyed or even seen the land before concluding the biggest real estate deal in history.

President Jefferson proposed to find out. He got an appropriation from Congress to send a military-exploring party from St. Louis up the Missouri River, hoping it would connect with another river that would lead them to the Pacific coast, and he appointed his personal secretary, Merriwether Lewis, and Captain Clark of the small but bold U.S. Army to take charge of this expedition.

Before the astounding cross-continent thrust of Lewis and Clark, America was discovered bit by bit. One great surprise after another turned up while people were looking for something else. The bigness was revealed slowly. English colonies along the Atlantic coast were content to linger on the coastal plain for a hundred years. It took over two hundred years and five generations of Frenchmen to make the great end run from the Gulf of St. Lawrence to New

Orleans. But Lewis and Clark, under pressure of an excited popular curiosity and spurred by a young nation of reckless energy, rose to leadership on the level of supermen. They crossed unsurmountable obstacles to journey from the Mississippi River to the coast of Oregon and report back to Washington in three years. Thus two of the biggest and most fantastic wildernesses, the Far Grass and the Monster Mountain, in America were discovered in one fell swoop.

Lewis and Clark found the soul of truth in the tall tales about the Far West which people had been hearing. On their way up the Missouri they saw rock formations like the towers and castles of the giants. They had seen the country of giants, mountains with huge glaciers, ravines a mile deep, and bigger trees than any man had ever seen before. They were not chased by snakes which rolled like hoops, but they had to dodge fierce rattlers that poured from the cliffs and boulders of the mesas. And as for the millions and millions of giant animals (the cattle of the giant Indians) grazing across an endless, treeless plain—they certainly beheld that spectacle!

During the next fifty years the Far Grass Wilderness was going to breed its own race of men—cowboys, buffalo hunters, Pony Express riders, saddle men who could take a mustang across the prairie at an average day and night speed of ten miles per hour. But there was no such breed of prairie men the day when Lewis and Clark left their base camp on the Mississippi and vanished for three years into the sunset.

They organized a party of twenty-five soldiers, two interpreters (Frenchmen from the north wilderness trapping country with a smattering of Indian language), and some expert hunters to bring in the food, also a colored man named York who was Lewis' slave, and an Indian girl. This good-sized party needed tons of supplies for an unknown time completely cut off among unknown dangers. Their requisition list included one cannon, guns, pistols, ammunition, spears, knives, metals in all forms, blacksmith forge and hammers, tailoring equipment, carpenter's tools for building boats and houses, staple foods and cooking equipment, medical supplies, and a load of "trading money" such as bright-colored cloths, hats, knives, beads, mirrors, little bells, and all sorts of gewgaws to buy friendship from savages who might want to drive off the white trespassers in their primeval wilderness.

They built a bateau (flatboat with a keel) fifty-five feet long with an enormous square sail and twenty-two oars, also two little piraguas with square sails and six oars each. Such craft could sail only before the wind, so they waited for a day with a tail wind and set sail up the Missouri hollering and shooting off guns "under three cheers from the gentlemen on the bank." Thus the classic Lewis and Clark Expedition embarked as though they were about to sail across a sea. The next generation would substitute prairie schooners for sailboats.

The squadron rounded a bend in the river and it was hardly out of hearing of the huzzahs from the gentlemen on the bank when the wind changed, the current slapped them against a sand bar, they got caught on snags, and they were forced to stop and camp for the night. The Missouri River, with its swift and treacherous currents, its shifting sandbars, banks that are constantly undermined and caving in, tricky winds, snags, shoals, and willow thickets standing halfway across the river in muddy water, does not offer first-class sailing. This is especially true if the boat is heavily overloaded, with a square sail that is hard to tack where a whirlpool takes hold of the bow and a crosscurrent slams the stern into a sand bar. Moreover, when men must constantly leap overboard and push and pull the boat, wet and cold, up to their waists in water, it is not enjoyable sailing.

That water was the wilderness home of the alligator gar, the most ferocious and the biggest fresh-water fish in America. This nine-foot monster had the skull of a dinosaur and the jaws of an alligator. It could take and eat a man fast—it had waited thousands of years for these men to come along.

But the Missouri with all its snags, shoals, tumbling banks, and whirlpools never quits. It comes from out of the faraway and swirls, splashes, and creeps across a thousand miles of plains and prairies. But also the two captains didn't quit. They and their soldiers, hunters, interpreters, and York rowed, pulled on ropes, stood in the water and pushed, fought their way step by step, mile by mile, week after week, month after month, for a year on the river which Lewis noted in his journal, "They deemed endless."

Thirteen months after the start one of the soldiers, McNeal, "exultingly stood with a foot on each side of the rivulet and thanked his God that he had lived to bestride the mighty Missouri." Two miles farther Lewis reached the source of the Missouri, a spring of ice-cold water issuing from the base of a mountain. They had crossed the Far Grass Wilderness and found themselves staring at the white peaks of the Rocky Mountains.

With no maps, no knowledge of passes, ravines, or waterfalls, no way to fight snowdrifts or knowledge of where to look for trails through the forests of giant trees, the supermen faced the Monster Mountain Wilderness and tried to figure out a way to go beyond to the headwaters of the Columbia River. This was an order from President Jefferson. They did this impossible feat and returned by the same route to tell the tale, mostly thanks to two members of their party.

One of the French interpreters had brought along an Indian wife, a Shoshone girl, sixteen years old, who had been captured in the Rocky Mountains by the Blackfoot Indians, brought over to the

Lake Superior area, and sold to the Frenchman. Her Indian name was Sa-ga-ja-wea, which means "Bird Woman." Indians were named after the animals and elements of the wilderness—chiefs for strong and fearful animals, like "Sitting Bull," and squaws for gentle creatures like fawns and birds.

Sa-ga-ja-wea was shy, little, and sweet, and perhaps the least member of this party of dauntless men, but she was destined to be one of the most indestructible and daring members of the party.

While snowed in during their first winter in North Dakota, Sa-ga-ja-wea had a baby. At the same time her French interpreter husband compelled her to work hard without a pause, scraping skins, bringing water, digging roots, and so on. She moved heavily, doing what she was told, no complaint, no comment, her face dispassionate, showing neither joy nor sorrow, as though all this slaving was unimportant to her.

One day Clark saw her huddled in a corner, blanket over head, the most miserable, dejected-looking person in camp. He ordered one of his soldiers to give her a sip of tea and some stewed fruit. She did not thank him, did not speak, but from that day on she watched Clark with a bit of astonishment. Her attitude toward him was that of his faithful dog.

One morning in March they looked out from behind their snowdrifts, saw blue sky and a wedge of ducks headed north. Spring comes suddenly to the prairie. In the Rocky Mountains a few months later when they knew not which stream to follow, which ravine would let them squeeze through, where to find trails in the dark forest, where the headwaters of the Columbia were hidden in a maze of mountains and forest, it was Sa-ga-ja-wea (who had been carrying her baby on her back those hundreds of miles) who then stepped up and pointed the way. She was a Shoshone and this was her homeland.

Some time later they met a band of Indians prepared to kill them. At first sight the Indians ran away before anybody could speak to them, but Sa-ga-ja-wea suddenly jumped up and ran forward, call-

ing out strange syllables, and burst into tears. The young Indian chief was her brother!

Lewis wrote in his diary, "The meeting of those people was really affecting, particularly between Sa-ga-ja-wea and an Indian woman who had been taken prisoner at the same time with her and who had afterwards escaped and rejoined her nation."

After that the Indians who had come so close to murdering every last member of the party helped them to find the headwaters of the Columbia River. They built canoes and started on a long and dangerous trip down the Columbia, starving, cold, wet, and among savage Indian tribes who were bent on killing them every time they made camp. One night the treacherous Indians pretended to be friends, sitting around a campfire, holding the white men in conversation while other Indians surrounded the party in the darkness, preparing to take their scalps.

In this terrible danger the negro York scrambled to his feet. Indian fashion, he began to show off with rough play. He had tremendous muscles and could perform unheard-of feats of strength, such as pushing over a good-sized tree, lifting a horse—or picking up a husky Indian and throwing him over the crowd, a feat which made them all laugh. The bulky negro told the Indians he had once been a wild animal but that he had been caught and tamed by his master. They blinked at him through their war paint and grew silent and afraid. York, who was as tired and hungry as any man there, knew that he must dance and holler, leap into the air, and toss Indians around, keeping them spellbound all night if need be. It was desperate work. At last the meeting broke up at sunrise through the sheer exhaustion and stupor of the Indians, and York and the white men got some peaceful sleep and slipped off.

The explorers, hunters, and trappers who trailed westward by the hundreds across the Far Grass Wilderness on the heels of Lewis and Clark soon came to know and love the distance. It was the biggest and best dimension of America. It offered men the widest and purest freedom they had ever known.

The prairie is like the sea in the way the whole dome of the sky comes down to a clean circle of the horizon in which a man finds himself standing in the exact center. It is like the sea also in the way the weather suddenly changes from gentle and friendly to dangerous and violent. It has large weather—great winds, tornadoes, thunderstorms that shake the ground, blizzards that suddenly make nothingness of earth and sky, and raging fire storms, in which ghosts of flames roar and run over the horizons, brandishing torches that make hundreds of square miles of prairie glow red.

It took men awhile to get used to this fearful wilderness. One of the great explorers, Zebulon Pike (Pike's Peak is named after him), was doing a bold job of discovery at the same time as Lewis and Clark. Pike was the first man to describe the prairie in Kansas and Nebraska and he called it "a desert—a barrier—placed by Providence to keep the American people from a thin diffusion and ruin." Pike, along with many others who first saw the prairie, evidently thought that the young nation would be much better off settling in the Green Woods Wilderness east of the Mississippi.

From the Mississippi the prairie gradually slopes upward across a thousand miles until it is about a mile high at the base of the Rockies. Since this upward slope is very gradual, the prairie looks flat all the way across. The eastern part of the prairie down in the Mississippi Valley is wetter, but as it gets higher and higher westward, it becomes drier and drier. The high, dry part of the prairie which lies against the wall of the Rocky Mountains is known as the High Plains. Here there is little rainfall. The air is dry. Nights are cold. The ground is arid with desert touches of sagebrush and prickly-pear cactus.

In the mountain wilderness that walls the west side of the High Plains there are deep snows, torrential streams roaring out of glaciers, and dark forests of giant trees. This is because the mountains have intercepted clouds riding the westerly winds and bringing moisture from the Pacific. They dump their rain and snow on the mountains and there is not enough moisture left over when they reach the plains to build forests of trees. It may be a hundred miles from one tree to the next. The only true prairie tree is the cottonwood (a kind of poplar) which is not a forest tree but needs the bright light of a full sky and has roots which plunge so deep that they can collect water from thirty to forty feet underground. Two or three cottonwoods grow by a spring. A straggling line of cottonwoods follows the bed of a river.

These few tall trees were rare landmarks that appeared like a mirage on the horizon, signaling a camping spot for the pioneers who crossed the prairie. Even if the spring or the bed of the river was dry, a cottonwood tree said that water was near the surface. They could dig a hole where, in an hour or two, a few cups or buckets of water would collect. But a few cottonwood trees standing alone in the dim distance only emphasized the vastness of the blanket of grass of the Far Grass Wilderness.

One man who explored west of the Mississippi in the early 1800s turned back when he was halfway across, thought he was lucky to get out of it alive, and wrote his mother: "To the traveler who traverses for several days these prairies and barrens, they are uninviting and disagreeable. He may travel from morning until night and make good speed but on looking around he fancies himself at the very spot whence he started. A dull uniformity of prospects spreads out immense . . . no running brooks, no sound of woodland music."

But why is there no forest in the eastern, wetter part of the prairie? Why are the outriders of the Green Woods Wilderness, such as bur oak and box elder, stopped from spreading westward by the American prairie? The answer is that a peculiar grass matting created the prairie as a strange and different wilderness.

Prairie grasses hold their long, slender leaves straight up in crowded masses. This permits sunlight to slide down the length of every grass blade, which greatly multiplies the amount of light energy that plant receives. One acre of prairie grass offers ten acres of leaf surface to the sun. Since the grass does not have trunks and branches to build, the food energy made by this light-catching apparatus goes into the roots. Roots of prairie grass may be five to twelve feet deep, and they grow at great speed, pushing down perhaps a half inch every day!

But the miracle of these roots is the way they form a tangled network, instead of plunging down with a single taproot as does a tree. This network is so compact, has so many millions of branches, that with its microscopic hairs the total length of a root system packed inside one cubic inch of prairie soil may be four fifths of a mile long. One of these grass plants may grow fifty-four miles of roots in eighty days. That is at the rate of a hundred miles per year!

In winter all the life of prairie grasses retreats into the roots, entirely underground. This is the perfect way for a plant to survive on the prairie, and the prairie grasses have evolved this way of life through thousands of years, slowly, while mountains were pushed up and glaciers retreated and the wide slope of the prairie was flattened.

The roots of prairie grasses, although in a constant life-and-death struggle with each other, have an exclusive franchise for the prairie soil. They shut out competition which includes that of the seeds of trees than cannot penetrate the tight sod of the prairie grasses. Few other plants could grow upon the primeval prairie wilderness so long as these amazing grass roots were unbroken by a plow.

This masterpiece of prairie life wins on another count. Prairie grass not only retreats underground in winter, safe from furious freezing winds and tornadoes, but also it is fireproof. Between the meager rains of spring and the blizzards of winter a drastic drought strangles the prairie in late summer and fall. The grasses turn red and dry, covering the prairie with inflammable straw. Then those ghosts of the prairie fire light their torches and the roar of the fire storm is heard. This does not hurt the prairie grasses; they are all roots, deep, moist, rich. They live in a vault in the ground which they have built for themselves. Trees and shrubs could not survive —a forest fire is terribly destructive—while a prairie fire has little effect on the grasses that will burst out fresh and green again in the spring.

When a prairie fire comes along, every living thing above ground must either run or dig or die. For example, what happens to a man on a horse was described by George Katman in 1832: "The hell of fires are driven forward by the hurricanes which sweep over the vast prairies of this denuded country. Before such a wind, the fire travels at an immense and frightful rate and often destroys on their fleetest horses parties of Indians . . . not that it travels as fast as a horse at full speed but impediments render it necessary for the rider to guide his horse in the zigzag paths of buffaloes until he is overtaken by the dense column of smoke that is swept before the fire, alarming the horse, which stops and stands terrified. The burning grass wafted in the wind falls about him, kindling up in a moment a thousand new fires, which are instantly wrapped in the swelling flood of smoke that is moving on like a black thunder cloud rolling on the earth with its lightning's glare and its thunder rumbling as it goes."

This tells us what kind of animals had to be created to live on the Far Grass Wilderness. They must either run or dig, and there can be no climbers!

The pronghorn antelope has a beautiful slender body with every part and dimension designed to make it one of the fastest running wild animals on earth. The pronghorn can sprint a mile a minute, and on a long run it can average forty miles per hour. Two pronghorns may start a race on impulse at any second. A little pronghorn is born, staggers to its feet, and starts running within twenty-four hours after it is born. Little pronghorns play tag by tearing off in one direction for a quarter of a mile and then darting off in another direction for half a mile.

Standing on the prairie, pronghorns lift high their heads on long necks; slowly revolving them, they tune in on every foot of the circle of the horizon with three senses. Tall ears can pick up the footstep of buffalo or the scurry of a coyote a long way off. Deep

sensitive nostrils are wide and moist and quiver, picking up the most delicate scent passing in the air. Large round eyes, steady and keen, detect and study everything that has the slightest motion all the way to the horizon.

The great distances of the prairie give a sense of being little and alone. When Washington Irving visited the prairie in 1832 he wrote, "To one unaccustomed to it, there is something inexpressibly lonely in the solitude of a prairie. The loneliness of a forest seems nothing to it. There the view is shut in by trees and the imagination is less free to picture some lovelier scene beyond. But here we have

an immense extent of landscape without a sign of existence. We have the consciousness of being far, far beyond."

The same sense of loneliness makes prairie animals live in herds or groups. The bigger the crowd, the more comfortable they feel. Pronghorns and buffaloes have their herds. Coyotes have their packs, prairie dogs their cities.

It might seem that pronghorns which bounce and streak across the grass with lightning changes of direction must be strong individualists who cannot live in a herd. But the pronghorn herd is one of the most remarkable groups of wild animals in the world. It is scattered far and wide over the prairie, yet each member is a sentinel for the whole herd. Five miles may separate one animal from another in the same herd, but they are together. This is due to their wonderful system for signaling to each other.

The rumps on the rear of each animal have large patches of long hairs, called rosettes. When things are quiet in the vicinity and there are no pronghorn alarms and excursions, the rosettes on the rump lie down like the rest of the animal's fur. But sooner or later comes a suspicion of danger. The pronghorn head jerks up; the animal freezes for a second, checking the scent, the sound, the movement in the grass. If it repeats, the animal bounds off in the opposite direction. It does not utter a sound, but the long hairs of the rosettes on the rump stand erect and flash white like a powder puff. When another pronghorn sees this, he also erects his rosettes and takes off. The signal passes from one to another, and quickly white flashes dot the prairie as the scattered pronghorns bounce off, all running toward the same part of the horizon.

And fast and far they should go, if the alarm was set off by a motion in the grass where a coyote was sneaking. The coyote is a little, fluffy, gray-furred, wild dog with a special yearning to enjoy the graceful pronghorn body for dinner. Although half the size of a wolf, coyotes were always called wolves by the first people who crossed the prairie.

The coyote is the second fastest runner on the prairie, making

about forty miles per hour on a sprint and twenty-four miles per hour on a distance run. This does not outrun the pronghorn, but the coyote, one of the cleverest animals in any wilderness, has worked out a strategy. Two, sometimes three or four, coyotes take their stations along a course where they plot to make a pronghorn run a race of death.

The first coyote pops up below the pronghorn, drawing its lips back from its teeth as though grinning. At this fearful sight the pronghorn flashes its rosettes and streaks off with the coyote in pursuit but falling farther and farther behind. Then, when the pronghorn is far ahead, coyote number two takes up the chase, and so on. The poor pronghorn zigzags back and forth between the coyotes. The desperate burst of speed is tiring. Finally the spent pronghorn slows to below twenty-four miles per hour and the coyotes close in.

But the pronghorn has a fierce battery of weapons to use when cornered. His hoofs are very sharp and he can kick with lightning strokes. A little wild dog may be left a bleeding carcass. But other coyotes pay no attention to their fallen comrade and hurl themselves at the neck of the pronghorn. Their only concern is with a good dinner. The other pronghorns also pay no more attention to the incident. They are safe over the horizon. So life and death go on in the Far Grass Wilderness.

The prairie wilderness is equally generous with places for animals which live vertically. Within and underneath the grass sod are cool, moist depths of soft earth where many champion diggers drop their shafts. Among these the pocket gopher, with swollen shoulder muscles as a power plant, and using its foreclaws as a fast mechanical digging machine, is a nimble excavator.

The pocket gopher has an odd way for avoiding the need to turn around in its tunnels. It has sensitive whiskers out in front when going forward and sensitive hairs on its tail when going in reverse; thus, underground, it runs forward and back with equal ease. The animal is named for the bulbous fur-lined pockets on each side of its head. These pockets have flaps opening to the outside—unlike the puffy cheeks of a chipmunk. The pocket gopher cuts grass into three-inch lengths, which it bales up and stuffs into its cheek pockets. Then it plunges into its tunnels with the two fat loads of hay for fodder and bedding.

Kangaroo rats are slow diggers and do not run long tunnels like pocket gophers. They build mounds perhaps fifteen feet across and four feet high riddled with tunnels. This architecture protects the labyrinthian home from flooding in a cloudburst. The kangaroo rat comes out of its pueblo only at night to collect grass, seeds, and husks. Instead of running like an ordinary rat, this animal's long hind legs act as powerful springs, so that it can travel with eight-foot leaps—exactly like a little kangaroo. When terrified by the staring eyes of an owl, it goes so fast it seems to be shivering and wringing its hands while running erect on its hind legs.

The dry corridors, stocked with seeds and choice grass tips, attract a miscellaneous crowd. The kangaroo rat may find it is sharing its mound of tunnels with lizards, snakes, centipedes, scorpions, spiders, crickets, beetles, ants, and millipedes. We don't know how they all get along together, but viewed from above the surface, the kangaroo rat's mound looks like a peaceful dome of earth on the prairie floor.

As for the champion digger, two trophies must be awarded—one for the fastest, the other for the farthest.

No other animal in the world can dig faster than a badger. The badger is broad and flat with stubby, bowlegs and is pigeon-toed. While searching through a prairie-dog town, he appears to be clumsy and lazy, but if the shadow of a big animal like an antelope, a buffalo, or a man falls on him, he digs so fast that he fades away into the ground. As he uses all four claws, the dirt splashes out for yards around, and in a few seconds the tail is vanishing into a turmoil of dirt. The badger's living quarters may be six feet deep at the end of a thirty-foot slanting tunnel.

The badger hunts underground. It digs so fast that it can pursue the pocket gopher, field mouse, land squirrel, mole, marmot, burrowing owl, mouse, wood rat, lizard, and prairie dog beneath the surface of the prairie. It never hunts on the surface; it never eats grass or other vegetations. It is a fierce hunter of underground prey —but always where the ground is especially deep and soft, as in the knolls and ridges of the Far Grass Wilderness.

Compared to the ill-natured badger, the prairie dog is a comical little animal with fat cheeks and a twinkle in his eye. Pioneers who discovered the prairie-dog cities far out on the lonely prairie found the "squirrels" amusing company and often held their fire just to enjoy a laugh.

In the primeval prairie wilderness the underground cities of prairie dogs, with populations in the millions, stretched for miles and miles through well-worn tunnels. Each prairie-dog family owns a mound three or four feet high surrounding the entrance to its tunnels like the rim of a volcano. The mound is both a dike that keeps out a rush of cloudburst water and also a lookout tower.

The entrance shaft goes straight down, sometimes as far as sixteen feet. When a prairie dog, sitting on its haunches on top of the mound, catches sight of anything that moves, other than clouds and waving grass, he dives headfirst and vanishes in a split second.

On the way down the long shaft the prairie dog brakes his fall with his body, which just fits the tunnel, and thus arrives gently at the bottom without bumping his head. But usually the prairie dog arrests his dive about four feet down, where he has hollowed out a guardroom to sit in. After waiting there quietly for a while, he stretches his neck, peeks out, and takes a good look around. If the danger is past or it is a false alarm, he climbs out and resumes activities on the surface of the prairie. The activities consist of grazing on grasses, seeds, and roots. A prairie dog never stores food in his burrow, and if he is forced to stay below for many days in cold or stormy weather, he simply lives off the fat of his body.

Although each prairie-dog family has its own establishment, prairie dogs never live off by themselves. They must have neighbors and enjoy the life of a big city. Their mounds resemble giant doughnuts, scattered far and wide across the prairie. Each mound has a prairie dog sitting up on his haunches on guard when the coyote alarm has sounded in the city.

But the prairie is so generous with mileage for its runners that the coyote pack may be many miles away, plotting a relay race of death with a herd of pronghorns. At such time about 20 per cent of

the prairie dogs will be sitting up on their haunches, craning their necks, on guard, while 80 per cent of them have their heads down, stuffing themselves with grass and seeds on the prairie spaces between the mounds.

But even grazing prairie dogs are tied into the alarm system of the big city. One feeds for about ten seconds and then automatically sits up and looks around for two or three seconds. At all times about one out of five is on guard, while four prairie dogs are feeding close by. This efficient alarm system distributes the guards evenly throughout the city, and it works for every community, whether the population is a few hundred or in the millions.

In the lower eastern areas of the Far Grass Wilderness the grasses are tall. In some places a man on a horse will be entirely hidden when riding through them, and if the horseman is out looking for lost cattle, he may have to stand on his saddle to spot them by the motion of the tall grasses. In contrast to this, up on the High Plains there seems to be almost no grass at all. But a bright green flush appears on the High Plains in early spring and runs rapidly with the thawing from south to north. This is the wonderful buffalo grass.

The blades of buffalo grass are only a couple of inches tall but so dense that hundreds of blades grow in a square inch. Because of massive root systems deep in the ground, buffalo grass is unharmed either by trampling hoofs or massive grazing. A grazing animal can chew off this grass and it springs up again unharmed, ready to be eaten a few days later. Thus the tremendous energy of this short grass oozes up through the prairie floor from underground food storage in the roots, spreads far and wide across the High Plains, where it is converted into the heaviest, strongest wild animal of all the American wildernesses. The short-grass country is the mother-land of the buffalo or American bison.

Standing there with sagging head, which looks too big for his body, the buffalo seems clumsy, tired, unhappy. But the head looks much bigger and heavier than it is, with big eyes staring out from the midst of a huge mane and with a full beard dangling under the chin.

It is true that the forepart of the buffalo is heavy—to his advantage. His normal position is with head down, nose in the grass, grazing. He never lifts high his head and sweeps the horizon with his eyes, alert for trouble, like an antelope or a horse. He does not have to lift his head for browsing among tree branches or the tops of bushes like a moose or a white-tailed deer. He is an animal fortress which no other wild animal on the prairie dares to attack. Wolves slink out of mountain ravines and onto the prairie for a buffalo dinner. But they dare not attack a buffalo in his prime; they follow the herd at a little distance, waiting for a feeble buffalo, about to die of old age, to drop behind the rest of the herd.

So the massive buffalo body enables the animal to live an easier, more comfortable life with head down. Yet this posture does not hinder him from traveling.

Buffaloes do much traveling. The herds follow the green grass north in the spring and south in the fall. Even then they do not have to hold their heads high and choose a path or detour around enemies lying in wait. Through the centuries they have followed well-worn trails that run north and south for hundreds of miles across the Far Grass Wilderness. These trails are worn deep in the sod, like

grooves, perhaps a foot deep, and along these the animals pass in single file. Even the file leader does not have to look far ahead. He simply walks in the groove while the others stretch out behind, also in the groove, each buffalo pacing his gait to the one next ahead.

This is a comfortable and effortless way to travel, but what about a stampede? What about running? In the primeval wilderness the buffalo never had to flee from another animal, but he did have to take to his heels before a prairie fire. Strange as it seems, the extra weight in the forepart makes it easier for this animal, which may weigh a ton, to gallop thirty-five miles per hour, almost as fast as a pronghorn antelope can run. The giant actually becomes light-footed by seesawing on his front legs. The huge shoulders are packed with muscles eighteen inches thick that work the front legs with fast strides, at the same time serving as the fulcrum of this monster seesaw. When the head goes down, the hindquarters come up, making the hind legs light and able to work at high speed, pushing the animal along, kicking up the dust like a pair of powerful paddle wheels. In this action the light hind feet are lifted high and swing forward together, crossing the front legs as with racing dogs.

Bull buffaloes sometimes fight duels by putting their heads down and colliding with a frightful crash. This happens in the mating season when the bulls are fighting over the cow buffaloes. And it happens when a younger bull, having grown to full strength, challenges an old bull for leadership of the herd. This natural habit of the buffaloes to charge and toss proved dangerous to a man on a horse when they appeared on the prairie. A buffalo could toss a horse and rider six feet in the air. A horrified witness reports that he saw a horse and rider lifted to the horns of the monster, who then carried them three hundred feet at full speed, suddenly stopped, and tossed them away.

But nature had made the buffalo an individual fighter. It was always when standing alone or separated from the herd that he became enraged and his eyes blazed red and he finished off a horse and rider. They never learned to charge as a herd but only to stampede.

Men on horses could stampede them by shooting off guns. Then the plains which had been still and empty suddenly began to ripple like a dark brown fur rug undulating across the horizons. The thunder of the herd rolled across the prairie. Bulls bellowed; cows moaned; the air was thick with dust; the ground trembled; little calves, bewildered, looking for their mothers, were trampled underfoot by the bulls that rushed headlong over them.

In the heart of Montana, where the Yellowstone River cuts a gorge in the plain, there was a hideous monument to the buffalo herd, called Buffalo Jump-off. The gorge is invisible from a few feet away because it is cut straight down from the floor of the plain with vertical walls that drop about fifty feet to the banks of the river. This was a favorite spot for Indians to stampede a herd. Those in front had plunged over, and the others, blinded and crazy, followed like a roaring cataract of monsters; and part of the wonderful old prairie life suddenly became a mountain of dead, hot debris. Here at the foot of the cliff an immense pile of whitened buffalo skulls, backbones, ribs, and leg bones partly blocked the course of the river. This was all that remained of thousands of buffaloes who had plunged over the cliff.

The buffaloes of the high plains were countless, and it seemed there would always be plenty of them. That was the way it looked to the men on horses who enjoyed the stampedes and the hunting of the big animals who galloped like seesaws. It was thrilling—the roars of the beasts, the thunder of their hoofs, the dust-fog filled with monstrous dashing forms, the bursting speed of the horse, the reports of guns, the yells of Indians.

A man who crossed the High Plains in 1832 wrote: "As far as my eye could reach, the country seemed absolutely blackened by herds." About the same time another man wrote: "We were suddenly greeted by a sight which seemed to astonish even the oldest among us. The whole plain, as far as the eye could discern, was covered by one enormous mass of buffalo."

As late as 1871 Colonel R. I. Dodge, driving a light wagon between two forts on the Arkansas River, encountered a herd of buffalo twenty-five miles long migrating to the north. His horse and wagon threw part of the big herd into panic, and he found them "pouring down upon me in one immense compact mass of plunging animals, mad with fright and as irresistible as an avalanche." Lucky for the colonel, his horse was a quiet old beast "so that their wildest, maddest rush only caused him to cock his ears in wonder at their unnecessary excitement." Standing his ground with his horse, he fired off his rifle as fast as he could. This caused the leaders, when they were a few feet away, to swerve slightly, opening a narrow wedge in which the colonel and his horse and wagon stood while the roaring buffaloes poured past.

It is estimated there were sixty million buffaloes on the prairie wilderness at the beginning of the nineteenth century. In 1847 the Hudson's Bay Company, the biggest fur company in Canada, took one hundred thousand buffalo robes out of Montana alone. In 1873 five million buffaloes were stampeded and killed. In 1905 there were fewer than a hundred of the giants wild in the United States.

Then, at the vanishing point, the American bison was snatched from becoming as extinct as the woolly mammoth and the giant beaver.

Today there are a few thousand buffaloes in quiet herds grazing in parcels of the high plains which have been given to them. They do not follow the flush of green from Texas to Montana in the spring, as did their ancestors. They do not make the prairie roar and shake with their stampedes. But they keep their heads down, because that feels most comfortable, and they kick up their heels and enjoy a seesaw gallop occasionally.

Lewis and Clark's round trip electrified the country. But the excitement was not about the Far Grass Wilderness. It was about the mountains on the distant side where superb game was plentiful and fortunes in furs were free for the getting. And now it was known that the Pacific coast had been reached beyond the mountains, where ships in world trade were coming and going. This was the grand prize which had been torturing the imagination and tantalizing Americans on the Mississippi frontier.

But Lewis and Clark showed that it was a discouraging, long distance across the middle of North America. They proved that it was impossible to make the trip by boat with portages because immense ranges of snow-capped mountains, one behind another, stood across the path. Thanks to the Indian girl, Sa-ga-ja-wea, however, Americans had reached a tributary of the Columbia River just across the mountains and used a boat to slide down the last three hundred miles on swift currents to the Pacific.

The route surveyed by Lewis and Clark was impossible for ordinary travelers, with its mountain avalanches and waterfalls and impassable snowdrifts in winter. To traverse this took a party of twenty-five men, hand-picked for daredevil toughness, led by two utterly fearless captains who would choose death rather than turn back. (And the Indian girl with the baby on her back had single-handedly kept them from choosing death!)

Before setting out, these men had spent all winter camping out-doors on the east shore of the Mississippi, toughening themselves, learning how to survive in the bitter cold, how to make a fire by rubbing two sticks together, becoming dead shots with a gun. Then who could follow this up? Who could be excited about the long trail across the prairie which was blazed by Lewis and Clark?

This challenge was accepted even before Lewis and Clark got back to Washington to publish their report. It was accepted by an uncommon breed of men who suddenly came into being—the Mountain Men. They were the sons of the daring pioneers who had packed their mules and crossed the Alleghenies to settle in Tennessee and Kentucky and the Ohio River Valley. This second generation of wilderness pioneers felt the urge to go far beyond their fathers' cabins in the Green Woods Wilderness. Now that they knew there were mountains over the western horizons loaded with game and lakes and streams and big timber, they must go there regardless of weeks of danger and suffering to get across the prairie. Such men were prepared and ready to go alone or with a friend or two. They were excellent shots. They had all the skills and strength of their woodsmen fathers. Moreover, they were fired with the excitement of a young nation which had become independent of Europe only twenty-five years before.

In all history there had never been a situation like this. A people had just taken over a fresh, new continent and explored its forest wilderness for a thousand miles to what they thought was its western boundary at a great river. Then all of a sudden a new and even bigger vision was presented to them. In one year the western boundary that had seemed so final melted away, and they were given a vision of another frontier, a thousand miles westward. This new frontier would double the distance across their country. Instead of a river it was a tremendous mountain range with fabulous valleys where the pioneer descendants of pioneers could be free and get rich.

Everybody, including the government in Washington, was

thrilled when the Mountain Men went forth. The situation was unprecedented. From ancient Rome to the Spanish conquest, no nation had an opportunity to double its homeland except by conquering a neighboring country on the field of battle or by building an overseas empire. That the "unoccupied" wilderness west of the Mississippi might be peppered with Indians didn't matter, any more than it mattered in the Green Woods Wilderness. This was true if we assume as they did then that Indians were wilderness wild men, usually referred to as savages, with no more title to the prairie and the mountains than buffaloes and bears.

The Lewis and Clark route along the Missouri River curved far to the north to North Dakota and Montana and penetrated the mountains through northern passes that were high and dangerous and blocked with snow in winter. But south of this route the vast Far Grass Wilderness was still a big blank.

At the same time the Mountain Men were saddling their horses and heading west across this unknown empty space along personal trails. They were not out to survey the land. They were fired by the desire to get across what everybody considered a wasteland, not fit for settlement, and to reach those mountains abounding in game.

Army detachments under orders from Washington were dispatched to map this vast western vacuum. These were led by soldier-explorers of the same type of daring leadership as Lewis and Clark. They kept daily records of directions of rivers, distances, heights of mountains, locations and names of Indian tribes. Out of these records, made through fifty years and thousands of miles of travel in untrodden areas, the maps of America's western wildernesses emerged. The heroic soldier-explorers who led these army expeditions became names in American history.

One of the first was Captain Zebulon Pike who, in 1806, was ordered to explore the southern prairie by going up the Arkansas River to its source in the mountains. Pike set out in rowboats, not sailboats. After rowing for five months some five hundred miles up the Arkansas, the party met a band of Osage Indians with horses which they had obtained from Spaniards farther south. Trading boats for horses, Pike followed the banks of the river into Kansas. At long last boats were discarded as vehicles for crossing the prairie. From that time on the favorite way to cross the Far Grass Wilderness, used by both Mountain Men and soldier map makers, was to ride along rivers on horseback.

The Arkansas River led Pike across the Kansas prairie and into Colorado, and across Colorado to the Rockies. This was a special triumph, because one of the greatest needs was a *southern* trail across the prairie to the mountains. After many days following the Arkansas River, still keeping on the plain, Pike turned southward, following what he took to be the hoofmarks of a party of Spaniards that had gone that way. Presently a cloud of dust appeared on the horizon and a group of murderous Pawnee Indians came whooping and surrounded the small party of soldiers. The Indian chief ordered Pike's batallion to turn around and threatened to kill them if they went any farther.

This aroused the soldier in Pike. Nothing could have made them turn around after that. He made a speech to the chief: "The young warriors of his Great American Father were not women, to be turned back by words. They would sell their lives at a dear rate and later other American warriors would come who would gather our bones and revenge our deaths on the Pawnee people." With these words Pike saluted the Indian chief, motioned his men to mount into their saddles, and gave the order—*forward, march!*

A few days later, Pike writes, "at two o'clock in the afternoon I thought I saw a mountain to our right like a small blue cloud. . . . In half an hour, the mountains appeared in full view before us and our party with one accord gave three cheers to the mountains. . . . Their appearance can be imagined by those who have crossed the Alleghenics, but their sides were whiter, as if covered with snow or white stone."

It was late November, and the mountains were indeed white

with deep snow. Pike spotted the highest peak, higher than anything, he thought, which the mind of man could imagine. The soldier who was under orders to make a map of the unknown wilderness promptly set out to climb the mountain, thinking it would be an advantageous place from which to sketch hundreds of square miles of rivers, valleys, lakes, and mountains. But Captain Pike's mountain-climbing party did not get very far. Cavalrymen do not have the headgear or the footgear or the know-how to climb an almost three-mile-high peak covered by snow and ice where there is no trail and no man has been before.

"Marching through the snow about two and one half feet deep, silent and with downcast countenances," they finally turned back "for the first time in the voyage discouraged." But Pike's Peak, Colorado, still bears the name of that brave cavalryman who first saw it and tried to climb it.

So now two routes were surveyed across the Far Grass Wilderness. Lewis and Clark's was extra long, detouring far north with the bend of the Missouri River and leading into mountain passes that were not open in winter. Pike's, along the Arkansas River, led to no mountain pass, and a traveler was forced to turn south on the Santa Fe Trail and trespass in Spanish-held land. (Indeed, on his return Pike was taken prisoner by the Spaniards and held in Santa Fe for a month before he was released.) It was apparent that a third trail was needed, across the middle of the prairie.

The Mountain Men meanwhile were getting across to the mountains in their own independent ways. But they did not keep a diary and report to Washington. They carried no surveying instruments and made no maps—except the maps they drew for each other with the point of a stick in the sand. A Mountain Man navigated by the seat of his pants in the saddle, the trigger of his muzzle-loading flintlock, and the nostrils of his horse.

Though a Mountain Man never wrote letters, he did a lot of talking when he dropped into an army post. When fact was sifted from tall stories, he supplied much information to the government survey parties about the vast unknown areas of the prairie and mountain wildernesses. One such tip-off was that the Platte River could be followed across what is now Nebraska and Wyoming to a usable pass in the mountains.

The Platte comes out of the west across the most desolate solitude of the High Plains and flows into the Missouri River 450 miles above St. Louis. The trouble is it doesn't flow much. It had not cut a deep channel; it is a weird sort of river for such a long one, a half mile wide with shallow water between mud banks. It almost dries up entirely in late summer. Lewis and Clark noted the mouth of the uninviting Platte on their way up the Missouri, but they passed it up to sail, pole, and pull their boats northward on the larger Missouri River. From appearances nobody would guess that the shallow Platte flowed all the way across from the mountains. But the Mountain Men said—just try it. Leave the boats on the Missouri and ride horses along the Platte.

So fifteen years after Pike, Major Stephen H. Long was ordered to follow the Platte across the prairie into the Rockies, taking along a squad of soldiers and a twenty-three-year-old geologist and botanist named Edwin James. These map makers started their trip of discovery into the wilderness in an entirely new kind of vehicle.

At the same time that Pike was peering at Pike's Peak and failing to climb it, Robert Fulton landed in New York bringing a steam engine from England, and soon side-wheelers were plying the Hudson. By 1820 somebody had designed a shallow-draft steamboat with paddle wheel at the stern where it would not be damaged by scraping against riverbanks. Long's party embarked on the first such rear-end paddle-wheeler at Pittsburgh. Thus the elegant Major Long sat in a chair on the deck under an awning, surveying the river banks for a thousand miles as they steamed down the Ohio to the Mississippi, then up that river to St. Louis, where they gained the Missouri, and enjoyed the ride upstream to the mouth of the Platte.

The design of Long's paddle-wheeler was cleverly calculated

to spread awe and terror among the Indians. An eyewitness described it in a letter from St. Louis after Major Long arrived in that town. "The bow of this vessel exhibits the form of a huge serpent, black and scaly, rising out of the water from under the boat, his head as high as the deck, darted forward, his mouth open, vomiting smoke, and apparently carrying the boat on his back."

Saying good-by to his stern-wheeler at the mouth of the Platte, the major's party mounted horses and followed the big shallow river clear across the high plains to the Rockies without anybody being murdered by savages or trampled under a buffalo stampede. They crossed the Continental Divide through a pass which later became the famous South Pass.

The Continental Divide is a line that runs along the Rockies where a drop of water falling on one side flows westward into the Pacific and another drop, on the other side, flows eastward into the Atlantic by way of the Mississippi River and the Gulf of Mexico. The Divide is not the highest ridge. It climbs only a few of the highest peaks. South Pass is a fairly low place to cross the Continental Divide, with green meadows on both sides. Major Long's party must have crossed over South Pass without thinking of it as a great historical event. Doubtless he was guided that way by Mountain Men, but as there is no record of this, Major Long is given credit for the discovery of South Pass.

There were now three great trails across the Far Grass Wilderness into the Monster Mountain Wilderness. Major Long's was the best of all. It became the famous Oregon Trail, traveled by the forty-niners seeking gold in California and by stagecoaches and wagon trains. And forty years after Major Long went that way, the exultant Pony Express dashed back and forth in his footsteps along the Platte River and over South Pass.

In 1860 the Pony Express was the climax stunt for getting across the prairie while the Far Grass was still a primeval wilderness with great herds of buffaloes, with pronghorns signaling to each other across the horizon, with prairie-dog cities, and with Indians

ambushing and murdering the invaders. This was a carefully organized daring and imaginative plan to cross the worthless plains
as fast as possible. Never before or since has horseflesh carried
men and messages so far so fast.

The Pony Express was intended for business messages between
New York and San Francisco, although private letters could be sent
for $5.00 postage. Mail by stagecoach took a month. The record
run of the Butterfield Stage was twenty-two days, made by changing to fresh horses at frequent intervals and with drivers standing
up, whipping and hollering their way across the plains. The Pony
Express reduced the time to an average of ten days in summer and
about twelve days in winter. This was incredible speed in those
days—like breaking the sound barrier in the more recent era of
flying.

Such an achievement called for a station every ten miles, where
two men would be waiting with a fresh, impatient horse, saddled
and ready to go. Eighty Pony Express riders were in the saddle
at all times, day and night, forty flying east, forty west. The horses
were California mustangs, strong, wiry animals, able to cover ten
miles at full gallop, trained to follow the route even when a rider
fell asleep in the saddle.

The riders were small, wiry men, like jockeys, but they had to
know how to use a knife and be dead shots with a pistol. They
galloped without hesitation through country where Indians were
burning down the stations of the Pony Express, murdering the men
there and stealing the horses. A single rider could not stop to do
battle with a tribe of Indians, and his chances of getting through
depended mostly on his horse, which was faster than the Indian
horses.

Everything about the Pony Express was designed for lightness
and speed. The rider wore light clothes, with a tightly fitting jacket
and cap, and pantaloons tucked into his boots. The mailbag was
fastened to the saddle, and it never exceeded twenty pounds. Letters were on the thinnest tissue paper, rolled in oilpaper to keep

them dry in storms and when the Pony Express rider waded through streams. Each rider had thirty miles to cover with three changes of mounts.

The "swift phantom of the desert" streaked by the stagecoaches with only a shout in the night before a person could get his head out of the window. In the daytime the passing of a stagecoach and the Pony Express in the solitude of the vast naked prairie was an exciting moment. Mark Twain, who was a stagecoach passenger in 1861, describes the breath-taking moment when the Pony Express flashed by.

"We were expecting one along every minute. Presently, the driver exclaims, *here he comes!* Every neck is stretched further, every eye strained wider. Away across the endless dead level of the prairie a black speck appears. It moves. Well, I should think so! In a second or two, it becomes a horse and rider, rising and falling, rising and falling, sweeping toward us, nearer and nearer. Then the clatter of hoofs comes faintly to the ear—another instant, a whoop and a hurrah from our upper deck, a wave of the rider's hand but no reply, and man and horse burst past our excited faces and go winging away like a fragment of a storm!"

The Pony Express lasted only eighteen months, and then the telegraph line was put through and made an end to it. We read about it now as a unique and romantic stunt to get across the Far Grass Wilderness, but the Pony Express was a sensation to the people of its day.

When the first Pony Express arrived in San Francisco in the middle of the night, cannon boomed all over the city, bonfires were kindled in the streets, candles appeared in windows, the crowds carried torches and lanterns in the light of which flags were unfurled. They sang songs and crowded up to tie ribbons on the panting pony or to pluck hairs from his beautiful tail for souvenirs.

CHAPTER IX

THE MONSTER
MOUNTAIN WILDERNESS

ACROSS the last hundred miles of the high plains mountains appear suddenly like clouds edging the horizon. The dim apparition where clouds and snow blend with blue mountainsides enlarges with every hour's travel, while sharp, immovable peaks along the broken crest grow clearer. The thrilling sight across the plains breaks a long monotony. A man whips his horse, which steps out at a bit faster pace; the word is passed along the army column; soldiers who have been swaying half-conscious in the saddle look up and make a gruff, happy remark to the man on the next horse; the man high on the driver's seat of a covered wagon rouses from a half-nap and sends his long whiplash spinning out over the six horses' heads in front of him.

The men who first crossed the prairie in the Montana-Wyoming area probably dismounted at the base of the mountains, built a campfire, and had antelope for dinner. In search of a way up they may have spent a couple of days exploring a canyon where a stream came tumbling down. Sooner or later an Indian turned up who would point out another canyon a few miles away, or he might show the newcomers a place where trails of wolves and bear went up into the mountains along the bank of a stream. Somehow men and horses got up into the Monster Mountain Wilderness.

Then the first white men picked their way step by step through this marvelous wilderness. They didn't even know what they would find behind a boulder or a tree a hundred feet ahead. It might be a beaver pond or a grizzly bear or an ambush of Indians with their bows raised to the kill-white-man-at-the-next-step position.

Other American wildernesses are within themselves much the same in appearance throughout their length and breadth. The Green Woods Wilderness is an almost unbroken expanse of leaf-dropping trees from the Atlantic coast to the Mississippi River. The North Pine Wilderness is a blanket of spruce from the mouth of the St. Lawrence sweeping across Canada to beyond Lake Superior and north to the Hudson's Bay area. The desert is the same kind of place from the Gulf of Mexico to California. And the one word which the first explorers used for the Far Grass Wilderness was *monotonous*.

On the other hand, the Mountain Wilderness is a world of contrast and variety, of abysmal valleys, black canyons, giant-tree forests, dizzy ledges where bighorn sheep and Rocky Mountain goats stand like lordly lookouts. Everywhere among the valleys and mountains surprising vistas of meadows and hidden deserts, forests and streams are revealed. All this had a peculiar fascination and irresistible lure for the men who first saw this wilderness.

The Mountain Men were purebreds of the primeval American wilderness like the woodsmen of the Green Woods Wilderness, such as Daniel Boone and Davy Crockett. They burned with curiosity and yearned for the timeless, free life of the wilderness, and they learned a strategy of survival from the wild animals

and Indians. But the men who followed the deer and Indian trails over the Appalachian Mountains were settlers who came to clear a corner for themselves in the Green Woods Wilderness and raise families.

On the other hand, the Mountain Men were not settlers but trappers and traders, always on the move, with no permanent home. They followed the beaver and elk along mountain streams, across valleys, through forests, over snowbound passes which appeared on no maps and where white men had never penetrated before. The mysterious corners of the wilderness were their personal hunting and trapping grounds.

The Mountain Man's map was in his head in the form of landmarks—a blaze on a tree, a fork in a stream, the face of a cliff, the position of a boulder, the outline of a mountain against the sky. The Mountain Man came to know intimately every mountain range, pass, crest, canyon, valley, stream, trail, camping place with grass, Indian lodge, and spring in the dangerous and dramatic wilderness where he ranged far and wide.

Here a man is not closed in. Even in the tall timber there is no blinding underbrush, but the ground is more or less clear, with a springy carpet of needles where one can walk freely among the giant columns. Sometimes there is a tight squeeze in a canyon. Then suddenly a tremendous view opens up of clear distance with snowy peaks above or a shimmering valley below.

The thrill of the unexpected was heightened by the wild beasts that lived in the hide-outs of the Monster Mountain Wilderness, although they increased the threat of every tree and rock. To meet this danger, and for a food supply as well, the Mountain Man looked to the long knife in his belt and never took a step away from camp without his single-barreled, muzzle-loading flintlock.

In the days of first discovery a man with a gun was an unknown object to the wild animals. When he sat quietly by his campfire, roasting choice cuts, a bear or elk or wolf might wander into the circle of the firelight. Wolves, that seemed always to be waiting just out of sight around the camp, after polite hesitation would barge in to claim the carcass which the man had thrown a few feet away.

A man, awakened by cold in the middle of the night, glanced over to see how his fire was doing. A large gray wolf was sitting quietly before it, eyes closed and head nodding in sheer drowsiness! The man watched for some time without disturbing the beast, then closed his eyes and went to sleep again, leaving the wolf

to the quiet enjoyment of the blaze. But a deep-sleeping Mountain Man was apt to wake up to find that the wolf had chewed off the straps of the saddle which he was using as a pillow.

An amazing fact about the Monster Mountain Wilderness is its vertical dimension—it is two miles deep. A man could follow a trail for a mile and seem to be standing still on the same spot on a flat map.

The lower valleys have ponds and streams, willow and aspen groves, and grassy meadows which are reflections of the Green Tree Wilderness and contain the homes of beaver, deer, and raccoon. Other valleys are high, very dry, and wide open for runners as on the high plains. Here coyote and antelope run, small herds of buffaloes graze, and here also prairie dogs, gophers, and badgers dig.

High, wide mountain slopes and canyons are the dominion of the biggest trees in the world—Douglas fir, ponderosa pine, western white pine, and the colossal sequoia among them. Forests of these tremendous trees cover the mountains like a great fur coat. This is the home of the American elk, called *wapiti* by the Indians.

Only the buffalo is bigger and heavier than wapiti. Comes a time in the fall when the bull elk leads the females of his herd to a high place where, standing on the crest of a cliff looking out over the forest, he fills his lungs with an enormous breath of mountain air and raises his muzzle toward the sky. Then, just at sundown, the bugling of the great elk echoes from mountain to mountain, as though he were letting the whole world know who owns this wilderness.

Somewhere through the giant-tree forest the panther is gliding. His long, beautiful body, twenty-six inches high at the shoulder, and mostly muscle, elongates to seven feet when he leaps. The mountain panther can broad-jump thirty feet from a running start. He can pour himself off a thirty-foot ledge and land lightly on his toes. If he crouches on a rock beside the elk's trail, the bugling

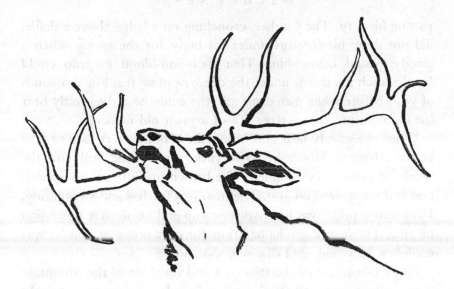

giant is doomed by the swift silent cat that springs suddenly as though shot from a gun. The elk's head snaps back, breaking the neck, and the elk carcass is punched twenty feet off the trail by the blow.

The grizzly bear treads softly among the giant trees. This brown brute of the American wilderness is the greatest of all meat-eating animals on the continent. He may weigh three quarters of a ton, and when he stands up—this is "the bear that walks like a man," for a big grizzly may tower twelve feet.

The grizzly knows that elk and deer can be cornered in canyons, and rabbits, raccoons, and beavers can be turned into dinner with a gentle pat. Wolves and panthers may glide out of reach, but who cares? An abundance of fresh meat increases the grizzly's girth and strength. But also, he likes to eat berries and roots, and he can swallow a beehive with all the honey and buzzing bees inside. The grizzly also loves to lie out on a log snoozing in the sun and, reaching down a forepaw, grab little fish to eat between naps.

Indians thought they wasted too many arrows on that thick grizzly fur coat, so they usually stepped aside to let the big bear pass on his way. The panther, crouching on a ledge above a defile, did not draw his forelegs under his body for the spring when a grizzly passed below him. That flesh-and-blood torpedo could hardly reach the throat under the deep, rippling fur. For thousands of years before white men came into the wilderness, the grizzly bear led the undisturbed, carefree life of a gruff old monarch.

When the grizzly bear and Mountain Man first met face to face in the Monster Mountain Wilderness, time stood still and the trunks of giant trees trembled. The brown brute knew no opposition and recognized no gun. The man was fearless and swaggering. His greatest pride was his marksmanship and his dearest possession his rifle. The man knew he had time for only one shot, but he was confident he could send that one shot home.

Hugh Glass, one of the strongest and toughest of the Mountain Men, following an elk trail with a friend, came upon a grizzly quietly turning up the turf with his nose, sniffing for roots. The bear ignored them, so they took steady aim from close by and with a single explosion sent two balls crashing into the side of the animal. The surprised brute jumped with all four legs off the ground. Then, snorting with pain and fury, he charged the men. *"Damit, Bill!"* roared Hugh. "We'll be made meat of!" The two men bolted across a hundred yards of level ground to jump off a bluff into a ravine. But Hugh tripped over a stone, rolled on the ground, and, scrambling to his feet, faced the bear who had risen on his hind legs and towered above him.

Hugh knew no fear and drew his pistol in one hand, his knife in the other, prepared to fight with these and his wits. As they closed, blood was streaming from the bear's nose and mouth. Then with one blow of his paw he knocked Hugh's pistol to the ground, and fixing his claws deep in the man's flesh, they rolled to the ground like two wrestlers—the monster grizzly on top.

Bill, frozen with horror, watched while Hugh plunged his knife again and again into the bear's belly. Flesh was torn from Hugh's ribs, exposing the bones, and he was blinded by blood from a flap

of his scalp that hung down over his eyes. In a few seconds Hugh
became unconscious and the knife fell from his hand.

Then Bill sprinted for camp as fast as he could go, to tell the
other men about the death of Hugh Glass. An hour later, returning
to the scene, they found the bear stark dead, lying on top of unconscious Hugh, who was hardly breathing. They moved the bear's
carcass and beheld Hugh, bloody and torn, lying there as good as
dead. They stripped him of his buckskin shirt and breeches, took

his felt hat, moccasins, shoulder strap and leather pouch with flint and tinder, and his flintlock. Then they dug a grave partly under his body so that he would topple into it as soon as he stopped breathing. After that they went their way and resumed their activities, setting the traps, trading with the Indians, visiting forts. Wherever they went they told the story of the heroic end of the great Hugh Glass.

Months later Bill was relaxing around the fire with a group of Mountain Men, when they saw a gaunt figure approaching on horseback. His face was twisted with scars; one ear was gone; the arm that held the bridle was lame and queer in the way it moved. They didn't recognize the stranger. Then, reining in his horse before them, a hollow voice said, *"Damit, Bill!* You thought I was gone under that time, did you? But hand me my horse and gun, my lad. I ain't dead yet by a damsight!"

Hugh Glass told them what happened after dizzy consciousness returned. He could not get to his feet, so he crawled to a spring for a drink and to some bushes where the berries were ripe, where he chewed leaves, twigs, and berries into a mush. He then crawled for days and days—he did not know how far—until he reached the Cheyenne River. There he managed to roll some logs into the stream and, lying out on them, he floated for more days and nights down the river. The water bathed his body and gave him drink, and he chewed things along the bank. At the end of unknown time he crawled up the riverbank at a trader's fort—*eighty miles* from the place where he won the duel with the grizzly bear.

Jim Colter, son of a pioneer settler, was twenty-five years old, living on the Ohio River, when Captain Lewis came along looking for recruits in 1803. He picked up Jim, who agreed to enlist as a private in the army for $5 a month to join the Lewis and Clark Expedition into the unknown. He went all the way to the Pacific coast and back with Lewis and Clark and turned out to be one of the most popular and good-natured men on the expedition.

No suffering ever got him down. There was no situation he could not meet. They could depend on his bringing down game with a single shot, and a few minutes later he would have a good fire going and the best cut of meat roasting to perfection. He showed the other soldiers how to smoke hides and sew up jackets and pants with sinews, how to make fur hats and moccasins. And Colter had such a personality that nobody was ever jealous of him.

While homeward bound, reaching the place in North Dakota where they had spent the winter on the way west, Jim asked for a discharge so that he could go back to the mountains. Lewis and Clark honored his request because he had been such a great help. He was the only man permitted to leave the expedition before it returned to St. Louis. Thus this soldier turned into a Mountain Man.

A weird adventure was in store for Jim Colter. This man who had won the respect of everybody in the Lewis and Clark Expedition, whose honesty was beyond doubt, was destined to be called the biggest liar of all Mountain Men who ever lived—quite a distinction.

Colter built a boat and retraced the course up the Missouri to the mouth of the Yellowstone River. He recalled how the captains and the Indian girl, Sa-ga-ja-wea, had seen the Yellowstone River, which came from the southwest, and how they had much discussion there and how finally it was decided to continue due west on the Missouri. But this time Colter was alone and made his own decisions, so he left the Lewis and Clark route at this point and followed the Yellowstone into totally unknown mountain areas.

He went southwest on the Yellowstone for 225 miles. Then, on foot, with only a Mountain Man's long knife and flintlock, and all his worldly possessions in a thirty-pound pack, he followed the Big Horn River south and from there headed west into unknown country. He saw the headwaters of the Colorado River. He was one man against the mountains and all its wild beasts. Living by his ingenuity, taking the course of the sun across the sky, day after day, week after week, he crossed five hundred miles of terrific mountain wilderness. He came to appalling precipices and somehow found a way to scale them or descend by narrow ledges. He wearily climbed unknown mountain ranges and crossed snow bridges. He looked into mysterious abysses as he dauntlessly struggled on and on. This was perhaps the most exciting one-man sight-seeing trip in human history. But the day came when Jim Colter turned around and headed back.

Instead of continuing on the roundabout trail by which he had come, he decided to head north to try to find the headwaters of the Yellowstone River and follow that river northeast back to the Missouri. It was due to this short cut that Colter, in 1807, stumbled across that amazing corner of the mountain wilderness which we now call Yellowstone Park.

This hardheaded Mountain Man saw things that might have made him wonder whether he had died in his sleep and awakened in a conglomeration of mountains, forests, and canyons haunted by demons.

The weird area was hidden behind mountains when Lewis and Clark passed it by on the north side. It was hidden behind mountains when Colter, going west, passed it by on the south side. No well-traveled Indian trails went through it. Indians avoided the place. They told Captain Clark that beyond the mountains was a place "where their children could not sleep; a region possessed of spirits which no man could approach." The Lewis and Clark party laughed—just another Indian superstition!

Why didn't reliable Jim Colter bring back his story of the Yellowstone region to the Mississippi frontier? He never wrote, but he liked to talk. He met Captain Clark in St. Louis a few years after his Yellowstone discovery, and Colter's route appears on the official Lewis and Clark map of 1814. Noted on the map are a "boiling spring," a "fossil mountain," and the words "hot spring brimstone." These were merely incidental marks on the map, and there is no further mention of the many outlandish wonders.

Captain Clark seems to have had complete faith in Colter as to the route he took. But did he play down as just a tall story the sights which Colter said he saw?

Everybody else played it down, thinking that Jim had become as big a liar as other trappers. When he told about that wilderness of hissing geysers, steaming hot springs, churning mud volcanoes, the great falls of the Yellowstone, 310 feet high, and its Grand Canyon, fourteen hundred feet deep—and particularly the brimstone—they laughed it off. They called it "Colter's Hell." Jim Colter received a lot of joshing about it around the campfires.

Perhaps Jim Colter would at least have tempted somebody else to go and look, except that a year after he discovered the Yellowstone wilderness he had a harrowing adventure which was just as unbelievable when he reported it later. This was an escape from savages that was "obviously a lie." But—in later years, by piecing together prattle from Indians who were eyewitnesses and a careful survey of the ground where it occurred—it was proved to be true!

Colter was exploring a stream in Montana with another Mountain Man named Potts. They were paddling along, each in his own canoe, when a band of bloodthirsty Indians appeared and ordered them over to the bank. Greatly outnumbered, they had to obey. When Potts's canoe grounded, one of the Indians grabbed his rifle, but Colter stood up, wrested the rifle away, and gave it back to Potts, who was so mad he pushed out into the stream and shot the Indian dead. The next instant, while Colter looked on horrified,

Potts was riddled with arrows and bullets. The Indians then tore his body apart and threw the pieces in Colter's face. Then, boiling with rage, the Indians planned a devilish torture for their captive who was still alive.

Jim was seized, disarmed, and stripped entirely naked. The Indians then went into a huddle, like a football team planning the plays. Nearby the ground was open and flat for about five miles to another stream. With gestures and shouts the Indians told Colter to run across this open ground. As he went, they goaded him on faster and faster. He couldn't believe they were letting him go, but when he saw several hundred young Indians throwing off their blankets and leggings for a race, he knew that the prize was to be his body and scalp.

So Jim Colter found superhuman strength and ran! Off he went with a desperate burst of speed, putting every ounce of his strength into the dash. When he had covered half the distance to the brush and trees on the riverbank, blood gushed from his nostrils. He was growing weaker. Looking over his shoulder, he saw that he had outstripped the oncoming warriors who were brandishing spears and whooping some distance back—all except one savage, who was far ahead of the pack and catching up with Colter.

Colter knew he couldn't make it against that killer, so he waited, naked and defenseless, for the final lunge of the savage's spear. Then a sort of miracle happened. Colter dodged; the Indian tripped on a rock; the head of the spear broke off, and Colter, seizing it like a dagger, stabbed the Indian to death. This astounding turn of affairs gave Colter fresh energy. He covered the last two miles in a daze of furious speed and disappeared in the brush. But he had won only a few seconds of grace.

He found himself on the bank of the stream, and here, a few paces away, Colter saw a dome of twigs and sticks in the water. This man who trapped beavers knew a beaver house when he saw one, and he knew it had an underwater entrance. If the beavers were old and large size, that entrance would be big enough for him

to wriggle through. And so it was! He dove underwater, came up to the beaver platform beneath the dome of twigs, and, squeezing in, he lay there, trying to stifle his thumping heart and panting lungs, listening to the yelling savages beat the bushes, as they searched up and down the banks on both sides of the stream and scrambled over the top of the beaver house. At long last they went away, while he lay bleeding. Two hours later they came back.

By nightfall the Indians finally gave up. It was quiet and very dark. Colter slipped out and swam silently for a timeless distance downstream. After that he followed the river for seven days and nights, living off the roots of plants until he arrived at a fort. There a trapper friend gave him food and a drink and listened to his tale with great good nature.

For twenty years after Colter, "Colter's Hell" was still a joke among the Mountain Men. They used it to spark a good story, as a sort of "see if you can top this one." Then, in 1830, the Yellowstone story suddenly took on fresh color and excitement due to a colorful liar named Jim Bridger.

Jim started his Mountain Man career by discovering Great Salt Lake in Utah. With a party of trappers he crossed the Continental Divide at South Pass and kept on westward to the Bear River in southern Idaho. At first they followed this northward. Suddenly it makes a sharp turn and flows in the opposite direction, south. That night in camp an argument arose about where that river was going. It didn't seem to be headed toward the Columbia River any longer; perhaps it flowed directly into the Pacific Ocean farther south? They made a bet, and Bridger, with three others, offered to explore all the way to the mouth of the Bear River to settle the matter.

After some seventy-five miles, a short distance in their terms, their river ended at a big lake in a glaring desert. Bridger dismounted for a drink of water, but taking a great mouthful, he yelled and spat it all out. Jumping to his feet, he said, "Hell! Here we are on the shore of the Pacific!" They hurried back to tell their friends, who were still camped up on the Bear River. The news that an arm of the Pacific reached close to the Rocky Mountains spread from Mountain Man to Mountain Man and then to the outside world. But a year later somebody went all around the shore in a canoe and could find no outlet—it was a lake. Bridger had discovered Great Salt Lake.

Bridger was fascinated by the mysteries of the Monster Mountain Wilderness. And he had the reputation as teller of the tallest tales of his time. Starting in 1830, he made a number of trips alone into Colter's Hell and saw astonishing sights that Colter missed. But when he told the facts nobody believed him. He had the same trouble getting people interested that Jim Colter had.

Bridger said that he had seen places where volcanoes shoot out huge columns of boiling water; where sulphur and brimstone burst through the ground and flow in streams; where mountains are rent asunder with cracks thousands of feet deep, and where the wilderness is so spooky that not only Indians but most wild animals avoid it. When he was jeered at and egged on with, "Jim, you can do better than that," he decided to try.

He said that, riding along one day, he came in sight of an elk, took careful aim, and fired. To his amazement the elk continued peacefully browsing. Bridger crept nearer, took most deliberate aim—but no result; the elk kept right on grazing. A third and fourth shot left the elk completely unconcerned; it seemed not even to hear the report of the rifle. Exasperated, Bridger decided to use

his rifle as a club when, rushing at the animal, he crashed into the side of a mountain made of transparent glass. On the farther side the elk was quietly browsing. Moreover, the curve of the glass acted as a telescope lens, so that the elk, instead of being only a few hundred yards away, was actually twenty-five miles away! Bridger's story was inspired by Obsidian Cliff, made of volcanic glass.

Another Bridger discovery was an ice-cold spring at the top of a very high mountain, from which the water flowed down over smooth rock, going faster and faster, until the water was boiling hot when it reached the bottom, due to friction with the rock. It is reliably reported that Bridger thought this was a plain matter of fact.

His discovery of Alum Creek was reported in true Bridger style. Fording the creek one day, he rode several miles out and back. But the return trip was only a fraction of the distance going out, and also he noticed his horse's feet had shrunk to mere points which sank into the ground so that the animal could hardly hobble along. Upon investigation he found that it was the alum in the water, which was so strong that it had the power to pucker distance as well as the feet of his horse.

Speaking of the alum in that creek, a journalist who visited Yellowstone in 1877 wrote: "This stream is so strong with alum that one swallow is sufficient to draw one's face into such shape that it is almost impossible to get it straightened out again for one hour or so."

It is a geologic fact that Amethyst Mountain, 9,400 feet high, contains the solid stone fossils of sixteen forests, one on top of another. The lowest, at ground level, was growing when the Age of Reptiles was drawing to a close. It was buried by lava when a nearby volcano erupted. Thousands of years later a fresh forest was growing on top of the first, when the volcano let go again and forest number two was buried. This event was repeated sixteen times.

This wilderness wonder seems hardly less astonishing than Bridger's story about the marvelous Yellowstone fossils. He told how a great medicine man cursed a certain mountain, so that from that time on everything about it became petrified. According to Bridger, stone elks and bears stand around like real live animals. Waterfalls and their spray are arrested in motion and stand still, all petrified. Wild flowers are crystallized, and birds soar with wings spread motionless in flight—and even the sun and moon shine with petrified light!

Bridger first discovered this petrified area when, approaching his camping place from a different angle, he found the way blocked by a deep chasm. It was a long way around, and Bridger and his horse were bone-tired. Riding to the brink to reconnoiter, he found that he could not stop his horse, which moved ahead at a steady gate, trotting out over the edge of the chasm as though on an invisible bridge. Presently he found himself on the other side, safe in camp, ready to cook a hip of venison for dinner. His amazement did not last long, because he quickly realized that the chasm, close to the petrified mountain, was simply a place where gravity was petrified, like every other natural object that had been there when the place was cursed.

Thus through the years the myth of Colter's Hell grew. Occasionally other trappers and a few personal expeditions went for a look, but the outside world refused to take their stories seriously until an official government scientific expedition was sent to find out all about this nonsense concerning the Yellowstone wilderness. After that a Chicago newspaper editor said that Jim Bridger had told him all about those wonders thirty years before. He had prepared an article based on the Mountain Man's description and then suppressed it after he showed it to a man who said he knew Jim Bridger. The man told the editor he would be laughed out of town if he printed any of "old Jim Bridger's lies."

So it was that this part of the Monster Mountain Wilderness was too wonderful to believe. The marvels of the Yellowstone were generally unknown until more than sixty years after they were first seen by Jim Colter. And these spectacular sights were not officially accepted in Washington until 1870!

A towering forest of sequoia trees in the High Sierra Mountains carries the silence and twilight of a cathedral. There are no patches of sunlight and shadow, so that it does not have black corners. Sunlight filtering through the ceiling several hundred feet high is transformed into a dim glow, tinted cinnamon-red by the tree bark. The floor is a needle carpet with a clean, swept look, with here and there a fallen branch like part of a giant's skeleton lying on it. The wood, so long as it is alive in the mountain air, is as indestructible as granite. The bark, with no resin like pine bark, is fireproof and may be two feet thick. Deep furrows in this bark run up the tree trunk, lined with a kind of felt where rough edges of bark have shredded.

The "big tree" (as the mountain sequoia is called in contrast to

the "redwood" sequoia on the coast) cannot be burned down like a pine forest in a fire. But it may be fired like a sort of skyrocket. A ground fire smoldering among the needles or debris on the floor can spark the shredded bark in a furrow. This touches off a series of sparks and tiny blue flashes, which dart up the huge trunk faster than the eye can follow. The felt in the furrow acts like the fuse of a firecracker by which a small flame on the ground jumps three hundred feet up into the top of the tree. There dried twigs, cones, and needles are touched off like fireworks and torches in the sky.

Because the big trees grow on mountainsides and in canyons more than a mile high, a thunderstorm, instead of stabbing them with lightning from above, may collide with them. Then, while wrapped in black clouds, the top of the tree is knocked off by a thunderbolt, while most of the tree below is left unscathed to live on through the ages. On rare occasions when the giants are buried in a thunderstorm, instead of being struck by lightning or set on fire, the whole colossal tree suddenly explodes and vanishes. A few of the largest limbs are thrown off, but the rest is shattered to bits. But usually the big trees are as calm and silent as the infinity of time which created them.

One does not see a big tree as a whole, or at a glance, but only the base of the broad, shadowy column. At the ground line the trunk folds under, making a black shadow that seems to detach the base of the tree from the earth. The big column seems to be balanced lightly in the air. You can hardly think of it as alive. It is too wide, too silent, too immovable. In a forest of big trees there is no hurry or flutter, no wind, no sound. A dog's bark is muffled. A person whispers.

It is surprising that this wilderness of silent giants was unknown and unexplored until years after the wildernesses to the north and south had been surveyed by the army explorers and crisscrossed by the Mountain Men.

In 1852 a man named Dowd was a member of a construction gang building a canal at the foot of the High Sierras. Dowd was

hunting through forests in the lower valleys to shoot some game for dinner when he saw a grizzly bear. This man's rifle was more powerful and the grizzly more afraid of him than in the early days of the Mountain Men. So, when wounded by a bullet, the great bear, instead of charging the man, took off up a canyon.

Dowd thought the bear would collapse any minute, so he pursued the animal on and on, up and up. After a considerable climb he found himself in a forest of the big trees. The bear was forgotten. He stood in amazement. According to his own words, he felt, "Surely this must be some curious dream!" He stretched wide his arms on a massive trunk. Looking up, he saw the columns disappear high above. He paced the distance around one tree—it was over a hundred feet!

When he told the men back in camp what he had seen high up in the mountains, they suggested that he sit down, eat his dinner, and forget it. He was fooling nobody. Dowd, of course, was in the same position that Jim Colter and Jim Bridger had been with their Yellowstone stories. So Dowd decided to make up a real lie to get the others to come and take a look.

A few days later he found a chance to climb up again and make sure that it wasn't just a dream. Returning to camp that evening, he said that he had killed a huge grizzly bear high up in the mountains and needed a party of five or six men to help him fetch it down. The men understood that a big grizzly was valuable from head to tail, and a party was organized to climb the mountain and get the carcass.

As Dowd led them higher and higher, they grumbled but kept on until they reached the big trees. Then they also forgot about the grizzly! Nobody would ever believe this!

This was the official discovery of the big sequoias of the High Sierras, the greatest tree spectacle in the world. There are vague rumors that others may have seen them before Dowd, but if so, they were too starved or tired or lost to give a clear report.

Before men came with gun and poison, the condor who floated above the giant forest knew no enemies. The gaunt old bird crouches on a limb hundreds of feet up, or on a rock projecting from the cliff of a thousand-foot canyon. His head is squat on his shoulders. He leans far over, holding it down like a dejected giant. His fierce, keen eyes search the wilderness below, inch by inch, for a carcass. He never attacks a live animal. He likes meat ripe, and somehow he knows when death occurs, even miles away.

Taking off from a mountain ledge, the condor lurches forward and falls into space while unfolding his ten-foot wingspread. The sharp drop gives flying speed while he sets his wings to catch the warm currents of air coming up the mountainsides from the valley. Then the condor gives a couple of slow flaps to adjust his position and soars away. Riding the air currents of the mountains with motionless wings, the condor scans hundreds of square miles of his wilderness for a ripe carcass. He maneuvers gracefully, weaving among the clouds and mountaintops. When something worth investigating is spotted, he turns with a quick, downward spiral and goes into a zooming dive with wings half open so that they act as rudders instead of brakes. If then he sees eagles or coyotes busy with the carcass, it is not ripe enough and he can wait. The big wings extend and he rises gracefully, higher than the point where the dive began.

A condor is usually seen circling slowly overhead, and he has an odd way of appearing and disappearing suddenly. Look away for a few moments, and when you glance again he is gone. You catch sight of a faraway speck racing sixty miles an hour over the horizon. You do not see the big bird return; but a few minutes later there he is again, circling lazily overhead as though he had been there all the time.

Twenty-three years after Dowd showed his friends the big trees instead of a grizzly bear, a most unusual man climbed into the big tree wilderness leading a small, wild mule. He was John Muir, famous explorer of the Rocky Mountains. Until John Muir came, men who plunged into the Monster Mountain Wilderness were either fighting to get through to California or they were after wealth of gold or fur. But John Muir came to find primitive beauty, to discover the wealth of space and time, to hold his breath in the hush within the giant forests, to share the power of a storm in the tree-tops, and to discover what life was hidden within the mists of waterfalls.

John Muir went on foot, carried as little as possible, depended on campfires for warmth, "that so I might be light and free to go wherever my studies might lead."

Brownie, the little mule, was his only companion. The animal was "tough as a nut, untirable, low and narrow, just right for squeezing through brush, able to climb like a chipmunk, jump from boulder to boulder like a wild sheep . . . but many a time in the course of our journey he was jaded and hungry, wedged fast in rocks or struggling like a fly in a spider-web, his troubles were sad to see."

At long last a man *felt and enjoyed* the raw wilderness—as it was created by the ages. In a terrible mountain storm, instead of crouching behind a boulder, he climbed a tall tree. He said that he never before enjoyed such an exhilaration of motion. "The slender tops flapped and swished in the passionate torrent, bending and swirling backward and forward, round and round, tracing indescribable combinations of vertical and horizontal curves, while I clung with muscles firm braced. In its widest sweeps my treetop described an arc of 20 to 30 degrees without breaking a fiber. I was safe and free to take the wind into my pulses and enjoy the excited forest from my superb outlook. . . . The sounds of the storm corresponded gloriously with this motion. The profound base of the naked branches and boles booming like waterfalls; the quick, tense vibrations of the pine needles now rising to a whistling hiss, now falling to a silky murmur. . . .

"Most people like to look at mountain rivers but few care to look at the winds, though they become at times as visible as flowing water. When winter winds are making upward sweeps over the summits of the High Sierras, the fact is published with flying snow-banners a mile long. Then yonder it descends in a rush of water-like ripples and sweeps over the bending pines. Detached plumes and leaves now speed on level currents, now whirl in eddies, or escaping over the edges of the whirls, soar aloft on grand, upswelling domes of air."

John Muir tells us that as he gazed on this scene, "all the so-called ruins of the storm were forgotten," and the wilderness appeared fresh, joyous, immortal.

It took somebody like John Muir to discover the little wilderness bird that lives inside waterfalls. The water ouzel is more attached to water than a duck or a stormy petrel of the Atlantic. It is born on a log or a boulder in a stream. It never flies overland but with whirring wings follows every curve in a stream with lightning rapidity. Coming to a waterfall, it dives into the white torrent, or darts abruptly upward, or follows the curve of the water over the cascade as though this were the bird's toboggan slide.

The ouzel's nest is made out of the green and yellow mosses which coat wet logs and stones near a waterfall. The nest is a foot across, huge for a small bird, and formed with a dome of moss and an arched doorway near the bottom. This wilderness hut keeps fresh in the spray and it is landscaped by rock ferns and grasses that spring up around the mossy walls or in front of the door which drips with crystal beads.

John Muir said of this surprising mountain bird:

"Among all the countless waterfalls I have met in ten years' exploration in the Sierra, whether among icy peaks or in profound canyons, no waterfall was found without its ouzel. No canyon is too cold for this little bird; none too lonely, provided it be rich in falling water. . . . You will find it flitting about in the spray, diving in foaming eddies, whirling like a leaf among beaten foam balls; ever vigorous and enthusiastic. . . . The ouzel seldom swims more than a few yards on the surface for, not being webfooted, he makes slow progress, but by means of his strong, crisp wings, he swims or rather flies fast under the surface.

"One stormy winter morning I observed an ouzel perched on a snag out in the midst of a swift, rushing rapid, singing cheerily . . . he suddenly plunged into the current, leaving his song abruptly broken off. After feeding a minute or two at the bottom (and when one would suppose that he must be swept far downstream) he emerged just where he went down, alighted on the same snag, showered the water beads from his feathers and continued his unfinished song!"

Crater Lake in the Cascade Mountains of Oregon is the remains of a wreck which turned that part of the wilderness inside out. The appalling event that took place five thousand years ago created a peaceful, dark blue lake in a vast bowl that looks like the crater of an old volcano. Crater Lake is five miles across and surrounded by twenty miles of cliffs brightly colored by yellow, green, and red rocks. The lake is two thousand feet deep, the deepest fresh-water lake in the United States today. It is more than a mile high, and it has no beach; the surrounding cliffs continue down to a great depth. There are no fish, and the water is so transparent that a white plate can be seen a hundred feet down.

The series of events which created Crater Lake began millions of years ago when deep cracks opened in the granite crust and volcanic gases rushed out. This relieved the pressure on fiercely hot materials that had been compressed under the solid rock which caused them to change from solid to liquid and pour up through the cracks in the form of pasty, red-hot lava. Thousands of lava flows spread in sheets one on top of another like a heap of griddle-cakes, until they built a vast plateau of black volcanic rock in some places over a mile in thickness.

In the course of time this plateau became one of the largest volcanic fields in the world, with towering cones. Some of the highest are today called Mt. Rainier, Mt. Hood, Mt. Shasta, and Lassen Peak, which was rumbling and fiery as recently as 1914. But greatest of all the volcanoes of the area was Mt. Mazama, tower-ing twelve thousand feet—yet it does not appear today on our maps!

During the Ice Age, Mazama was a silent mountain monarch, dazzling white with an immense glacial dome. Giant glacial fingers from the crown ran down canyons in the side of the mountain, filling them with ice a thousand feet deep. The volcano looked dead, its days of lively fireworks ended. Then, about four thousand years ago, things began to happen to Mt. Mazama.

While Mazama towered serenely, its high slopes and rugged canyons sparkling white in the sunlight, irresistible forces were building up deep beneath the mountain. Four miles down, red-hot, pasty lava was squeezing through old cracks. During thousands of years of the Ice Age the pressure of that lava slowly increased. With Mt. Mazama sitting on top, her crater and vent holes plugged by rock, the lava below opened deep subterranean cracks and spread sideways. So great was the heat and pressure that rocks not only cracked, but they shattered and melted, creating a big reservoir of lava in which gas was dissolved with explosive potentialities, like carbon dioxide in a bottle of pop.

As years passed, the pressure in the reservoir kept mounting. Something had to give. At long last lava plugs in old vents leading to the top of Mt. Mazama were blown out and plumes of white vapor appeared in the blue sky above the ice dome. Steadily the escaping gases increased, pulling up furious lava that boiled and spilled over.

The top of the mountain turned bright red, while the slopes below were still pure white with ice. Mt. Mazama was waking up. The escaping gases, instead of subsiding, became noisier and more terrific. Suddenly there was an awful sound, as though the sky were being ripped off, and a full fountain of pumice mounted from the red summit.

For weeks and weeks the weird fountain of hot dust, stones, and gas bubbles poured up, darkened the sky, and drifted across the land. Mt. Mazama turned the wilderness, with its waterfalls, its snow, and its pine forests, into a gray, dead, empty landscape by burying five thousand square miles under six inches of gray dust.

Twenty-five miles away the inhabitants of an Indian village stared, terrorized, at what was going on. But the pumice blizzard was only a mild prelude to what happened next.

A day came when the breathy rush of the pumice fountain was followed by heavy rumbling and roaring, and the ground shook. Fragments of rock torn off the mountain—some of them weighing tons—bounced lightly in the pumice fountain. Then a black cauli-flower cloud smothered the mountain, blotting out everything except rapid-fire lightning flashes all through the cloud.

Hidden deep within the black cloud, accompanied by an infernal uproar while the wilderness for miles around trembled, the top of Mt. Mazama collapsed. The ancient rocks on the proud heights cracked and crumbled. They toppled inward, melted, and flowed downward *inside* the mountain. There seemed to be no end to this internal avalanche. A long time afterward, when the sky was clear again and the last echo of the rumbling and exploding had died out, only the base of Mt. Mazama was left standing; its upper half had disappeared. It did not blow off—*it had collapsed into the chamber left by the escaping gases!*

Seventeen cubic miles of solid rock vanished. In their place we see Crater Lake, as it was left by the wreck of Mt. Mazama. This was a long-kept secret of the Monster Mountain Wilderness, un-known until 1880.

CHAPTER X

THE SAND AND ROCK WILDERNESS

THE Sand and Rock Wilderness appears motionless and filled with a great silence. There are no forests to make the wind roar and whistle. No animals calling to each other. No crashing waterfalls and splashing brooks.

Vast is the Sand and Rock Wilderness, with the Great Basin to the north and southward three deserts (the Mojave, Sonora, and Chihuahua) side by side across southern California, Arizona, and New Mexico. The triple seas of sand spread over the long border, deep into northern Mexico, and run down the mysterious Mexican peninsula called Lower California. It was in these areas that white men first ran into the Sand and Rock Wilderness some 340 years ago.

Only twenty-five years had passed after Columbus when by sheer luck the Spaniards discovered the capital city of the Aztecs, murdered Montezuma, and plundered that rich civilization of gold and pearls. This met their expectations regarding the gold of Asia, and it whetted their appetites so that they listened to Indian stories of more riches to the north.

In armor, on their horses, and with fifty bedraggled Indians to carry the baggage of each white man, they trailed for thousands of miles over the sands and around the volcanoes of northern Mexico. We can only guess at their sufferings when their armor became too hot to touch.

Another expedition reached the Gulf of California which separates Mexico from the 750-mile peninsula. Seeing blue water to the horizon, they thought they had reached the South Sea off Asia. Now they could travel by water, so they lost no time building boats to sail north and find the rich cities.

Instead of the ocean leading up the coast to China, they found themselves on a dead-end road. Instead of forests, lush valleys, and wealthy cities to conquer, they found burning heat, glaring sand, and dead volcanoes. Their only reward was to discover that this queer sea contained vast oyster beds. The Spaniards were able to buy pearls with "sea-biscuits that were so full of maggots they could run around the ship's deck on their own legs." The half-starved Indians looked on the maggots as delicious fresh meat.

The Spaniards built a fifty-ton ship to cross, as they thought, the open sea; it was equipped to sail for months on a voyage of discovery. Then they sailed laboriously northward on and on, "but slowly, as there was little wind and intense heat." They had plenty of time to collect the biggest cargo of pearls that a ship ever held, but they ran out of sea and spent a month in a broiling sun on a sand bar.

This was the head of the Gulf of California. They were utterly baffled until the captain climbed a volcano and saw water opening up to the northeast. So they had discovered the Straits of Anian, the much sought, often found, always lost waterway from the Pacific to the Atlantic! (The water was a shallow inland sea in the burning desert where Imperial Valley is today.) The crew were delirious with joy. They could now sail northeast triumphantly back to the Atlantic, their fame and fortune secure. The discovery of the Straits of Anian would bring them even more credit than finding rich cities.

They put forth superhuman efforts to get their ship through the swift currents and shallow waters between the sand bars. They struggled far enough to reach a point of no return. Finally, hopelessly grounded, the sorcerer who lured them into this trap caused the water to recede from the keel "as if by enchantment." At last they left the ship with its cargo of pearls upright, to sail into eternity with its keel buried in the desert sand.

Spaniards who sailed west from Mexico across the Gulf of California, instead of north, saw the mountains on the big peninsula of Lower California. They took this to be an island. It was discovered at the same time that a thrilling book was a best seller in Spain, appealing to the spirit of discovery and superstitions of the time. The book re-created the old legend of the Amazons as warlike women who lived on islands "at the right hand of the Indies, very close to the Terrestrial Paradise, abounding in gold and infested with many griffins." The Amazons were led by Queen Calafia who lived on the island of Calafornia. The Spaniards who saw the big peninsula thought this must be Queen Calafia's island. Their leader, Jiménez, called the mystery island Calafornia. It was to prove a bitter disappointment to Spaniards who didn't know they were lost in the American wilderness. But the name stuck.

With visions of gold they hurried over and approached the beach gingerly, armed to the teeth, as they did not belittle the military power of the Amazons. But what they found was a murderous desert where even thorny cactus does not stand upright but crawls on the sand like huge, vicious snakes.

In dry valleys up on the mountains they found Indians living in squalor, barely subsisting among rocks under the hot sun. They were as near to being animals as any wilderness people in the continent.

These people thought that the desert of Lower California was the whole world and they themselves its sole inhabitants. For they went to nobody and nobody came to them, and each little group remained within the limits of its own district. They must have been a miserable relic whose ancestors, a few thousand forgotten years before, had migrated southward from upper California or fled across the gulf from Mexico. They became prisoners of the desert mountains of the peninsula where there were no trails to lead them out and only water was visible to the east and west.

Those Indians were very serious about their ancestors. One family group said they were descended from a bird, another from a fish. Some traced their origin to a particular boulder, while others were proud to be sons of a bush.

The first Spanish visitors also found that in Queen Calafia's California rattlesnakes were the real rulers of those desert mountains. Their capital city was a cleft in high granite walls, containing a pool with ten thousand barrels of clear water at the foot of smooth, vertical rock. The pool could be approached from only one direction, where a sandy ledge led down to the water's edge that a man might follow for a drink.

But rattlesnakes also must drink, and they enjoy clear, cool water. For twenty miles in all directions there was no other place to stop the thirst, and somehow the squirming serpents managed to travel many miles across sand and rock to reach the cool liquid and raise big families there.

The Indians feared the place and looked for distant paltry springs where they could drink. But one day a Spaniard who had wandered far across sand flats and rocks, insane with thirst, found himself in the vicinity of the big pool in the cleft of the rock.

Those who searched for him a few days later found his footsteps in the sand and saw how he had halted and moved restlessly about, waiting for the sun to set. Looking from a rock above, they studied how he had picked his way down the ramp of sand littered with deadly snakes and evidently squashed their coiled and squirming masses underfoot as he ran to get a drink of water. And he had that last cool, refreshing swallow for which he was ready to pay with his life where countless fangs awaited him. They saw his body lying there. The gentleman from Spain only wanted a drink of water in the desert.

After that the Spaniards called the water tank "Hell-Awaits-You." A close friend of the man told how he went back years later and looked down at the skeleton still stretched out on the sand among the rattlesnakes. He was riding a hinny (a little mule) which can smell snakes a couple of miles away. "The hinny stopped, sniffed the air and glanced back at me as if distrusting my common sense. A mile from the tank I left her loose, that she might find her way back to camp if I died on my trip. Wrapping my legs to the knees with folds of buckskin and with a long stick in each hand, I approached the rocks and looked down on the pool. His head turned its eye-sockets toward me and an arm-bone twitched. It was only playful snakes inside his skull which caused empty eye-sockets to glare at me; but the shock nearly cost my life."

The visitor to Hell-Awaits-You was so startled when the eyes in the skeleton blinked at him that he stepped back quickly, slipped, and fell on a big rattler. "Just in time, I grasped the snake's tail and flung it over the cliff. That I did not follow the snake into the pool was due to Saint Appolinario, to whom that morning I had vowed a pearl for the cure of my toothache."

Crazy for cities to plunder, bigger and richer than Montezuma's, the Spanish conquerors bribed and browbeat the Indians to tell them where the other cities were. Every rumor pointed in one direction—*north*. Go north, you Spaniards, and there you will find not one city but seven! And along their streets are rows of shops buzzing with workers of gold and silver. There are houses four stories high. These are the Seven Cities of Cibola, in the province of Quivira. It takes forty days' traveling through a desert to reach them. This is all very clear and definite. Why delay?

We shall never know whether the Indians spun this yarn to speed the Spaniards on their way with the fond hope that they would commit suicide in the desert or whether the Seven Cities of Cibola was a tribal myth out of the northland. Probably it was both. Mexican Indians near the old Mayan and Aztec civilizations could easily believe the talk about the Seven Cities.

In 1530 an Indian from northern Mexico who was the personal slave of the viceroy of New Spain told him that he personally had seen the Seven Cities and that they compared with the cities in Mexico. This settled the matter. Seized with avarice, the viceroy, Nuño de Guzmán, organized an army of four hundred Spaniards and twenty thousand Indians to go and take the cities. They were soon scorched and parched and brought to a halt somewhere below the Rio Grande. Cuirasses and helmets turn into ovens at the touch of the sunlight that shines there.

After Nuño de Guzmán died, the serene call of those Seven Cities might have been forgotten—perhaps delaying the discovery of our marvelous southwest deserts for more than a hundred years —except that Cabeza turned up! He had been on his great circle tour for eight years, from Texas through New Mexico and Arizona, to the Colorado River and down to the Gulf of California. When Cabeza appeared, walking among his cheering Indians, his countrymen promptly asked him about the Seven Cities. He said that he had not seen them himself, but that Indians had told him about seven great cities with houses four and five stories high a few days' march from where he had been.

When Cabeza's hearsay confirming the Seven Cities reached the ears of the new viceroy, De Mendoza, he resolved to succeed where De Guzmán had failed. He selected three hundred Spaniards of noble birth for the honor of taking part in Spain's greatest conquest. They took along eight hundred Indian slaves and hundreds of spare

horses and pack animals. To make success a certainty, Spain's famous soldier, De Coronado, was made captain-general of the expedition.

Coronado set forth with banners flying; but by the time they reached Arizona (somewhere near Douglas), the wilderness "got" them. The gentlemen horsemen had to turn into muleteers. They had to learn how to make campfires out of cactus and eat mesquite beans. "As Coronado came to where the desert begins and saw that there was nothing good, he could not repress his sadness; notwithstanding the marvels promised further on."

It is written that after fifteen days more of toiling through the desert they were about twenty-five miles from Cibola (in Pueblo Indian country) and there they met the first Indians. As these were the first white men the Indians had seen, they fled with outlandish yells and hoots. Coronado's men were "so surprised, some saddled their horses the wrong way."

By sheer never-stop, never-say-die leadership, Coronado conquered the Sand and Rock Wilderness in a way. For some three years his men wandered far and wide across the Southwest, looking for the golden cities. They did find four- and five-story houses built by cliff dwellers and Pueblo Indians. It seems that Cabeza had spoken truly, for the Indians who told him about these houses must have thought them grand and elaborate in their simple terms. But there were no streets lined with shops which were filled with workers in gold.

Coronado staggered out of the desert broken in health and wealth, a defeated man. But he had planted the Spanish flag all over the Sand and Rock Wilderness!

Some five hundred miles north of the sand bars at the head of the Gulf of California, an astounding event occurred in the heart of the Sand and Rock Wilderness. A party of Spaniards had been traveling twenty days across a desert plateau without finding water. The few pints left in the deer bladders which they carried were hot and stale. Suddenly they caught sight of a river just a mile away. But though they struggled three days to reach it, they could never touch its water. The river they saw was *a mile straight down* under their feet—at the bottom of the Grand Canyon.

That happened in 1540—seventy-five years before Champlain discovered the Great Lakes, eighty years before the *Mayflower* arrived in Plymouth Harbor—when a party of twenty-five horsemen, wearing breastplates and helmets, stood on the brink of the Grand Canyon and cursed their luck. Captain Cárdenas was an important man. He personally owned "twelve horses, three sets of Castilian armor, two pairs of cuirasses, and a coat of mail." But with it all he could not get a single drink of water from that river in the Sand and Rock Wilderness.

The report of the expedition says, "They came to the gorge of a river. From the brink, it looked as if to the opposite side it must be more than nine miles by air line. They spent three days trying to find a way down to the river which, from above, appeared to be only six feet wide. The descent was found to be impossible, for at the end of three days, Melgosa, Juan, and another, they being the lightest and most agile, undertook to clamber down. They kept descending in sight of the men left above, until they were lost to view.

"They returned without being able to reach the bottom because of great obstacles. For what from above had appeared to be easy, proved rough and difficult. They said they had gone only a third of the way down. But from the place they reached, the river must be as wide as a mile. Men above estimated small rocks jutting from the wall of the canyon as high as a man. They swore that when they reached them, the rocks were taller than the highest tower of Seville."

How did it happen that Captain Cárdenas found himself standing on the brink of the Grand Canyon in northern Arizona when all wildernesses to the north, east, and west were as yet unseen by white men?

It was another of those wild-goose chases like planting a ship under full sail in the desert sand near the mouth of the Colorado River and that other baffling excursion when they found the odd people, cut off from the rest of the world in Lower California.

After Cárdenas tried in vain to get a drink of water from the Colorado River at the bottom of the Grand Canyon and turned his back in disgust on that spectacle, 329 years passed until a man went through the Grand Canyon in a boat.

The deepest crack in the earth's crust was created by special conditions which existed in that area and nowhere else in the world. The combination was:

1. An eternal length of time—in this case, several million years.

2. A husky river flowing all that time, with an unfailing volume of water—in this case, the Colorado River, fed by waters from the Rocky Mountains in Wyoming and Colorado.

3. The land through which the river flows lifting steadily higher in pace with the rate that the river cuts down through its rock. This remarkable thing occurred with the whole area rising to become a plateau a mile high.

4. A desert dry region, so that frequent rains do not wear down

the sharp edges of the cut and form a sloping valley. Dryness is the nature of the Sand and Rock Wilderness.

So the chasm was created, filled with magnificent colors of rocks in layers like a sliced, multi-colored layer cake. Trails of trappers led to its brink, where men stared down into the dark, mysterious depths, where a tumbling, angry, heavy, roaring river looked like a silent, silver thread. Then, like Cárdenas, they turned away lest they die of thirst within sight of water.

It was August 1869 when Major John W. Powell and nine companions launched two little boats, the *Emma Dean* and the *No-Name*. Five men in one boat got through, but a nineteen-foot falls snatched the *No-Name* and smashed it to kindling. The place still bears the name Disaster Falls.

Of this daring expedition a mile down in the depths of the earth, Major Powell wrote: "The great river sinks into insignificance, dashes its angry waves against the walls and cliffs that rise to the world above. . . . We have an unknown distance to run. What falls there are we know not. What rocks beset the channel we know not. What walls rise over the river we know not."

He noted how the place was so deep, the walls so high, that clouds floated below the summits of the cliffs and played around thousand-foot columns of rock. "We hear a great roar ahead— sound grows louder and louder as we run—we find ourselves at the top of a long, broken fall, with ledges and pinnacles of rock obstructing the river. The descent is eighty feet, and the rushing waters break in great waves on the rocks and lash themselves into a mad, white foam."

The Sand and Rock Wilderness is so old and unchanging that it bears the marks of events of past ages as though they occurred yesterday. Trunks of large trees are scattered like jackstraws across a desert in northern Arizona. From a distance they look as though they had just been felled; but they will not be used as timbers for a house or logs for a campfire because they are solid rock.

Those forest trees were growing 160 million years ago in swampy land. Then mountains pushed up and cut off winds bringing rain from the Pacific. The swamp dried up and the trees died, tumbled down, and sank into the mud. In the course of time the trunks were buried three thousand feet deep under the sand. Down there the wood cells became filled with minerals dissolved out of the sand, and this turned the tree trunks into agates streaked with beautiful mineral colors.

In a recent era the covering of sand where these trees were buried was washed away by torrents of cloudbursts and blown away in desert sandstorms. It is thus that these trees of a bygone age reappeared on the desert floor. The agate trees are jewels cast up out of the ancient sand and rock wilderness, lying there like trees carelessly thrown down only last year instead of millions of years ago.

Seventy miles west of the Painted Desert, where the agate trees lie, there is a round hole in the sand and rock wilderness. It is so deep that if the Washington Monument were standing in it, the top would be below the rim of the hole—which is 570 feet deep and three miles around. Fifty thousand years ago a tremendous piece of iron fell out of the sky, and, striking the Sand and Rock Wilderness, it dug this hole out of solid rock in a split second. A shattering explosion echoed in the canyons of the Painted Desert, and a dazzling flash lighted up twenty thousand square miles of sand and rock.

It is a good guess that rattlesnakes trembled in their dens, horned lizards dived into their holes, kangaroo rats jumped higher than they had ever jumped before, and Gila monsters, fleeing in terror, ran for the first time in their lazy lives. But no wilderness people witnessed the crash of this visitor from outer space for it all happened before the Indians came to build their pueblos in the wilderness.

The force of the blow blasted and vomited four hundred million tons of rock and bent the surrounding layers of rock upward more than one hundred feet. At the same time it buried a ball of iron and nickel weighing more than three million tons a thousand feet deep under the rocks. That gift of metal from the sky is still there—

the ball is too hard to drill through and too heavy for a bulldozer to move it.

The awful crash which left this scar that time does not erase was only a trifling event in the ancient Sand and Rock Wilderness. A minute after it happened timeless serenity returned.

One evening in 1901 a young miner named Jim White was returning to his shack in the foothills of the Guadalupe Mountains of New Mexico. Climbing among the rough stones, he caught sight of black smoke curling against the pink sunset sky a mile or so away. This was strange; he knew of no camp in that place. Hurrying over to see what was going on, Jim came to a ridge and looked down on the spookiest sight he had ever seen. Instead of spiraling black smoke from a stranger's campfire, he beheld in the dim twilight millions and millions of bats rushing out of the mouth of the cave. He had discovered Bat Cave.

Twenty years before some cattlemen had muttered something about seeing bats, but it took a man with curiosity to get excited about them and explore further. In days that followed Jim White saw myriads of bats pour out from underground just at sunset and return just before dawn to disappear into the same cave. Entering himself in the daytime, he found a huge cavern room draped with bats hanging head downward from the walls and ceilings like black clusters of grapes.

Passing through Bat Cave, Jim entered a maze of mysterious corridors which led into a series of big rooms deep in the rock. Here were fantastic crystal sculpturings of all shapes and sizes. Some hung down from the ceiling like fancy stone icicles. Pedestals rose from the floor, decorated with crystal forms as colorful and delicate as flowers. Arranged along the walls or standing apart on ledges were rocks with iridescent colors, twisted and tortured and spiraling. All this had been waiting there, unseen and unknown—like an exhibit of eerie sculpturing from another planet.

After that discovery Jim White devoted his life to exploring the

marvelous desert cellar. He followed twenty-three miles of galleries to a depth of more than one thousand feet underground. He discovered a rock chamber thirteen hundred feet long and six hundred feet wide, with an arched ceiling two hundred feet high. This he named, in the plain language of a miner, the Big Room.

In later years Jim White, the man who discovered the world's largest limestone cavern under the floor of America's Sand and Rock Wilderness, was appointed chief ranger of the Carlsbad Caverns National Park. Even today the great cavern has not revealed all its secrets. There are cracks between crystal columns and dark recesses behind frozen stone icicles; and there are holes in walls where the beam of a flashlight disappears in blackness, leading into corridors where no foot has ever trod. And below the one-thousand-foot level there are even deeper levels with corridors and dungeons and strange crystal treasures still undiscovered. Nobody knows how big this palatial cellar is.

The Mountain Men who first crossed the Rockies, arriving at the westernmost pass, stared down at a purple and yellow wilderness that blended with the sky and seemed to have no far side. This was the Great Basin that includes the Great Sandy Desert of central

233

Oregon, Great Salt Lake, and most of Utah and Nevada. The Great Basin offered many kinds of torture to the people who first tried to cross it on the way to the Pacific coast. A floor of lava rock with sharp edges tears the feet of horses; square miles of the largest sand dunes of the continent are heaped up along the western face of the Rockies in Colorado; and here is an immense sagebrush desert, with a flat, gravel floor, no spring, stream, or water at all, but gray wormwood and sagebrush, their quivering dry branches sounding like death rattles.

The tough men who first came to the edge of the Great Basin were used to hardship trails. Sand and rock, fierce sun, and gray bushes could not stop them; but they were puzzled and surprised when they followed disappearing rivers.

The Rocky Mountain's snow fields, glaciers, and lakes deliver much water to west-facing canyons, headed west toward the Pacific Ocean. But rivers in the Great Basin never reach the sea. The water sinks through the porous floor of lava gravel, or evaporates in hot sand, or goes into a lake without an outlet. Blue water in the Great Basin can be a tragic deception. In many places lakes stand motionless for hundreds of years without the refreshment of running water, while they dissolve the elemental mineral salts out of the sand and rock and turn bitter salty. Many lakes have evaporated, leaving a glaring white patch of salt crust.

This weird desert called the Great Basin played many terrible tricks on the people who first tried to follow its disappearing rivers and drink its blue bitter water. But one of the most surprising and dangerous tricks is the cyclone-cloudburst that brings too much water.

A man is wrapped in his blanket by a sagebrush campfire on the bank of an arroyo (dry stream bed). The gulch is utterly dry and stony, but an experienced Great Basin man knows where to find a tin cup of water under a boulder here and there.

The night is clear, with no cloud in sight. The man sleeps soundly until three o'clock in the morning, when an alarm clock goes off inside him. He sits bolt upright, listening to a deep rumbling and roaring sound up in the mountains miles away. It seems ridiculous, with the sky so full of bright stars and the air so still, that any storm in the distant mountains could matter. But there is no more sleeping that night. It is time to pack the horse and get moving. In an hour a wall of water will come boiling along the arroyo faster than a man on a horse can run before it.

The unique cyclone-cloudburst of the Great Basin begins as a small, dense black cloud held close against a mountainside, just below the top and at the head of a canyon. The cloud is at that one spot only, and everywhere else the weather is clear and beautiful. The cloud does not expand much, but quickly it grows denser and denser and tighter like a clenched fist ready to strike. Suddenly it bounces and tumbles. It dashes itself against the rocks. Then it straightens up and begins to move slowly like a giant spinning top, with its lower point touching the ground. This is no dust cloud; it is almost solid water. As it roars down the mountain it tosses around rocks weighing tons and mounts a flood that roars out of the canyon thirty feet deep.

There is another place of dreadful splendor in the Sand and Rock Wilderness. It is the deepest valley in America and the most deadly. It is a glaring, harsh link between the two great regions of the Sand and Rock Wilderness, with the Great Basin to the north and the Mojave Desert to the south.

Death Valley was a vacuity in the North American wilderness until it was discovered in a tragic way in 1849. Unlike other wildernesses, which were first entered by explorers, soldiers, or trappers, Death Valley was discovered by family men with their children, together with some careless, carefree boys out for adventure.

It was the year of the forty-niners. Dust hung over the High Plains, where creaking, cumbersome covered wagons headed for California along the Platte River trail. Crossing the Great Divide at South Pass, they came down into Salt Lake City, a base for rest and wagon repair and stocking up with supplies. Families from towns back East met each other and got together in parties, employing experienced guides to conduct them by various trails across mountains and deserts to California and Oregon.

Came a time when a large party was organized to follow a trail for weeks and weeks, southward and westward, to reach southern California in the vicinity of Los Angeles. This was the famous Sandwalking Company in charge of a Mormon elder named Captain Hunt, who had come back to Salt Lake City from southern California after the Mexican War. Many groups combined in the Sandwalking Company, totaling two hundred people, more than one hundred wagons, and five hundred horses and oxen. When they were en route the wagons were scattered along the trail for some twenty-five miles as they rumbled along, following Captain Hunt.

Somewhere in the dust of this great caravan were seven wagons with all the possessions of the Bennetts and the Arcanes—including two-year-old Charlie Arcane and three Bennett children ranging from two to seven years and their dog Cuff.

During the first week people were in high spirits, with plenty of provisions in the wagons, fresh meat on the hoof, and Captain Hunt knowing where to find rivers and springs for camping places. In the evenings parties of young men stirred things up with horseplay and competed for laughs as they visited the campfires of the groups scattered across the valley. These parties called themselves the Hawkeyes, Jayhawkers, Buckskins, Bergamasters, and Wolverenes. The Jayhawkers were the noisiest, especially when they elected a captain of their own, named Doty, who had to be initiated.

One night a stranger named Williams dropped in. Where was the man from? Where was he going? What was the news? A crowd gathered around and Williams did a lot of talking. He said he knew a short cut that would save five hundred miles to southern California. This was interesting, for Captain Hunt had warned them that the trail ahead would take many weeks of travel, climbing mountain passes over sharp, volcanic stones and across sun-parched deserts. Five hundred miles shorter! No wonder they listened to Williams. He showed them on their charts where to turn directly west to find the short cut. No, he had not gone that way himself, but he had heard about it from Indians, and he was happy to pass along the information in case it would be helpful.

Captain Hunt was dead against it. He argued that no white man had ever been over that cutoff. There were many bitter arguments around the campfires all that night.

Under Captain Hunt's orders the wagons got under way the next day and continued south. But a day or so later they came to the landmark where Williams had said they should turn to the right for the cutoff. When Captain Hunt looked back along the miles of the column, he saw team after team turn off to the right. Perhaps half the wagons left him, and among those that turned off were the seven wagons of the Arcanes and the Bennetts.

A couple of days of trackless travel changed the minds of most of the defectors, who turned back and rejoined Captain Hunt. He probably slowed down to give them a chance to catch up. But the twenty wagons of the Jayhawkers and the seven wagons of the Arcanes and Bennetts did not turn back; they continued west. In two more days they reached a point of no return.

As they crept on, the few stunted old trees grew farther and farther apart; there were no clumps of moist grass, not anything green. The mountains and valleys ahead looked even more stark and barren. They saw a high butte twenty miles to the south and they all waited while a man went to climb it. When he came back he said that all creation was in sight, and from anything he could see, it would not afford a traveler a single drink in the whole distance or give a poor ox a mouthful of grass.

Hot, tired, worried, with only the water in their kegs, they broke out in violent quarreling about what direction to take. Small groups among them separated and went in different directions. Two men who owned one wagon fought over it and settled the duel by sawing the wagon in two.

In a later year, a surviving Jayhawker told what happened to a group of nineteen men who broke off by themselves. They were caught in the north end of Death Valley where they burned their wagons, ate their oxen, and a few struggled through to survive just barely. Others went around a rock called Poverty Point and were never seen again. He told how at one place they spotted a bush and a few blades of grass and found a little pool of water under a boulder. "Jack West swallowed all he could hold and then told the boys to kill him for he would never feel so good again."

A few words, scribbled at the time, tell what the Sand and Rock Wilderness did to those men:

"South, 28 mile, no water, 10 o'clock at night—thence west 10 mile, no water—then south 12 mile, no water—then southeast, 8 mile, got weak—then due south 20 mile, no water—left wagons, packed cattle, 6 days wandering. Fish from Iowa died. Ischam died same day in evening. Robinson and McGowan died. Offered Brian $5 for biscuit but he refused. Old man Townsend left. Richards found water. . . ."

The writer added that one man lay down at the water Richards found and was dead before he could take a drink.

The night that Williams turned up and talked too much, the families with little children were presented with a terrible dilemma. The long column of the Sandwalkers under Captain Hunt was creeping slowly on a roundabout route. They visualized the weeks ahead, how they would be dragging across the hot southern desert with only stale water in their kegs to drink and gnawing on bacon for the daily fare. There would be no more fun of caravan life. It was a question how much the children could take bumping along in a stuffy wagon all day, when it would be too hot to get out and run on the sand with Cuff.

A man named William Lewis Manly helped them to make up their minds. Manly was one of the most popular adventurers of the West, and also he had prestige because of an exploit a few weeks before joining the Sandwalking Company. He had gone over South

Pass to the Green River where he bought an old ferry boat. Then he did the "impossible" by riding this several hundred miles down through the canyons of Utah, almost to where the Green River flows into the Colorado. He got below the place where the name *Ashley* had been painted on the canyon wall twenty-five years before.

Manly had become a friend of the Arcanes and the Bennetts. He was interested in the children; they all looked to him for help and advice. Manly said that he was taking the Williams' cutoff with the Jayhawkers and *why not come along?*

Who wouldn't under the circumstances? There would be Manly and another free lance they liked, named Rogers, and the boys were gay and energetic company. So it was that the two families who managed their seven wagons independently followed the wheel tracks of the Jayhawkers to the brink of Death Valley.

As the Jayhawkers grew more desperate they pushed ahead faster and faster, Manly and Rogers with them, until out of sight of the Arcanes and the Bennetts. But when they fought with each other, they left marks in the sand that told the story to the party with the little children that came along a day or so later.

After the burning of the wagons, feasting on oxen meat, and drinking of oxen blood, Manly and Rogers had pushed ahead with the nineteen Jayhawkers, leaving the Arcanes and Bennetts behind.

They struggled over the Funeral Mountains into Furnace Creek Wash, where they found the fresh-water spring that saved their lives.

Manly told later how they thought their sufferings were at an end. They expected to see at last a green California valley. Instead they stared down into a glaring white blank far below. They were seeing the floor of Death Valley, 280 feet below sea level. Manly tells how he noted far ahead the peak of a high mountain covered with snow (Mount Whitney, outside Alaska the highest mountain in the United States). He thought of the cool snow and the wonderful fresh water that rushed from it. But with that hideous, burning salt crust to cross, the snow was as out of reach as if it were on the moon.

Manly and Rogers knew that the best chance to survive was to push on with the Jayhawkers and cross that terrible valley as fast as possible. They also knew that without their help the Arcanes and Bennetts and their children would die. When the boys started down Furnace Creek Wash, Manly and his friend turned back to find Mr. Bennett's party and lead it to the spring.

After that, for forty days and nights, this cruel place in the wilderness held these people in a grip of death.

Somehow they tumbled, slid, and bumped their wagons down Furnace Creek Wash a couple of thousand feet to the bottom of Death Valley. The white and blistering crust was so hard a wagon made no visible track on it. They found themselves trapped there, between the steep Funeral Mountains at their backs and the cliffs of the Panamint Mountains ahead. They tried to go south to get around the steepest mountains, but the feeble oxen staggered; their feet slipped on the crust and they could not drag the wagons over the rough salt. Then they headed west (the valley is only six miles wide at that place) into a canyon.

Mustering a few surviving oxen, all concentrating on one wagon, they pushed and pulled and forced it high up. They had to get over that mountain to live and they had to have a wagon to carry the children and the water kegs and what was left of bacon and grain. With Manly's encouragement they found superhuman strength— and at the top of the canyon they found a vertical cliff! They had to turn back and toil down those hard-won rocks, half tumbling, with that wagon and its dying oxen, and return to the glaring floor of the valley.

Manly got them back to Furnace Creek Wash where they were within reach of the spring. The pitiable little group went into camp, utterly exhausted. There seemed to be nothing left to do. They looked at each other in an awful silence. One mother told later of that retreat back across Death Valley. "It was always the same . . . an awful silence. . . . The pitiful, delirious wails of the children were worse to bear than the killing thirst. Every step I expected to sink down and die. I could hardly see."

In desperation it was decided that Manly and Rogers should go ahead alone to find a way out and bring back food. Mr. Bennett guessed they would be back in fifteen days at the longest. So an ox was killed to fill their knapsacks, and the two men started off while those behind waved hats and bonnets as they disappeared from sight.

Fifteen days passed and nobody returned. Bennett declared that Manly would come back if he were alive. Day dragged after day while they lived on a tiny bit of rice and tea that was left, to vary the diet of stringy meat from oxen who were shrinking with starvation before their eyes.

On the twenty-fifth day they were lying under the wagon, half dead, half sleeping, hope gone—when a gunshot broke the desert silence.

Manly, who stood holding a smoking gun about a mile away, tells how he was sure they were too late. He saw no signs of life. "Then a man came out from under the wagon and stood up and looked around, didn't see us in the glare, then suddenly he did see. He threw up his arms high over his head and shouted *the boys have come!* Then other bare heads appeared from under the wagon . . . they caught and embraced us with all their strength. Mrs. Bennett fell on her knees and clung to me like a maniac. Not a word was spoken."

Manly and Rogers had climbed through trailless canyons and across deserts where no white man had been before, struggling across two hundred miles from Death Valley to San Fernando (just north of Hollywood). There they got a white horse, a brown horse, and a little mule. Loading these with supplies, they turned around and started back across the Mojave Desert, headed for Death Valley again. Eight days later the horses walked with drooping heads; prickly cactuses and thorny mesquite punctured their feet and legs. Bunch grass seemed to make them thirstier. Their tired steps grew slower and slower. The men dismounted and led the horses, which now carried only saddles. One day they saw water, and they rushed to it and cast themselves on the ground at it. The water was heavily salt.

The little mule was lively and sharp-witted and cropped every spear of grass. He was now carrying most of the load, with the men bearing what they could. They buried a bag of wheat under a boulder, to find it on the return.

They were an odd team—two men on foot, stooped under bulging knapsacks, two horses with empty saddles, a little mule stepping along briskly under an overloaded pack. For ten days they picked their way across the trackless Mojave Desert. Every step had to be chosen carefully to avoid stumbling over rough boulders or brushing against a jumping cholla cactus, which drives fierce needles into the flesh at the slightest touch; they had to give a wide berth to the Joshua trees which looked like mad giants brandishing great fistfuls of ten-inch daggers.

They could not pick up their own footsteps where they had stumbled along, so tired and desperate, a few days before. But they kept the northeast course toward that awful valley, staring ahead for a glimpse of the Panamint Mountains. When they were about fifty miles away they saw the mountains through the yellow haze. Perhaps they were too late. Manly and Rogers spoke a little louder

to their horses, tried to quicken their footsteps. They had to reach those people without an hour's delay, with their four small children waiting for them, huddled together at the bottom of the hideous oven beyond that mountain sky line.

When they finally entered a canyon of the Panamints, the little mule started up without a pause; but the horses' heads now almost touched the ground, and as they started climbing among the rough rocks, the poor animals stopped at every step, gathering strength to take the next. Manly thought it would be impossible to get the women and children back over the mountains and across the desert without the horses, but now they had reached the end of their trail.

Manly later wrote about it: "We removed the saddles and placed them on a rock. After a few minutes' hesitation—minutes crowded with torrents of wild ideas and desperate thoughts—we left them to their fate and moved on." They could not spare the ammunition which had to be saved for long-eared desert rabbits. "Just as we were passing out of sight they neighed pitifully after us. One who has never heard the last despairing, pleading neigh of a horse left to die can form no idea of its almost human appeal." Then they saw the white horse charge head on against a white cliff and commit suicide.

The little mule kept going, her bulging pack, like a phantom ball, bouncing up and down, up and down, as she stepped steadily among the rocks.

243

Manly and Rogers were upset by the loss of their horses and aching and weary from climbing with their loads. The men had no breath for conversation, but one muttered, "Ain't she good!" And the other gave a faint grunt. It was their vote of confidence in the little mule.

Many hours passed, with the mule leading the way up the mountain, finding a path with little hesitation, zigzagging between boulders, jumping and stumbling over smaller ones. The crest of the Panamints was only five hundred feet above when, over the top of a boulder, they saw the mule's load stand still. The canyon had narrowed suddenly, and the loose stones among which it was possible to pick a path had disappeared. The little mule was waiting at the base of a ten-foot wall. She turned to look at the men inquiringly, it was their turn to take the lead.

Ten feet is a trifle among mountains that rise ten thousand feet. The men could manage to climb the wall, but they couldn't boost up the mule. So they brought stones and built a ramp for the animal. Over the top of the wall, climbing was fairly easy for a few hundred feet, and then suddenly they came to a cliff standing at the head of the canyon. The cliff was broken by a ledge that slanted across its face from bottom to top. The men thought they could traverse this narrow ledge, but what about the mule?

While the animal nipped on bunch grass and wiry twigs of sagebrush, the men crawled up along the ledge on hands and knees. At one place for about twelve feet it narrowed to a shelf *scarcely four inches wide*. Below this narrow place there was a sheer drop of fifty feet. Manly dared to try it and reached the top where the ground sloped gently to the crest of the pass. He wrote: "It was all I could do to cross the shelf and it was impossible at that place to build a foundation to widen it to make a ramp for the animal."

The men knew that if they could somehow get the mule across the shelf, they could reach the crest from where easier slopes descended into Death Valley. They worked along the ledge, breaking off all projecting rocks and sending loose rocks crashing down, especially along the four-inch shelf, until every loose piece on the shelf itself was removed. They unpacked the mule, tied the ropes together, to make two lead lines, one in front and one behind. Manly was out in front and Rogers behind, with the mule between. They kept the lines taut to balance the animal and give her confidence. Let Manly tell the story:

"Without a moment's hesitation, the little mule tried the ledge. Carefully and steadily she went along, selecting a place before putting her foot down. When she came to the shelf she leaned gently on the rope, never making a sudden start or jump, but cautiously as a cat, moving slowly along. There was now no turning back for her. She must cross this narrow place over which I had crept on hands and knees, or be dashed to death. When the worst spot was reached, she stopped, looking back as well as she could. I called encouragingly and talked to her. Rogers wanted to holler at her, and frighten her across, but I thought it was better to talk to her gently, and let her move steadily.

"The lives of helpless women and children hung in the balance. This was the climax time of all the trials and hardships. As I watched the little mule, I burst into tears and was not ashamed of my weakness. Rogers said softly, 'Come.' I gently pulled the rope. She smelled all around and looked over every inch of the ledge, then took one careful step after another—until, calculating the distance, she made a spring and landed on the rock beyond!

"There could be no more hopeless moment than the one just passed. We would push on now and get through to the people. We would save them all.

"It was a strange canyon. The sun never shone into it where the little mule crossed the shelf. The rocks were a peculiar yellow color. That night the mule was turned loose she ranged and searched for food, finding only scattered bunches of sagebrush. She picked at them here and there and then at dark came into the camp and lay down close to us."

Two days later Manly and Rogers, leading the little mule loaded with supplies, halted one mile away from the silent wagon where there was no sign of life. And Manly fired the gun.

Excitedly Manly and Rogers unpacked the flour and beans from the mule and took two golden oranges from the sack for the children. After a day of food and rest they all set out together for the two-hundred-mile trip across mountains and deserts to San Fernando.

Without horses they made saddles and bags out of the canvas top of the covered wagon for the women and children to ride the two remaining oxen. The oldest boy and girl, George and Melissa, sat on the back of one ox, while the two-year-olds, Charlie and Martha, stood in cloth pockets that dangled on each side of them. The two mothers rode the other and last surviving ox. They headed across Death Valley for a roundabout pass which Manly and Rogers had taken on their trip out of the valley. All went well for a couple of miles, then a strap slipped and the oxen bucked and bawled. The ladies tumbled off their ox and caught the children, and when it was found that nobody was hurt, they rolled on the ground, holding their sides with hysterical laughter. That was the first laugh they had had for a long time.

On the second day the party reached the crest of the Panamints. They halted and looked back at the bright-colored mountains and the blazing white valley floor far below. In Manly's words: "We took off our hats and then, overlooking the scenes of so much trial, suffering, and death, we spoke the thought uppermost, saying, *'Good-bye, Death Valley!'* Ever after it was called Death Valley. Ours were the first visible footsteps and we the party which named it the saddest and most dreadful name which came to us from its memories."

CHAPTER XI

THE WEST COAST WILDERNESS

A PHANTOM wilderness once ran for five thousand miles from Bering Strait to Lower California. For four hundred years after white men first saw the Pacific coast, this wilderness fought against everyone who trespassed in it. Wilderness people killed them; fog and rain hid anchoring places; sand bars and rocks trapped and wrecked ships; steep mountains and impenetrable forests blocked the way, and deserts confronted them with barriers of heat and thirst. The discoverers of the West Coast Wilderness came upon it at far separate times and places, from four points of the compass, and each thought he was discovering a different part of the world.

Juan Rodríguez Cabrillo, sailing from Panama in June 1542, was destined to be the first white man to see our California coast. He found plenty of Indians, especially on Catalina Island and the islands of the Santa Barbara channel, and he traded with them trinkets from

247

Old Spain for fish. His chief problem after coping with storms was how to get enough to eat in that desolate world. Like Columbus, Cabrillo had no idea what he was looking at—it didn't matter because it looked worthless, anyway.

Of course, Cabrillo crossed no ocean and he kept land more or less in sight on the starboard rail, but a lookout, staring at horizons to the north, can feel just as much dread of the unknown as one looking at horizons to the west. The ocean which Cabrillo explored had even more demons than that of Columbus.

Cabrillo had two little ships, home-made in Panama, frail and unwieldy like Chinese junks. Their crews were small. They had no charts and only meager provisions. Moreover, the crews who had been stumbling around in a strange, tropical jungle were highly superstitious. They thought that the world was square, not a globe, and that their ships would fall off sharp edges into hideous space where the crew would be seized by demons.

Consider how long they had been cooped up in their rickety little craft, tossed in mountainous seas, blinded by fogs, whipped by gales! It took three months to go from Panama to the area of San Diego. From there they sailed north for forty-five days more, reaching a calm place where they saw big tree trunks floating in the water and thought that this must be near the mouth of a river. But the logs blocked the way, they were unable to find the river, and there was no wind to push them.

There is no certainty where the spot they saw the floating tree trunks was, but from his logbook it is calculated that Cabrillo went the whole length of the California coast and that the river was the Eel River near the Oregon line. If so, Cabrillo was the first white man to see the colossal tree trunks of the redwoods in Humboldt County. But they were floating in the water and he never put foot in the forest, delaying the discovery of the redwoods three hundred years.

Fate played another trick on Cabrillo. At the end of his resources where the big logs were floating in the water, he ordered his two ships to put about, and they started on the long trip back, desperately looking for a safe harbor where they could anchor and rest. They caught sight of the headlands of the Golden Gate as stern, forbidding mountains barely visible through the fog and put to sea to clear this dangerous land, missing the discovery of San Francisco Bay, one of the world's finest harbors.

What was Cabrillo looking for? Why was he so disappointed? It was the same old illusion—gold and riches—that had sent Columbus across the Ocean Sea and lured Coronado to stagger all over the Sand and Rock Wilderness. This was the time when all Spain was excited by the Seven-Cities-of-Cibola fairy tale. Cabrillo's voyage was part of that quest. The viceroy had sent Coronado to find the Seven Cities by land, and ships north in the Gulf of California to find a water route to them. When the first ships were stuck in the desert sand, two more were built to sail west and north, outside the big amazon island (Lower California). This was Cabrillo's project.

Cabrillo was a great and daring man who gave his scared crew wonderful leadership. But Cabrillo was unable to do any real exploring because he had such miserable ships in such foul weather. The land he saw was a constant menace to be avoided, "the coasts high and steep and with great difficulty could we land from tremendous surf." Nights were cold, mornings foggy. Cabrillo had no time to think of anything else but handling his ships and surviving.

On the way back he fell ill and they made a landing near Monterey. There, a month later, in January 1553, Cabrillo died, overcome by defeat in the midst of the wilderness. His people brought the two ships back to Mexico, in despair after a voyage of 283 days of fabulous discovery.

The reports of the survivors, who were sick and tired with the trip, postponed exploring in that part of the world by the Spanish for the rest of the century. There was no thought of discovering the west coast of a continent. Even though the land faced west, it was considered to be part of Asia which would curve northwestward and join the Orient. Anyway, this first glimpse of the California coast was checked off as worthless, and the Spanish turned their attention to South America where they were finding real treasure on the coasts of Chile and Peru.

After Cabrillo thirty-five years passed while the long west coast remained unknown and untouched. Then an extraordinary visitor turned up who spent the month of July 1579 on the coast just north of San Francisco Bay.

It was the time of Queen Elizabeth's reign, when England flowered with gallant deeds and challenged Spain everywhere on the seas. The Queen's Sea Dogs were, in fact, pirates who enriched the royal treasury by capturing Spanish ships around Florida and South America. John Hawkins, who put Ingram ashore on the Gulf of Mexico, was one of them. Among the buccaneers Sir Francis Drake was the greatest seaman and the most daring, and to him the Queen gave the supreme assignment of all. He was to sail around South America, through the Straits of Magellan, and to the Orient, with five ships. He could pick up treasure en route by overpowering Spanish ships on both coasts of South America.

What about the west coast of North America? There was no news of any wealth in that region. A rumor out of Spain was that the Spaniards had found it worthless. But nobody was sure whether or not that land was connected with Asia. So Drake had permission to see if he could find a northern water route leading directly back to the Atlantic. If so, that would be more exciting and important than continuing to the Orient. This was looking for the historic Northwest Passage in reverse.

During two years' sailing around South America, Drake lost all but one of his ships in storms and fights. That one was his flagship, the *Golden Hind*, which was so overloaded with captured treasure and survivors, including "25 tons of precious metals, besides 10 tons of cannon and arms," it was hardly seaworthy after storms had driven it far north where they saw dangerous rocks on the coast of Oregon. So Drake turned south to find a harbor where he could make repairs. He felt his way down the unknown coast in fog, storm, and cold, searching for a harbor.

At length Drake dropped his anchor in a little bay which was too exposed for ship repairs. Drake called it "unsatisfactory," and in a day or so they were on their way again. They did not quite hold out long enough to discover San Francisco Bay. They dropped anchor in a small inlet, just north of the Golden Gate, where they spent a month repairing the ship. Drake's log says: "It was a convenient and fit harborough . . . but nipping cold and continuous fog." Indians, excited to see white skins, made no serious trouble, but they crowded close and pilfered the party. So Drake built a stone fort to live in while they were fixing the ship.

Nothing is said about exploring in the area. They wanted only to quit that hostile, dangerous wilderness as soon as possible and sail back to England via the Orient. When their ship was ready, they vanished into the sunset, leaving only the stone fort—and one thing else—to mark the phantom visit.

Although Drake felt no real interest in the West Coast Wilderness, he left Queen Elizabeth's calling card. He nailed to "a firme post" a brass plate on which he called the land New Albion * and took possession of it in the name of his Queen.

That historic brass plate was lost for three hundred years until one Sunday in 1936, a businessman out for a walk near San Rafael on San Francisco Bay picked it up where it may have been dropped by an Indian. The plate bore the inscription just as Drake said, giving Queen Elizabeth title to New Albion, which today we call California.

The daring Cabrillo and the hasty Drake brought back no news from the west coast to stir the imagination. They left that wilderness where they found it—its secrets unrevealed, its nature unknown—

* Albion was the ancient Roman name for England, used as a genteel expression in Elizabethan times. It was coined from the Latin word *alba* for "white," when the Romans saw the white chalk cliffs of Dover. When Drake saw white cliffs on the California coast, the name came to mind.

an unexplored part of the world. And thus it continued for 165 years—except for a vivid glimpse of Monterey Bay by a remarkable Spaniard named Sebastián Vizcaíno.

This man had energy and imagination. He found he could get commissions and backing from a greedy government if he promised the sky. He offered to explore everywhere, build forts, make settlements, pay His Majesty the fifth part of all the gold, silver, pearls, precious stones, and mineral substances which he obtained and the tenth part of all the fish, cleaned and in barrels. His reports were replete with gold and pearls and handsome Indians and beautiful ladies wearing precious stones and wonderful forests for shipbuilding, surrounding magnificent harbors.

This fast operator made other explorers jealous by pretending to find such things, where they had found only squalor, dangerous coasts, and deserts, and they petitioned the King to cancel his commissions. But in those days it took many months for the mail to reach Mexico from Madrid, and by the time the cancellation arrived, Vizcaíno had already returned from the expedition he was forbidden to take!

Around 1600 Spain, defeated by England on the sea, was bringing its galleons to Mexico across the Pacific by way of a base in the Philippines. The ships making a landfall, beaten by the sea, the men tired, out of water after the long haul across the Pacific, were unable to find a quick, safe anchorage. One of their best galleons, the *St. Augustin,* was wrecked on the Lower California coast when unable to make harbor after bringing sorely needed supplies halfway around the world. In this extremity Vizcaíno stepped up and promised to deliver a fine harbor.

In despair the viceroy asked the King to forget all previous reports about the man's mistakes and boasting, urged that he be given three boats, crews, soldiers, and provisions for an expedition far north along the unknown coast until a harbor was found *somewhere.* So the day came when Vizcaíno was once again on his way, northbound along the coast of California, to bring back a harbor.

After eleven months he returned to Mexico, bristling with enthusiasm. What he said about the southern part of our west coast was well designed to make Vizcaíno one of the greatest explorers of history and set people on fire to follow in his wake up that coast. But nothing happened. Perhaps somebody working in the government files didn't like Vizcaíno. Somehow his report was buried in the India Archives in Seville, where these glowing descriptions of the California coast were lost for 283 years. In 1885 a researcher, probing the dusty dungeon of the India Archives, touched a crumbling document, its faded writing just barely legible—Vizcaíno's lost report!

It shows that, more than a hundred years after Columbus, the Spanish still thought this continent was part of Asia. In their minds the coast went northward and then curved westward, forming one land mass. They called the Pacific Ocean, the South Sea. Listen to Vizcaíno:

". . . concerning the expedition by Order of Your Majesty for the discovery of harbors of the coast of the South Sea. . . . The coast line trends onward to near Japan and the coast of Great China, which are but a short run away, and the same is the case for Tartary and the famous City of Quinsay. . . . I diligently explored the whole coast, not leaving harbor, island or bight without sounding.

"I discovered a port which I called Monterey, it is all that can be desired as a station for ships making the voyage to the Philippines, sailing whence, they make a landfall on this coast. It is sheltered from all winds, while on the coast there are pines from which masts of any size can be obtained, oaks, the rose of Alexandria, a great variety of game such as rabbits, hares, partridges and flying birds. . . .

"This land has a genial climate. Its waters are good. It is very fertile. It is thickly settled with people of gentle disposition, peaceable and docile, who can be brought into subjection to the Crown of Your Majesty. They have game such as deer larger than cows

253

and bear and many other animals. The clothing of the people consists of skins of the sea-wolves abounding there. They go to sea with 14 paddle-men at a side with great dexterity. I was informed by many I met of a thickly settled coast, that inland there are great communities and they are well acquainted with silver and gold."

Vizcaíno used his imagination. Monterey Bay is not landlocked. Many of the beasts and plants he mentions never existed in California. And he did not meet with the kind of people he describes. But some of the climate and delight and the abundant wildlife along the California coast comes through.

After that, for more than a hundred years, the marvelous wilderness from Bering Strait to Lower California vanished from the news as completely as though it did not exist.

The West Coast Wilderness pursued its age-old business for more than 150 years after Vizcaíno's report was lost. Then a different kind of explorer went north from Mexico to the California coast. Instead of men in medieval armor, looking for rich cities, they were missionaries. In 1769 Junípero Serra (Father Juniper), sweeping aside all fears about the dangerous, worthless country up there, led a band of friars to San Diego—walking all the way because he had a painful infection in his leg and couldn't sit on a horse.

Father Juniper pushed north along trails that no white man had walked before. In a few years he established twenty-one missions, each a day's journey from the next, all the way to San Francisco, named by Father Juniper after St. Francis, the patron saint of his Franciscan Order. Father Juniper's mission was the first settlement to overlook the Golden Gate.

But it was not very "golden" then. When the first ship to sail that coast for 172 years reached San Francisco, a priest on board the boat wrote:

"Sea wolves were about the vessel . . . the ship made a mile an hour. . . . Fog became very thick, a great deal of rain fell. . . .

The navigation officers could not get an observation. A heavy sea, it was impossible to celebrate mass owing to the rocking of the ship. . . . Land was described on the bow: Blessed be God and let Him be praised by all creatures."

It was the same old story. As late as 1774 they were staring at an unknown land and wondering what it was and having a hard time to get there.

A redheaded man named Juan Colorado, nicknamed "The Flame," also told what things were like in Father Juniper's time:

"An Indian, sent to deliver two loaves of bread and a letter, to a mission sixty miles away, hid the letter under a stone so that it could not see him eat one loaf. Therefore, the letter could not tell tales on him, since it had seen nothing. . . .

"A priest, who had trouble holding their attention, when preaching to some Indians, hung a hind quarter of deer about his neck, to make them concentrate on him. But the audience smacked their lips so loudly as they watched the meat that he could not be heard. . . .

"Indian children did not number their years. At three years old they were 'bug age' because they could catch bugs to eat. At four they were 'mouse age,' and at six, 'snake age,' indicating the wild animals they were able to hunt at those ages. When they were 'deer age' they were sought in marriage. . . .

"Great flocks of birds covered a bay and Indians put seaweed on their heads and tied cork-wood under each arm to float among the birds. Then, with hands outstretched on each side, they would quietly pull under water ducks that pleased them; and so they gathered ducks as one might pick figs from a tree. The Indians held the ducks under water until they were drowned and the flock, supposing they had merely dived for food, did not miss them at all. . . .

"Shoals, left bare at low tide, were covered densely by millions of geese, ducks, and snipes. Pelicans and cormorants filled the air, as if neither land nor water had room for them. Huge turtles lay asleep on the water. At certain tides, sandy beaches were hidden under infinite quantities of sardines, left there by retreating waves. The fish overflowed onto the land as a brimming bucket sheds its burden. We ate until we were completely full, but envied whales those vast bellies they filled with this delightful fish."

This may be the first mention of the mysterious grunions which appear all at once on southern California beaches by the millions out of mysterious depths of the ocean. They ride in and up the beach with the waves on a full-moon tide after sunset in June and lay their eggs in the sand. When the eggs hatch a month later, baby grunions by the thousands hitch a ride in the waves of another full-moon tide and vanish into the ocean after their parents. Nobody knows whence they come or whither they go.

The long, narrow West Coast Wilderness is one of the greatest battlegrounds for existence on earth. Trees along the coast and sea animals below the cliffs are particularly tough and stormproof, hammered out where pounding waves tear down volcanic mountains.

Sitka spruce, one of the toughest trees in America, emerges from the lava of Katmai in Alaska and runs down the coast to Oregon. It stands exactly on the crest, above the surf, receiving the full force of the powerful west winds of the ocean where they bounce up and curve over the top of the cliff. Sitka spruce is black and rigid but shaped by the air flow so that it takes the form of a torn banner flapping in the wind. The needles of this tree are terribly sharp and long and stab the flesh.

Canyons which open to the sea are loaded with deep dunes, their surfaces clean-swept by the crystal dust that has streamed over them for hundreds of years. Here and there on this shifting white surface lodgepole pines have taken hold. Their roots dive to measureless depths, absorbing nourishment from the pure crystal sand, holding their positions in the face of vicious attacks of wind and sand. Southward the Torrey pine lives on the steepest hillsides, in a yellow and otherwise treeless canyon. This amazing tree drops its roots straight down more than a hundred feet through soft sandstone, while trunks and branches twist and loop like wrestling serpents. Torrey pines are surviving remnants of a forest that has been in its death throes for ages in the West Coast Wilderness.

Behind these trees that front the sea, deep ravines and mile-high mountain slopes are loaded with huge, ancient, Douglas firs, two hundred feet tall, so dense they resemble giant wheat fields. The Douglas fir forest holds the darkness of night at noonday.

Other fir trees, known as true firs, are the sharpest, straightest tree spires in the world, with outer branches turning up like the roof of a Chinese pagoda. Enormous purple cones stand straight up in clusters at the peak of the fir trees. A squirrel climbs the dizzy height, cuts one off, and hurls it down. The big cylinder is shattered. The squirrel hurries down and carefully picks up, one at a time, the hundreds of seeds scattered on the ground.

The cedars of this wilderness form tapestries with their twigs and needles. The delicate fronds fold down the center, so that when lifted in the wind, they compress, and when dropping, they fan out. The gentle rising and falling of the cedars' foliage make it seem as though the forest is breathing. Alaska cedar has come down from the tundra to live in these forests. Its wide fronds have the nature of their ancestors that found a way to unshoulder a burden of deep snow by turning steeply down and then revolving and closing in toward the trunk. Alaska cedars look like collapsed tents.

The coast redwoods, related to the big-tree sequoias far away in the High Sierras, grow in damp, twilight valleys close to the coast where they are bathed in fog every night. These are the world's tallest trees, although not so massive as the big trees. A trunk, twenty feet through, supports tons of timber, drawn up three hundred feet, straight as a plumb line—one of nature's easy miracles. But nature did not hurry in creating the mighty redwoods. Some of them were growing in their present valleys in

Julius Caesar's time and kept on growing up during the Dark and Middle Ages. The Ancient World turned into the Modern—and the same redwoods are still there.

The redwood valleys catch fifty-five inches of rain from the Pacific each year—but it is the combination of fogs and cold nights that created these colossal trees. The fog that bathes them is condensed by the night chill in the upper branches of the tall tower. The fog is heavy and condenses fast, so there is tremendous dripping in this forest every night. This soaks into the ground where it is picked up by the roots and lifted up again hundreds of feet in the pipelines of the trunk. Thus fogs give the redwoods two or three times more water than they would get from rain alone.

Extreme tallness, by increasing the vertical fog-collecting area, makes their unique waterworks all the more efficient.

The ocean has been trying to tear down the west wall of the continent for thousands and thousands of years. The power of the attack is seen in the rugged look of the coast. In many places mountains at the edge of the sea have been undermined until the cliff toppled. Then the rocks were rubbed together, clanking back and forth in the charge and retreat of the waves until ground to sand. When the sand swirled away, the waves moved forward to pound the hard core of the mountain again.

There are many jagged little islands just offshore. They are the rumps of old volcanoes whose pyrotechnics ended long ago, now brought to the vanishing point by the mauling of the waves. All this seems to spell nothing but destruction and death where land which bears eternal trees at its crest is broken and in retreat, and the ocean wins every battle in the long run.

But extraordinary animals are created in the turmoil at the edge of the sea. Here are millions of cracks, crevices, estuaries, hollows, and secret corners. Seaweed jungles fill these places in the splash of waves and in the clear currents where little fish run.

Secret living places among the rocks and breakers also teem

with populations of lobsters, crabs, clams, snails, shrimps, and elegant abalones. They are well protected from the killer whales and sharks which hunt in deeper waters farther out. And a monster has come from down the coast of Alaska to live in a hide-out here among the breakers.

Midway on the coast of Oregon a headland juts out with two cliffs facing at right angles, rising straight up out of the water some six hundred feet. Anyone standing on this headland hears uncanny sounds. Heard in the fog, in the dead of night, one could easily be persuaded that Cabrillo's demons were somewhere below. The crash of waves, hunching their backs and hurling themselves against the cliffs, is followed by the rumbling and rolling made by stones bumping into each other in the retreating wave. At intervals muffled sounds of snarling, barking, and roaring animals come through from the cave of the monster Steller sea lions.

The rocks of the headland are formed like a sandwich with soft sediment rocks for the bottom and top layers and in the center a layer of basalt, which is the hardest, heaviest volcanic rock. When mountain-building forces inside the earth's crust raised up the headland, the layers were bent over in such a way that the hard, volcanic layer formed an arch in cross section. Then, for a thousand years, pounding waves hollowed out the cave by breaking down and washing away the softer rock within the arch.

The waves roll in, sweep through the chamber of the cave, which has a thirty-foot dome, and rush out through an opening in the cliff at right angles. The force of an incoming wave is broken by the rocks and a sharp turn within the cave, so that the currents gently lift and subside around big rocks and ledges to which they deliver a steady supply of seaweeds, little fish, and a generous menu of sea foods.

Nobody knows when the Steller sea lions moved in. But what a superb stronghold is this for a breeding place of sea lions, well hidden under the mountain from grizzly bears and panthers in the wilderness above.

Sea lions are as restless as the waves which created them. In the luxury of the big cave they are constantly in motion, diving off rocks and ledges and then climbing back. Even when sitting down they must sway their huge black bodies back and forth, with snouts pointed up while they snarl and roar. A bull Steller may be thirteen feet long and weigh a ton, but the female is half his size. When her children get settled on a rock beside her, she gives them a quick shove that sends them tobogganing down the slippery surface for a splash, and then she blocks their efforts to climb back up. It is probably a sea-lion swimming lesson.

Steller sea lions were not created to loaf around in a luxurious cave. Strength and bulk gave their ancestors a large share of the Pacific. They raised their families on wet rocks around the Alaska coast and then toured the ocean, riding the swells by turning wheels like dolphins and rolling like walruses. They feared nothing and everything feared them—except the killer whale which drove them into the cavern behind the breakers.

Nobody knows whether the sea lion has ever seen his famous neighbor, the sea otter. At times when the lions leave their cave and roll seaward to inspect their ancestral ocean, the sea otters, in the waves just beyond the breaker line, suddenly vanish.

The sea otter is as much a salt-water animal as a fish. He never leaves the waves, which he fits like a glove, to walk ashore and meet his cousin, the otter that turns somersaults in fresh-water ponds.

The pine marten and fisher, which run in the treetops, are also relatives of the sea otter. They are all descended from an unknown land-mammal ancestor. In the case of the sea otter, claws for tearing flesh turned into webbed feet for paddling, and limbs for running became forearms for reaching and scratching, holding fish, and hugging babies.

When there are no white crests on the waves, sea otters lie on their backs, white bellies up, bobbing in the waves. Then sea otter with its long, white whiskers and big, round eyes looks like a little old man floating on his back. In this dozy position, the otter holds his front paws over his eyes to shade them from the glare of the sun.

The tail is held straight up like an antenna erected for danger signals. The neck is double-jointed, so that an otter floating on his back can lift his head like a periscope to search the horizon for sea gulls that are attracted by white bellies. Also, the sea otter is ever ready to go below when the triangular fin of a killer whale cuts the water or a sea lion comes out of his cave and heads that way like a rolling tugboat.

The easygoing sea otter navigates without turning over, by sculling with his tail, his body pivoting back and forth as he goes. More speed is gained by undulating the body, and, if that is not enough, he can lower one or two hind limbs into the water to row fast. In a real emergency the sea otter flips over and, vibrating four limbs, he shoots through the water at ten miles per hour, riding up and down the waves as though on a roller coaster. If hard pressed, he shoots straight through a wave as though it wasn't there. And with a body as supple as water he can turn and dive without a splash.

The sea otter's favorite floating place is among seaweed, where he can reach out, help himself to food, and nibble all day long while hardly turning his head. But for a full-course dinner he folds his arms on his chest and undulates down at a steep angle, assisted by powerful kicks of the hind feet. Down he goes, maybe a hundred feet or more, where, in the dark depths, a super sense of smell leads him to the most delicious crabs and shellfish.

The wonderful abalone, six inches across, is clamped in place with a grip that a man needs a jimmy to break. The sea otter, using his teeth like pliers, easily pulls off an abalone and spirals back to surface, where the food is laid out on his broad chest which he uses for a dinner table.

These animals, poised in the strength of the sea, were in perfect balance among the shore waves for untold ages. Their exquisite fur coats got them into plenty of trouble when men arrived.

As late as 1740 the West Coast Wilderness north of the California-Oregon line was unknown. The era of discovery of the New World, which began with Columbus, was at a pause. European conquerors, buccaneers, and seekers of oriental treasure had become past history. Spain in the south, England on the Atlantic coast, France along the St. Lawrence River and down the Mississippi to New Orleans were replacing primeval wildernesses with farms, cities and governments.

Yet there is still no report, no word of bold discovery, no mark or name on a map in that part of the continent which will later be called the Oregon country and Alaska. This area was left over because it was too far north of Mexico, too far west of the Mississippi River. The first white men to see this wilderness stronghold came from the west and from a country which had played no part in the New World until now.

The icebound coast and snow-capped mountains which Vitus Bering saw to the east through storm clouds in 1741 resembled the coast which Eric the Red saw to the west through storm clouds around 1000 A.D. In both cases the weather was arctic, the scenery mysterious, and it was all in the day's work.

Vitus Bering was a Dane, raised on a grim farm in Jutland. He was no dreamer and adventurer; he had no yearning to discover anything. He had no interest in the New World—probably he never heard anything but vague rumors of it. But destiny had some fame in store for Vitus.

Exciting news came across the Baltic from Russia. Peter the Great was building a nation out of swarms of half-civilized tribes over there. He was even creating a navy. In 1703 word had reached Vitus that Peter was laying the foundations of a palatial new capital city to be named St. Petersburg. The next year twenty-three year old Vitus Bering crossed the water and enlisted in the Russian Navy. With that the young man disappears for twenty years, and when next we meet Vitus Bering he is a man in his forties who had just been ordered by Peter the Great to carry out a task almost too big and dangerous to think about.

Bering was to transport six thousand miles across Siberia all men, supplies, and equipment needed to build a boat. He was then to sail to the most northern point of Siberia to discover whether or not Asia is joined to America. We know that Bering got across Siberia and built the boat, but little is said about the endless days and nights fighting mud, snow, cold, in a primitive wilderness, to get thirty-three men and all that gear to the east coast of Asia. Vitus Bering seems to have had the character of a top sergeant. He was a man of few words, strong, tough, able to handle men, to get things done and carry out orders.

They built their boat, the *St. Gabriel,* sailed north in 1728, through what is now Bering Strait, missed Bering Island on the American coast, in fog and storm, and did not land anywhere. Bering decided that there was no more land northward and that Asia and America were not joined. He returned to St. Petersburg and so reported to Catherine I, who was then Empress of Russia, after Peter's death.

After that he disappears again, this time for about twelve years. Then Vitus Bering, sixty years old, is ordered by Catherine to return to the east coast of Siberia, to build two more ships and sail east to check up on rumors of an island or continent to the east.

Eastern Siberia was inhabited by Chukchi Indians who knew about the strait and the existence of land which we call Alaska. Around the time of Bering's first expedition a man named Popoff turned up in St. Petersburg who had been among the Chukchis near Bering Strait and had seen "ten prisoners from a large country across the water." They told him that the land over there was inhabited by a people with walrus tusks in their cheeks. They said "there were various animals and trees not found in Siberia." It may have been this curiosity-stirring report that made Catherine send Bering on his second expedition.

Again Bering carried out orders perfectly. He built the *St. Peter* and the *St. Paul*. Bering was on the *St. Peter*, and with him was a German naturalist named Steller (who gave his name to the monster sea lions). The *St. Paul* was captained by Lieutenant Chirikoff.

After they became separated in foul weather, Chirikoff, in the *St. Paul*, continued east, day after day. Evidently the continent was a good deal farther away than anybody had thought. Chirikoff, of course, did not know the lay of the land and that he was running parallel to the Alaska peninsula. But at long last they sighted mountains and forests in the vicinity of Sitka. This was exciting. It is one of the few times when there was any discovery to cheer about in connection with Bering's expeditions.

Dementief, the pilot, and ten men armed with guns and a cannon were sent ashore in the largest boat and told to return the next day to report. Chirikoff's journal tells how they waited six days and nobody returned, but they saw smoke over on the shore. Then he sent another boat with the boatswain in charge and three of his best men, the carpenter, the calker, and a sailor. They were ordered to fire guns according to a code signal, which would tell about the men on shore, as soon as they landed. No signal was ever seen or heard. The *St. Paul* lay to, everybody on deck on the alert, firing a cannon regularly every hour all night. Three days later the ship, in great danger in a rising gale, left for Siberia.

What became of the two boats and their men is one of the mysteries of history. It has been said that they were murdered by Indians. But American Indians in that place had never seen a white man and they would have run away rather than attack. Also, the party was well armed and able to take care of itself, and no gunfire was heard on the *St. Paul*. A theory is that both boats were lost in a peculiar tidal whirlpool which was found forty-five years later inshore where Chirikoff's men vanished.

Meanwhile Bering on the *St. Peter* had headed north and in a few days reached the Alaska peninsula, where he sighted a rugged, snow-capped mountain (Mt. St. Elias). They went into Kyak Island where a boat went ashore for water, while Bering stayed on board. Then they headed west and were overtaken by terrible weather, which forced them to spend the winter on an island. A month later Bering died there, in December 1741. Today that island bears his name—Bering Island.

Here occurred the last episode of this first expedition to the northwest American coast which was such a dismal failure to the men who took part in it. The *St. Peter* was driven so far up a rough beach by winter storms and was so badly damaged that it could not be launched again. The surviving members of the crew were in a desperate situation—shipwrecked on an unknown island, in an unknown world. But, as has happened many times elsewhere in other remote places in the wilderness, they managed to escape by superhuman effort. After the leader's death his men took their wrecked ship apart piece by piece, and with these fragments they built another boat half the size—in which, after incredible suffering, they returned to Siberia.

So the long Pacific Coast Wilderness shrugged off the first white men who looked at it. The Russians had discovered it by accident, and they did not know until years later what they had found. Chirikoff saw the great forest around Sitka, but when the wilderness swallowed up his two small boats and fourteen of his best men, he withdrew to Siberia. Before his death Bering had a glimpse of superb Mt. St. Elias between storm clouds, its white summit gleaming above forest and inlets, but he was sick and tired of it all and, without going ashore himself, he headed for home.

When the survivors of this dreary, tragic expedition barely made it back to Siberia, nobody was excited about the west coast of America. Bering would have dropped out of history and the Alaska coast been left undiscovered for another generation except for one find. Had Coronado's men returned to Mexico with gold from the Seven Cities of Cibola, it could hardly have created more of a sensation than bundles of nine hundred sea-otter skins which Bering's men brought back!

Those funny, good-natured animals that paddle around on their backs were rare in Siberian waters. When they were caught, their beautiful pelts brought up to one hundred kopeks, trading with the Chinese on the Amur River; and here were hundreds of these skins captured from waters around islands to the east. The cry, "*Look what Bering's men found!*" triggered a special kind of gold rush.

At that time a mixture of half-civilized Asiatics and Russians were hunting and trapping along eastern Siberian rivers. The fur trade was organized under a Russian officer called the *Woewod*, who wore a magnificent uniform. He also wore a scowl and got for himself and Russian friends a wealth of ermine, mink, and beaver by bullying, torturing, and murdering the natives. But sea otter! The *Woewod* ordered everybody to the Siberian east coast to build boats.

They built and sailed them at the rate of ten a month—it didn't matter that two out of five were lost. The Russians moved into the Aleutian Islands. Sea otters were so teeming they could be driven up through the surf by the hundreds and clubbed to death on the beach. Two Russians slaughtered five thousand otters in one year on one small island in Bering Sea. The next year they killed only one thousand sea-otters, which exterminated the animals on that island.

Reaching for fresh herds of sea otters, the Russians moved farther eastward along the Aleutians each year and arrived at the Alaska peninsula and down the coast to Sitka. Within thirty-five years after Bering the two-thousand-mile coast from Attu, the most western island, to what is now British Columbia was charted and well-known in Russia. When the sea otter stampede started, the Russians probably did not associate the Aleutian Islands with America and gave no thought to the Spanish, English, and French who were far away in the eastern and southern parts of the continent.

But echoes of great events in Alaska traveled across Siberia to St. Petersburg and from there to all the capitals of Europe. Countries which had been seeking sudden wealth in the new world for 250 years were jolted. The Russians had outsmarted them in a wilderness which they had not explored and which was not even on their maps.

Thus it happened that around 1775, the year of Concord and Lexington, Spanish and English ships, as well as Russian, were appearing on the northwest coast. Yet the prairie and Rocky Mountains were still unexplored.

A Spanish ship dropped anchor in a remote mountain-girt harbor at Vancouver Island. Two Spanish ships lay off the coast of Washington, within sight of the majestic Olympic rain forest. Three years later the great English Captain Cook, in his globe-trotting battleship *Resolution*, sailed from Vancouver Island through the Aleutians to Bering Strait, which he called "the hitherto unknown western extremity of North America." Ever since Bering the Russians had been under strict orders to keep that part of the world to themselves, to give nobody information, or tell people in Siberia where they had been. Secrecy was their policy while they plundered the sea of otters.

Among the ships which were meeting on the northwest coast, sparring over positions, and quarreling over who owned the continent, one country was missing. This was the United States of America, which was born just as the last piece of the jigsaw puzzle completing the outline of the continent was put in place.

Americans on the Atlantic coast had no interest in the Pacific coast. They were just beginning to feel at home in the Green Woods Wilderness and they had their hands full at Saratoga and Yorktown. The sea-otter bonanza and the question of who owned the west coast was left to European countries.

To people in Boston and New York, Oregon was more remote than China. Than China? That classic deception of the New World still retained its magic. The word "China" now caused the brand new Stars and Stripes to jump from Boston harbor over all the intervening wildernesses to the Oregon coast.

The ink was hardly dry on the surrender of the British at Yorktown when Yankee merchants put their heads together about oriental trade. They bought two ships—the fourteen-year-old, eighty-three-foot *Columbia Rediviva*, and a sloop less than half the size, the *Lady Washington*. The name of the larger boat (Latin for "Hurrah for Columbia!") was promptly shortened to one word by its crew.

The new United States lacked gold to buy spices, tea, and silk, so the captains of the two ships were told to pick up otter skins from the northwest coast en route to China. They were given a collection of rummage-sale knickknacks for trading with the Indians—snuffboxes, rattraps, jews'-harps, pocket mirrors, iron tools, and cooking utensils.

A young captain named Robert Gray commanded the little sloop, and a famous old explorer and soldier of fortune commanded the brig. A year later, after barely surviving big seas and snowstorms, going around Cape Horn, Captain Gray anchored his sloop on the coast of Oregon, months ahead of slow, old Captain Kendrick. When the *Columbia* finally arrived, she was in bad shape, with her topsails down. Gray offered to take her over and the two men traded ships. Thereupon Kendrick with his sloop disappeared into a cove among the Douglas firs, while Gray, with thirty men and ten guns on the *Columbia*, competed for otter skins with the European countries.

A few months later Gray sailed for China with his sea-otter gold. He called at Hawaii where Captain Cook had been killed when he discovered this volcanic wilderness a few years before. Gray was surprised to find a kingdom with charming people, instead of savages, who wore wreaths of flowers and fancy clothes. This was something they didn't know about back in Boston, so Gray shanghaied two young Hawaiians, named Atoo and Opie.

On August 9, 1790, after three years away, Captain Gray returned to Boston Harbor. He was the first American to sail around the world, and they gave him a rousing welcome: "A Federal Salute of thirteen Guns, and three huzzas from a great concourse of citizens."

Gray marched up Beacon Hill beside Governor Hancock—with Atoo on his heels. The Boston papers headlined the "Crown Prince of Hawaii" and described the boy as a "living flame clad in a crested feather helmet and a feather cloak of golden sunset in scarlet."

Gray told the Boston merchants what was going on across the continent in the fantastic West Coast Wilderness; how England, Russia, and Spain were disputing each other's claims in a land of countless inlets and islands, loaded with marvelous black forests. The coast was such a labyrinth that the anchoring places were endless and many were as yet unclaimed. Free-lance captains were taking personal possession of hidden harbors to build factories—the name they gave to storage places for sea-otter skins.

After only seven weeks' stay in Boston, Captain Gray and his Man Friday, Atoo, were back on the *Columbia*, with orders to pick up another load of sea otters. The list of things put aboard for trading shows how ideas about the wilderness on the west coast had changed since the first trip. This time Captain Gray took "woolen cloth, trousers, pea jackets, shoes, muskets, blunderbusses, 14,000 nails, 143 sheets of copper, over 4,000 chisels."

Eight months out of Boston, Captain Gray reached the northwest coast, well prepared to get a cargo of otter skins. The fine, primeval forests stood undisturbed along the west wall of the continent. Only in offshore waters and among the islands the gentle animals who feared no enemies were being massacred. Were they not numberless?

Captain Gray wanted to find some land to claim for the United States. It must have a good harbor, at least one that could accommodate the *Columbia*. He searched far up and down the coast but with no luck. The best harbors were all taken by other countries. Then he recalled that farther south he had seen what looked like a fine waterway running inland. He had tried to get in but was blocked by a strong tide rip and a line of breakers on sand bars. Other ships had passed the place by because of that dangerous reef. Now Captain Gray, as a last chance, decided to go back and try again.

He hove to off the sand bars and studied the winds and tides. It looked like a big river, and if he could get a full-moon tide with just the right wind, he might make it. It was worth the gamble. He put men in a pinnace, to row through, take soundings, and feel out a passage. Then, with magnificent seamanship, under short sail, the *Columbia* followed her pinnace between the sand bars. Presently they "stood in a large river of fresh water, up which we steered." They spent eight days exploring about thirty-five miles upstream; they landed, planted the flag, and claimed the area for the United States three thousand miles away. Finally, with a captain's affection for his ship, Captain Gray named this greatest river of the West Coast Wilderness "The Columbia's River."

When, months later, Captain Gray's news reached Boston, there were handshakings and toasts on Beacon Street; but elsewhere the incident received little notice. The country was excited about its new Constitution and the building of a new capitol on the shores of the Potomac. A harbor in a remote part of the world where foreign nations are catching sea otters—who cares?

Between Philadelphia, where Congress was meeting, and the west coast lay three thousand miles of wilderness. When Gray's anchor was splashing into the Columbia, Kentucky was being admitted as the first state west of the Alleghenies—and Kentucky was "way out west."

On the other hand, up in Montreal fur was the topic. When Captain Gray's news reached them they pricked up their ears. They were not bothered about American competition in the fur business just because the old *Columbia Redeviva* had been there. They felt that England's rights to the wilderness coast were safe in the hands of Vancouver, who was out there at the same time as Gray. However, Gray's report of a big river flowing out of the interior of the continent into the Pacific could be very important. Canadian fur traders had heard from both Cook and Vancouver how quickly and easily the sea-otter snatchers loaded their pelts and sailed straight over to the Orient, whereas it took the Canadians almost two years to make a round trip, sailing down the St. Lawrence River and around Africa or South America.

If only they could find a northwest passage through the Canadian wilderness! Their lakes and rivers extended on and on westward until lost in a vast wilderness maze. Now the mouth of the Columbia had been discovered. Where did it come from? Perhaps it could be reached by a short portage through a mountain pass? They were used to carrying canoes and heavy loads across portages.

The possibility of discovering the inland source of the Columbia and using that for a west exit out of the hunting and trapping wilderness was tantalizing. They were knitting brows over this question in Montreal, in September 1792, when a man arrived en route from London to the most remote and isolated spot in the north woods. The man was Alexander MacKenzie, and the spot was his personal fort on Lake Athabaska, west of Hudson's Bay.

MacKenzie was a partner in the North West Company, known as the Big Company. The Nor'Westers were the gentlemen adventurers and gamblers of the wilderness. They were out to capture the trade of all the Indian tribes in the great Canadian fur-bearing region. They had a swank club in Montreal, the Beaver Club, with the motto: "Fortitude in Danger."

Three years earlier MacKenzie had built his fort at the end of the white man's trail. From there he made the longest river run in history, through a wilderness unseen and unknown to white men. In a birchbark canoe he averaged forty miles a day on the full flood of a big river. He kept hoping it would turn west, but it held north. Grimly he kept on toward the top of the world. And then, after fifteen hundred miles of swift current, the river broke up in a delta of tundra flats and ice pans. MacKenzie could not figure the longitude and he was not sure where he was. There was no place to go except back. He retraced the fifteen hundred miles, paddling laboriously upstream (southward) to his fort, feeling that his all-out effort was a failure. He named the river which led nowhere the "River of Disappointment." Today that long river in the Canadian wilderness, which flows into the Arctic Ocean, is named after the frustrated man who discovered it, the MacKenzie River.

The daring trip on the River of Disappointment left MacKenzie angry at himself because he had fumbled the longitude. So he traveled all the way to London, where he spent the winter of 1791–92 studying astronomy and navigation. Now, back in his fort on Lake Athabaska, buried in a north-woods winter, he prepared to stab west through the heart of a trackless mountain wilderness. He would start when the ice first cracked in the lakes early in May, and he would not turn around until he reached the Pacific.

On May 9, 1793, ten men climbed into a specially built, strong, light twenty-five-foot canoe, to vanish into an unknown country for an unknown time and distance. They were two Scotsmen, Alexander MacKenzie and Alexander MacKay, six French-Canadian canoemen, and two Indians. They headed southwest on the Peace River and with eight men at the paddles forced the big canoe upstream against the current.

This was something different in American wilderness exploring. They had no illusions about finding gold or rich cities; they were not on the trails of fur-bearing animals; they were not lost in the wilderness and trying to escape; they deliberately plunged westward to find a way through to the Pacific Ocean, cost what it might in courage and effort.

Day after day, week after week, the brawny paddle strokes of the French Canadians and the two Indians drove against furious currents. At first, as MacKenzie says in his diary, they went through "a succession of the most beautiful scenery I have ever beheld." There were grassy terraces ending with broken precipices. Everywhere they looked they saw moose, elk, bison, and bear.

At one place rapids rushed at them between towering cliffs only a hundred feet apart. They dragged the canoe through by a 360-foot line, and at one place they had to cut steps in the face of solid rock to get around a shoulder. Again, they had to cut a trail through dense forest cluttered with fallen trees to carry the long canoe and baggage around a canyon where the river was nine hundred feet below, and they followed it only by the dull roar of the distant water. Holding on to a spruce tree, they leaned far out to get a look down, where the river appeared to be in a dark prison of stupendous cliffs. It charged at opposing walls like a caged beast and then fell back in foam and roar and whirlpool. Great trunks of trees, blocks of stone and ice were piled up and smashed in shapeless ruin at the exit of the canyon where they put the canoe back into the water.

Then came a hard decision. They stood at the fork of the Peace River at the base of the Rocky Mountains. Here the Finlay River, looking like the main road, led north with the smoothest water, and the Parsnip River led south, with rough, fast water to buck. Of course everybody, weary of wild, contrary water, urged that they take the north fork—except MacKenzie. He recalled that back in winter quarters an old Indian had told him about a fork like this. The Indian said that the south fork led, by way of a portage, to another river which flowed west.

MacKenzie decided to gamble on this advice, if, indeed, this was the place. Among grumblings and mutterings of the others he ordered that they take the south fork and fight their way up the Parsnip River. Twelve days later they reached a little lake, the source of the Parsnip. The hardest part lay ahead. Shouldering canoe and baggage, they climbed through a pass, crossed the Continental Divide, and found a small river going their way.

But there was no joy of shooting rapids. They took a terrible tumble down the small river, narrowly escaping a final smashup. MacKenzie named it the Bad River. Then suddenly they popped out of the darkness of the forest into the sunlight and found themselves on the Fraser River, which MacKenzie thought was the Columbia.

A few days later, when the Fraser was getting too rough to paddle, they caught sight of a big house on the bank. They had discovered the Carrier Indians, a mysterious semi-civilized tribe that lived in the depths of the Canadian Rocky Mountain wilderness. These amazing people had a twenty-by-thirty-foot log cabin with three fireplaces, rows of twig cots, and shelves to store dried fish. They had clever salmon traps with weirs that projected four feet above the water. They were astonished to see white men but were friendly. They told MacKenzie not to dare the dangerous river below but directed him back upstream a few miles to an unnavigable stream, which MacKenzie named the Black Water River, and told him to follow that downstream on foot.

Back at the Black Water River, MacKenzie's party left their canoe and heavy equipment. They shouldered their packs and for two weeks walked west down the Black Water, cutting a trail through the wilderness. The French Canadians carried ninety-pound packs and the Indians forty-five-pound packs, while the two Scotsmen went ahead to find the way, with their guns ready for Indians and game. The Indians they met looked at them with open-eyed astonishment and then ran away. They had to climb over another mountain range and at long last came down to the banks of the Bella Coola River where they found Coast Indians.

After a feast of salmon and berries the Indians took the MacKenzie party in their own canoes down the Bella Coola. These Indians proved to be "the most expert canoemen in the world." Even the French Canadians admitted it. Their bronze bodies, necks, arms, legs, and their paddles, in a beautifully co-ordinate motion, sent the canoe leaping among rocks and waterfalls at great speed. They could take a canoe over a high weir without shipping a drop. A day later MacKenzie's party was paddling in salt water!

MacKenzie's logbook describes this historic moment:

"The tide was out and left a large space covered with seaweed. The surrounding hills were involved in fog. Wind was ahead

from the west and very strong. As we advanced along the land we saw a large number of sea otters. We fired at them without success for the rapidity with which they plunge under the water. We also saw many porpoises (seals), the white-headed eagle [the bald eagle became the national emblem of the United States], gulls, and a smaller dark bird [double-breasted cormorant or little Baird's cormorant?]. . . . The tide fell 11½ feet; we kept shifting baggage when it came in . . . we ate a porcupine too big for the kettle so it was cut in pieces and every morsel was devoured."

Then came a dangerous surprise. Indians, armed with daggers, came in three canoes from down the coast to the mouth of the Bella Coola. The two Indians who had come all the way from MacKenzie's fort on Lake Athabaska became terribly upset. At the same time the friendly Bella Coola Indians said that a war alarm had been sounded by another tribe. To save their lives, MacKenzie's party must flee up the Bella Coola without a moment's delay.

MacKenzie tells how one of the young Indians entreated them to leave before arrows and spears began to fly. "In relating our danger, his agitation was so violent that he foamed at the mouth . . . my people were panic-struck . . . it was necessary to disguise my apprehension."

MacKenzie had reached his goal. He had stabbed clear through to the west coast. Why not leave at once in the hour allowed to save their lives? MacKenzie remembered his trip to London to study longitude and that he had brought a telescope and other instruments all the way back to this point for this moment. The fog was at that hour too thick for observations. He must wait overnight.

In the face of fear hysteria he picked out a high rock and ordered his party to use this as a fortress for the night. They slept there with two men always awake and on watch through the night. The next morning the clouds broke enough for a glimpse of the sun, and MacKenzie got his bearings. His latitude and longitude were so accurate that it was possible years later to find the exact rock where they slept that night. He was on Point Menzies on King's Island in a labyrinth of salt-water inlets, with the north end of Vancouver Island some fifty miles away across the water.

Now he was ready to leave, except that one thought troubled him. How would the people back at his fort and his friends in Montreal ever hear about this if they were wiped out by the Indians?

So MacKenzie took another hour for mixing powdered cinnabar

stone with hot animal grease to make orange-red paint. And he painted the face of the rock where eleven men had spent the night with these words in big letters:

ALEXANDER MACKENZIE
FROM CANADA BY LAND
THE 22 OF JULY, 1793

Then they entered their canoe and with swift paddle strokes vanished from the scene, to return by the route they had come, through a world of towering mountains, gigantic trees, and torrential rivers.

No man ever set himself a more dangerous goal or reached it with finer leadership and higher courage than Alexander MacKenzie. He was the first white man to cross the continent from coast to coast north of Mexico. But he did not find the headwaters of the Columbia River. He found no west exit direct to the Pacific coast from the dominion of fur, and his trail was so tortuous it could never become a travel route. MacKenzie's dash lighted the dark depths of the wilderness only for a split second of history, like a photographer's flash bulb.

A few steps inland from the tide line, the vast West Coast Wilderness remained as unknown as before MacKenzie's thrilling thrust to the Pacific until well into the 1800s.

On the morning of September 6, 1810, a crowd was gathered at the foot of Manhattan Island, watching two ships square off in a fair wind for a run through the Narrows. In the lead was the pride of the new American Navy, *U.S.S. Constitution*. Her high-angle bowsprit, extended by an extremely long jib boom, was like a finger pointing proudly and with high hopes toward a goal far beyond the horizon. The frigate was followed by a ship half her size, the sturdy brig *Tonquin*, under charter by a New York merchant named John Jacob Astor. A few miles outside the harbor the *Constitution* hove to, broke out her colors, and fired a cannon salute, while the brig acknowledged the courtesies with her signal flags flying, sailed past, and headed south.

A new kind of expedition was under way. The *Tonquin* was not out to explore unknown places; she was not taking a military party to possess new land; she was on the way to establish a trading post at the mouth of the Columbia River where Captain Gray had planted the flag eighteen years before.

Waving farewell from the rail of the brig, besides the crew, were twelve clerks for the future business office, thirteen French-Canadian canoemen, and three partners of Mr. Astor's company—Mr. McKay, Mr. David Stuart, Mr. Robert Stuart. The master of the *Tonquin* was Captain Thorn, a distinguished officer on leave from the U.S. Navy, and no ship ever sailed with a more honest man or a better seaman. But, also, no ship ever sailed with a harder disciplinarian, a man so stern and unyielding that he turned a business trip into a nine months' nightmare, ending in the worst man-made disaster ever seen on the west coast.

Since the ship was chartered by their company, the partners expected to enjoy some owners' privileges during the long voyage; but Captain Thorn asserted that the admiralty laws gave him sole command. He was utterly scornful of the landlubber Astor partners and their clerks. He ordered lights out in their cabin at 8 P.M. He would not let them open a box to get warmer clothing or supplies without his permission. When they took the whaleboat ashore during the long months rounding South America, they were to return to the ship instantly when the captain blew a whistle.

Once when one of the Mr. Stuarts and seven clerks were ashore on a desert island near the Straits of Magellan, the captain sailed away and left them when they were tardy returning. When the men on the island saw their ship putting to sea, they jumped into the whaleboat and bent to the oars with all their energy in a hopeless chase to catch up with the brig. They called and waved desperately, while their aghast friends on board saw them steadily falling farther behind.

Mr. McKay shouted at the captain and tried to call him to his senses. The other Mr. Stuart who was on the ship drew his pistol, told the captain to put about or he would blow out his brains. At that moment the fickle wind of the Straits of Magellan suddenly shifted to a head wind; the ship was stopped in her tracks; the whaleboat caught up. There is nothing in the record about what words were exchanged with the captain as the men climbed aboard.

So on and on the brig *Tonquin* sailed with Captain Jonathan Thorn weathering all storms, both those of the sea and those that shook the timbers inside the cabin.

Some six months after clearing New York they caught sight of the mountains of Owyhee above the horizon. Dropping anchor in the harbor of Karakakooa, near the place where Captain Cook had been murdered by savages, they waited with guns handy for hostile natives to appear. It was a place of wild and broken shores with overhanging cliffs of black volcanic rock. After a few hours of suspense the long surf-riding boats of the natives suddenly shot around a promontory, and they arrived alongside, laughing and friendly, with fresh fruits and vegetables to trade.

After that everybody had a good time except Captain Thorn. He loved pork and bacon, and when the natives offered no pigs, he demanded to see the king. But King Tamaahmaah * had moved to a small island called Woahoo. So now, while the Astorians were having a great time on Owyhee, the captain quickly blew the whistle to be on their way to Woahoo to find the king.

A few days later the *Tonquin* dropped anchor off a beautiful sandy beach they called Waititi, where long rollers curved smoothly up to a palm-fringed shore. Here they saw the king's two-story palace made of stone and wood. Captain Thorn proceeded immediately to his business, and after several days of argument King Tamaahmaah was persuaded to part with a few pigs.

The master of the *Tonquin* was then ready to weigh anchor and

* Kamehameha

279

be on his way. But he ran into some trouble at this island wilderness. It was hard to reassemble the partners, the clerks, the French Canadians, the chief mate, the armorer, the sailmaker, not to mention the crew, for the last long haul to Oregon.

They were busy meeting the savages on "the most beautiful island of the Sandwich group . . . 46 miles long and 23 wide. A ridge of volcanoes extends through the center, rising to lofty peaks, skirted by undulating hills and rich plains where native cabins peek out from beneath groves of coconut and other luxuriant trees."

They found the "islanders a comely race of a copper complexion. Men tall and well-made, with forms indicating strength and activity. Women with regular features and a lascivious expression . . . nineteen young women gave a dance for the partners."

As the *Tonquin* was not at sea, Mr. McKay now could assert himself as Mr. Astor's business agent. He remembered Mr. Astor's suggestion that they call at those islands far out in the Pacific, with an eye to future trading. So the partners arranged meetings with the king, while Captain Thorn strode the quarter-deck, boiling with rage because his whistle had lost its power.

At the invitation of the partners Tamaahmaah came aboard the *Tonquin*, wearing full regimentals with sword clanking at his hip (probably gifts from Vancouver who had called at Owyhee seventeen years before). He was accompanied by his three wives, very simply clad in *paus*. The partners wore Highland plaids and kilts, and the clerks invited to the meeting wore scarlet coats. They poured their best wine, displayed the American flag, and Mr. Mc-Kay explained that the three partners in plaids and kilts were chiefs of a very great tribe which would send ships there in the future and make the King of Owyhee and his people rich.

This volcanic wilderness, with its coconuts and king, gave the Astorians their first good cheer of the voyage. They could not know that it was also the last good cheer of their lives—that doom was waiting over the horizon.

When the *Tonquin* put to sea, twelve native Hawaiians were added to her crew, replacing men who had become lost in the island wilderness. Although the captain and the partners were now not even on speaking terms, about seven months after leaving New York, Captain Thorn brought his ship safely to the coast of the Oregon country. He hove to where a fresh west wind sent a tumbling sea against a sand bar, extending a sheet of foam across the mouth of the Columbia River, and ordered Chief Mate Fox to take the whaleboat with four French-Canadian canoemen and make soundings through the furious surf.

Just before they cast off, Fox whispered in the ears of the partners, "I am sent off without seamen to man my boat in boisterous weather on the most dangerous part of the new coast. My uncle was lost a few years ago on this same bar and I am now going to lay my bones alongside of his." They watched from the deck as the whaleboat became a speck, careening and tossing in the surge where the discharge of the river struck the incoming tide head on. The boat was never seen again.

After that Captain Thorn, under short sail, cruised back and forth for two days, waiting for a better tide and wind. Then he ordered Mr. McKay and one of the Mr. Stuarts to take the pinnace for soundings across the bar, with an able mariner, the sailmaker, armorer, and two Hawaiians. Three were drowned, but the two partners, the armorer, and one Hawaiian survived. After that Captain Thorn brought the *Tonquin* through the surf and between the sand bars into the Columbia River—to the place where he had been ordered to bring her.

They started to build a fort according to Mr. Astor's wishes, but before it was finished, the *Tonquin* put to sea with twenty-three of their company, including Mr. McKay and the chief clerk, Mr. Lewis, and, in addition, they took along an Indian from Astoria as interpreter. They were bound for Vancouver Island to get pelts for the new Astor trading post.

The *Tonquin* anchored where snow-covered mountains could

be seen and a tall black forest stood at the water's edge. A few canoes came out and Indians held up sea-otter skins. They seemed friendly, so Mr. McKay went ashore in one of their canoes to dicker with the chief.

The next morning business was buzzing on the deck of the *Tonquin*. Captain Thorn, who had taken over shipboard trading for Mr. McKay, had opened some of the boxes which the partners had been forbidden to touch. He spread out blankets, clothes, knives, beads, and fishhooks and gestured to the Indians to climb aboard with their otter skins and start trading.

But the merchandise did not move fast. The Indians kept demanding higher and higher prices, while Captain Thorn, who had set his prices, was not a man to haggle. He thrust his hands in his pockets and paced back and forth on the deck with jaws firmly set, which was his way of saying that they could take it or leave it.

Chief Nookamis paced back and forth with the captain, his pleas for a better bargain becoming jeers and taunts. Every time the captain about-faced, the insolent Indian thrust a beautiful big sea-otter skin under his nose. The end came suddenly. Captain Thorn snatched the skin, rubbed its juicy side in Nookamis' face, threw the Indian overboard, and kicked the piles of skins right and left about the deck.

The *Tonquin* was left alone, calmly riding at anchor, enveloped in mysterious silence all that night. The next morning swarms of canoes came out. The Indians appeared to have no arms and made friendly gestures. They held up their finest skins, not only sea otter, but marten, mink, and bear as well. Captain Thorn was gratified that they showed signs of doing business on his terms. He invited them all to come aboard.

Trading took an odd turn—the Indians seemed to be interested only in the knives. The Indian interpreter, backed by the Astorians, urged the captain to clear the decks and sail away. But Jonathan Thorn thought that his gruff, unyielding way of handling savages was proving successful. They were bringing superb skins and dealing on his terms. When the knives were gone they would want blankets and other things. Besides, he pointed out to the others, there were guns in the cabin to take care of any rascals that got out of hand.

Canoes kept arriving; the deck became crowded with Indians, and an hour later the captain changed his mind. He suddenly ordered six men aloft to make sail, prepared to weigh anchor, and roared out an order to clear the decks!

Indians who were stooped over, trading, snapped upright. There were a few seconds of utter silence as though a mysterious blow had struck the deck and people were collecting their wits. Then the air was rent with shrieks and hideous war whoops. Brandishing knives and war clubs, the Indians fell on the white men. Clerk Lewis was stabbed while still bending over some otter skins and, mortally wounded, he fell down a hatch into the cabin. Captain Thorn fought back with giant courage, laying two Indian corpses at his feet with a clasp knife.

Six men up in the rigging to set the sails stared down from the yardarms at the carnage on the deck. When they slid down the outer lines, two were promptly murdered. But the others got into the cabin where the guns were and where they found the sorely wounded Mr. Lewis. Shooting from the cabin door, they cleared the deck. The Indians leaped into their canoes and paddled away, taking with them the Indian interpreter.

After that, for a second night, the *Tonquin* rode at anchor in a fearful silence. Her unfurled sails flapped in the wind. Her chains clanked like ghosts in the dark. She was a dead ship—except for five men somewhere below decks.

During the night a dinghy pulled away from the *Tonquin*. It held four men who were desperately trying to row back to Astoria, 240 miles away. Mr. Lewis, almost helpless from loss of blood, remained in the *Tonquin's* cabin.

The next morning the Indians, seeing how the ship swung aimlessly, paddled cautiously around her. Remembering the gunfire that drove them off, they dared not go aboard. At length a man appeared at the rail; it was Mr. Lewis, beckoning to them in a friendly manner. Gradually they tested the situation, and then a few bold Indians climbed aboard. The man who had beckoned to them had disappeared. It looked all clear.

They saw a confusion of blankets, clothing, spilled boxes of beads and fishhooks among corpses. They went below and found heaps of treasures like bacon and sugar and cooking utensils. They searched everywhere, but there was no sign of the white man who had beckoned to them. This was a rare and exciting situation! They called to the Indians waiting in canoes, and the news quickly spread over to the shore. Indians came from every direction and swarmed through the *Tonquin*, yelling and leaping on deck for joy at the big loot of a fine ship, and her wealth of equipment and cargo.

When the ship was jammed with Indians, and her supplies and chattels were flying over the rail to outstretched hands in the canoes alongside, there was a sharp crack, a hot, blinding flash, and the roar of an awful explosion shook the forest and echoed far away in the mountains.

When the smoke cleared away the *Tonquin* had disappeared. The bay was covered with fragments of the wreck, shattered canoes, and Indians struggling in agony or making for the shore in panic. For days afterward limbs and heads and bodies were washed up on the beach.

A few weeks later men at Astoria, down on the Columbia River, while busy building their trading post, saw the Indian interpreter who had sailed north on the *Tonquin* approaching. He told them how all the white men had been massacred and about the astounding calamity in which more than a hundred savages were killed and many more mutilated. He said that for several days after the explosion surviving Indians sat mute and stunned while their women mourned and sobbed. He was held prisoner and was cowering in a corner when he heard a shout from the woods and four white men were brought in. On seeing them, those who had sat silent and downcast leaped to their feet and yelled. They called the interpreter out of his corner and asked him to interview them. The men who had slipped away in the night in the *Tonquin's* dinghy had gone ashore for water and rest some miles down the coast where Indians had tripped over them. A one-in-a-million chance of bad luck!

The Indian interpreter asked how they happened to be in the woods, and they told him how the five men in the cabin of the *Tonquin* that night had talked about cutting the anchor line and sailing away, but Mr. Lewis was badly hurt and they were too few to handle the ship. It was then decided to take the dinghy and row back to Astoria—they figured they could make it in ten days. Mr. Lewis was in agony from his wounds and said he had not long to live. He urged the others to go without him. He said that the next morning he would drag himself to the rail and beckon to the Indians to come aboard and when he saw them start he would manage to get below and crawl into the powder magazine where they would never find him. He would listen for their shouts, and when he judged that as many Indians as possible were aboard . . . he would set a spark to the magazine! After much argument and seeing Lewis' suffering, the others reluctantly agreed.

The Indian interpreter said that after the interview they put the prisoners to death by slow torture. In the excitement he escaped, as he knew his turn would be next.

Fourteen years after the *Tonquin* the Hudson's Bay Company had established a trading post of extraordinary size and splendor at Fort Vancouver (opposite Portland, Oregon). Manager Mc-Loughlin had enclosed eight acres with a heavy timbered stockade twenty feet high. In this he built a two-story baronial mansion with a smoking room to entertain all comers where the biggest heads of elk, moose, bear, and bison were mounted on the walls. There were two fireplaces where flames leaped and roared from logs it took three men to lift.

McLoughlin was six feet four, broad and thick, with a great forehead, overhanging brows, strong as an ox, and with a booming voice when he chose to turn it on. He was the king of old Oregon, which he ruled from 1824 to 1846, and his mansion was known far and wide as the Big House.

John McLoughlin always wore black and carried himself with dignity. Because of his white hair and eagle nose the Indians called him "White Eagle." He traded fairly, but one day when an Indian chief demanded payment for rocks taken for ballast McLoughlin seized the Indian, forced a stone into his mouth, and yelled, "Eat that, you rascal, and then I will pay you for what the ship eats!"

One day in April 1825 a three-masted brig, the *William and Ann*, was warped into McLoughlin's dock. She hailed from England, had rounded Cape Horn and been more than eight months at sea. She had just crossed the treacherous sand bar at the mouth of the Columbia after lying to for six weeks, not daring to approach the California coast in "gales a thousand times worse than around Cape Horn."

Everybody at the post, whites and Indians with McLoughlin towering among them, was gathered at the river's edge to help make the brig fast and see who would step off.

Down the gangplank came an excited young man—David Douglas of the Horticultural Society of London. Eight months of sea had bronzed his face and hardened him for the wilderness, but the clothes that he had just changed into were fresh out of a London shop. He wore spectacles on his nose; he lighted his pipe with a magnifying glass, using the sun's rays, and he enjoyed "an effervescent drink" (whiskey and soda perhaps?). When McLoughlin caught sight of this young man, he strode through the crowd and gave him an especially hearty welcome.

Until David Douglas arrived they saw forests, not trees, in the West Coast Wilderness. The forests were tall and dark; they contained fur-bearing animals and savages; they supplied logs for forts and cabins. But nobody noticed what kind of trees they were or anything special about them. One of the greatest trees in the world, with its homeland on the northwest coast, had not been recognized.

As the *William and Ann* sailed up the Columbia River, David Douglas was overwhelmed with the wilderness, unbelievably different from anything he had seen in England. "The scenery is grand . . . lofty hills well wooded with pines . . . mountains covered with perpetual snow." He was so fascinated by the dark forests which he saw from the ship's deck that he could hardly wait to plunge into them. Mr. McLoughlin cautioned him and gave him a woodsman's outfit with gun and knife, taught him how to treat Indians and grizzlies and how to use streams and animal trails to keep from getting lost. In the months that followed Douglas merged with the wilderness. He made many friends among the Indians, who liked his oddities and marveled at the way he could light his pipe in the sunlight without an ember.

Douglas collected samples of all the plants he found, pressing them in herbarium sheets to take back to London. In this occupation he might spend the whole day on his knees in one spot, and that drew great respect from the Indians. The man was performing the rites of his tribe. They gave him an Indian name which meant "Grass Man." Douglas made the most of this by declaring he was a great chief of a king in a faraway land.

Even when he wandered through shady stillness among tall straight trunks, he called the trees pines. He measured a fallen one —227 feet long and 48 feet in circumference. He considered them "the most striking and truly graceful objects in nature," but they frustrated him. He wanted to collect fresh cones with ripe seeds that grow near the tops of the trees. "I couldn't climb to get the cones. Buckshot didn't reach them. The trees are too large to cut down with a hatchet."

In the long run, of course, David Douglas got what he was after. When the Horticultural Society of London examined the cones and seeds, the buds and needles which he brought back, they recognized that a new kind of tree had been discovered, unlike all other evergreen trees. They gave it a complicated scientific name which means "false hemlock with yew leaves." We call it Douglas fir, and it is the most valuable forest tree on earth. The strength of its streaming grain is revealed by its use as tall masts and spars. The weight of the northwest wind leaning against a mainsail may make a ten-inch boom bend like a bow. But Douglas fir holds with the strength of the primeval wilderness.

When a man is fighting for life, soaked by snow and icy torrents, living on acorns, helpless in the face of grizzlies and savages, it is not the best time to take an interest in trees. But L. K. Wood, who told the world about the redwoods, was an unusual man.

Unlike Douglas firs, which are spread over mountainsides and along coasts in full view, this second tree wonder of the West Coast Wilderness is hidden in foggy valleys. The redwoods start just below the Oregon line and run south in broken coast ranges as impenetrable as any wilderness in our land.

In 1849 Wood had gone into the wilderness with a party of gold prospectors on the Trinity River just east of the coast ranges. They were having no luck in finding gold. They had pushed on and on, expecting to strike it rich always around the next corner. Now they were several hundred miles up the Sacramento River and it was fall. Torrential rains had turned all the rivers into furious floods, and the mountains were covered with snow. They suddenly realized that they could not get back to civilization until the following spring, while supplies of food would never carry them over the winter. How to live in winter was an old story for men experienced in the wilderness. But these gold miners were used to having a base of supplies with bacon, flour, and sugar, and people coming and going.

The map showed the coast line about fifty miles west. What lay between was blank paper. They asked a group of Indians who said that was enemy country and they had never been through it. But

Indians like to make white men smile by telling them things they want to hear. They spoke to each other silently with their eyes; then one said that the sea was not more than eight suns away and there was a large and beautiful bay with grasslands.

It was raining torrents on November 5 when twenty-four men followed a dim elk trail up a slippery, muddy mountainside, due west. Before nightfall mud turned to snow. All animal trail marks were gone. Up and up they struggled through snow to the knees. From the summit of the first mountain they looked out upon range after range of snow-buried mountains, between them deep canyons filled with roaring torrents. Most of the slopes were covered with dense, trackless forests. All this they would have to cross to reach the sea. It was impossible. Sixteen men dropped out and returned to the Trinity River. Eight, led by L. K. Wood, kept going.

During the next ten days they plunged on through swollen streams, climbing down ravines, crawling up the cliffs on the other side. All streams west of the ridges flowed north—and they were determined to keep to the "short cut" straight west. They were averaging two miles per day.

Then an insurmountable mountain loomed up ahead. It was too steep to climb, too high and snowy, and there was no pass in sight. They turned north, following a river that roared at its base. The next day they suddenly flushed seventy-five Indians in war paint. The white men instantly realized that this was their end. But the Indians, who had never seen a white man before, gave a yell, and warriors, squaws, and papooses all ran away. Some threw themselves headlong in the river and fled to the other side. The Wood party was debating whether to keep on down the river in the wake of the Indians when a huge grizzly loomed up. That settled the matter. They decided not to move an inch and to let the grizzly make all the decisions as to which direction to go, when, and how fast.

After that they followed tortuous streams northward, wading in icy water, stumbling among boulders, climbing mountain ranges whenever possible to get west. They lived mostly on acorns with occasional deer and elk meat.

Four weeks after seeing the Indians they were still on the way. But now it seemed that they were out of their heads. They were in a nightmare in which they were lost in a forest of gigantic trees. Such trees, of course, were unbelievable—but they felt real. Mr. Wood had an irresistible urge to linger among the amazing trees and study them. He measured one that had fallen. It had a diameter of twenty-two feet and paced to a length of three hundred feet! The other men cursed him for this delay over the trees. The whole trip was a nightmare and they were all stark mad, especially Mr. Wood, who was excited about the phantom trees. The river they followed at that time they called the Mad River.

On the fortieth day after they had started west for a trip of "eight suns" they stopped in wonder and amazement. They had "issued from the dismal forest prison in full view of the Pacific Ocean"!

The coast redwoods had been discovered.

During nearly half of the nineteenth century the West Coast Wilderness inland was a vast, remote, undisturbed area. Only individual hunters, trappers, and fur traders went into it. It was crossed only by well-armed parties prepared for life-and-death struggles with the wilderness, such as the Lewis and Clark and the Fremont expeditions. In the south horseback and pack-mule traffic followed the coast line from Mexico to San Francisco Bay, but north of that all transportation was by ship.

A square-rigger would take four to six months to go from New York to the west coast, depending on luck, weather, and the skill of the skipper. The only regular transportation was the annual Hudson's Bay boat between London and Manager McLoughlin at Fort Vancouver. It was this route that David Douglas used, and he was perhaps the first tourist to old Oregon not connected with fur or government business.

Eleven years passed after Douglas. This time McLoughlin came out of the Big House and strode down to the dock in some excitement. The cheering was louder; the people were crowding up to shake hands with the manager, and everyone was fighting to lend a hand helping to work the new ship arrival into dock.

She was the *Beaver*, seven and one half months out of London, across the Atlantic and around Cape Horn. She carried two masts square-rigged with towering canvas above yardarms and a fore and aft sail low on the main mast. This was the familiar brigantine rig of that time, but the ship carried in its cargo something which had never been seen on the west coast before. Heavy packages and crates in the hold contained the parts of a steam engine, and two huge paddle wheels lashed on deck looked very odd and mysterious.

The *Beaver* had been built in England. Her keel was elm; her huge timbers were oak; her over-all length was one hundred feet, nine inches; and she had two thirty-five-horsepower, wood-fueled steam engines, the newest and best. After test runs in the English Channel, the new-fangled steamboat parts were dismantled and stowed, and the *Beaver* was rigged as a brigantine and given a crew of twelve men for sailing to the faraway Columbia River. At Fort Vancouver they dismantled the sails, installed the engines and paddle wheels, and the first steamer ever to ply the coast waters of the Pacific brought a new era to the West Coast Wilderness.

Yet the primeval wilderness yielded slowly and only on the fringes, bit by bit. No wagons crossed the Far Grass Wilderness and the Monster Mountain Wilderness into California until 1844. These first wagons, of pioneers Townsend and Stevens, were blocked and left abandoned, buried in deep snow in the mountains until spring. Then Stevens and some helpers went back and brought a few of the wagons down into the Sacramento Valley. Otherwise there was no vehicle with spoked wheels in California as late as 1846. There were only heavy, two-wheeled oxcarts with solid oak wheels which creaked and rumbled slowly around.

There was no hotel worthy of the name in San Francisco until 1846, no lawyers, no resident doctors. Every ranchman knew how to set a broken bone and give first aid. Otherwise people in the growing hamlets at Los Angeles and San Francisco turned to doctors from the ships in the harbors.

But in 1843 "Dr. Joe Meeks" enjoyed a thriving practice down Sacramento way. Dr. Meeks turned up from the Rockies in a company of ruffians and gentlemen of fortune from Oregon. One of his first patients was a boy who had a toe cut off. Meeks stuck it back on with a poultice of mud, and it grew. After that he was kept very busy, and people who wanted him for childbirth or bone-setting were always sending for him where he hung around in the store.

One day a doctor from a ship in San Francisco came into the store, glad to find a fellow doctor to talk to. But something was wrong—medical words had no meaning to Dr. Meeks, and he scarcely knew one herb from another. He practiced herb medicine by grabbing a bottle and using whatever he found in his hand. So this was the end of Dr. Meeks who could not read or write. After that one of his companions from Oregon, who happened still to be around town, remembered that Joe Meeks had said, "Boys, when I get down to California among the greasers I'm going to palm myself off as a doctor."

A pioneer lawyer named B. B. Harris arrived in Los Angeles by mule pack from Texas in 1849. He stopped at a ranch on the edge of town where he saw how a wild horse could be broken as a saddle animal in a single afternoon by gently throwing it upside down on a bank of sand. Wildly kicking hoofs quickly subsided when the horse felt the peculiar pressure of soft, yielding sand against his back. Harris' journal says, "Thus, did we stumble on Rary's secret of horse taming which years after drew the attention of the whole world."

Lawyer Harris, on his trip to the coast in 1849, passed through wilderness little changed from Cabeza's wilderness. His journal closes with, "I confess that the trip at that time was dangerous even from wild beasts, let alone viler redmen. . . ."

It was early 1848; the villages around San Francisco Bay totaled a few hundred population and boasted two newspapers. These were merely bulletins with gossip columns, ship movements, arrivals of cargoes of whiskey, shootings in the local saloon, and speculations about the stranger walking down Market Street. The papers were bitter rivals, waging a battle of headlines over the hottest news of the day—the rumors from a few miles inland where they were looking for rocks with a yellow glint. One day *The Californian* had a scoop. The issue of March 15, 1848, carried this item:

GOLD MINE FOUND

In the newly made raceway of the saw mill recently erected by Captain Sutter on the American fork of the Sacramento gold has been found in considerable quantities. One person gathered $30 worth in a short time . . .

This item was published while Sam Brannan, owner of the rival paper, *The Star*, was out of town. He had ridden over to Sutter's mills to see what was going on and get the news firsthand. He had left in charge of his paper a young editor who thought it smart to pooh-pooh that scoop. For two months after the item came out, while Brannan was away, *The Star* ridiculed *The Californian*. "All sham! As superb a take-in as was ever got up to guzzle the gullible."

Within a few hours after those words appeared in his own paper, Sam Brannan galloped into San Francisco all travel-stained, his horse with mane flying and flanks heaving. It was a bright, sunny day when Brannan galloped up and down Market Street, waving above his shaggy head a bottle flashing with gold dust. He shouted over and over again, "Gold, *Gold*, GOLD! From the American River!"

The wilderness was beckoning again with gold, as it had to Coronado 350 years before. San Francisco "wiped itself off the map going up to the diggings." The hysteria spread eastward across the mountains and plains. The following year clouds of dust rose above the long trails as the wagon trains of the forty-niners poured into the West Coast Wilderness. The vast western wilderness had surrendered.

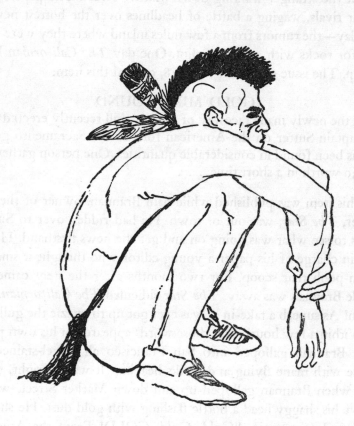

POSTSCRIPT

I HAVE just come out of the American wilderness where I have
been lost for about a thousand years. During this time I met
many vivid spirits who took me with them to share adventures in
unknown, untrod places.

In the beginning there were no vivid spirits, but ancient rocks
told of the birth of a continent of which I caught a glimpse in the
mists of time. It was blurred, but it had the general form of North
America. It was a tremendous rolling expanse of granite and black
volcanic rock with no sign of life. As I looked, cloudbursts deluged
the dead continent and many lakes gathered in low places. When
the sun shone, steam arose from the lakes and wet rocks, and I de-
scried in the steam coarse, grotesque trees in the valleys and around
the lakes and terrible lizards stalking among those trees, some of
them six times as big as an elephant. At long last the east and west
rims of the continent were thrust up by some mighty invisible force
to form mountain ranges, and at the same time the middle of the
continent rose, spilling off the water, and the terrible lizards began
to tumble and die.

Then before my eyes a marvelous change came over that continent. The sun shone pleasantly; white clouds sailed across blue skies; ocean waves slid up and back on sandy beaches; lakes sparkled and rippled, and rivers splashed with fish. Green woods were created and filled with songbirds, deer, and many animals. Dark forests appeared where squirrels were chased in the treetops and bears stared from behind trees and long-legged moose waded in the marshes.

Apart from these forests a vast prairie was spread out with a million head of buffaloes moving across it like a brown shadow. And in another place a deep, gray swamp with tall trees held some of the ancient primeval silence.

Then I caught sight of a brilliant desert made of yellow, red, and pink rocks where odd birds that couldn't fly ran after snakes that couldn't glide. And suddenly the air over this beautiful land was filled with ducks and geese, trumpeting swans and whooping cranes, whose formations marched in the air over the whole length of the continent.

The pageant of green and the colorful life were all the more astonishing because the continent had been so lifeless and nightmarish before all this happened. It appeared to me that a single tremendous miracle had taken place through the forces of the sun, moon, and winds and that everything was in delicate balance with those forces and with each other.

Time was not felt until I began to meet the vivid spirits who, like myself, had never seen such wonders before. I first espied them among ice fields, dim and ghostly in fogs off the northeast coast. It seemed appropriate that the first men to see the supernatural continent should look like men in a legend. Their great beards streamed like pennants in the wind as they arrived in long, swift boats driven by sails and also by oars. The leader was standing in the bow when he caught sight of a cliff with a spruce forest on top silhouetted against the setting sun.

Five hundred years later I stepped ashore with Christopher Columbus on an islet off the coast of Florida. Columbus said that, according to his charts, this was somewhere off the coast of India. Later I went with Amerigo Vespucci, exploring a long and mysterious coast. He was good company and got excited about the strange animals and plants. He thought it was a new continent, but he had no name for it and marked it on his chart: *terra ultra incognita.*

A man named Cabeza and I were lost together for eight years, trying to find our way out of Texas. That was one of the smartest men I've ever met. He did such clever tricks for the Indians that they worshiped him and gave him their best food instead of killing him. And I shall never forget that young English sailor, Dave Ingram. We walked together the whole length of the Green Woods Wilderness from the Gulf of Mexico to Nova Scotia. He couldn't read or write but he could live off the woods like an Indian.

Others who knew the animal happiness of the wilderness were the French canoemen, *les coureurs des bois.* In my estimation Peter Radisson was the greatest of them all. He could outwit the Indians on their own terms. The Mountain Men were the same kind. Such men were created by great and soul-stirring wilderness. The Mountain Men took the immense depths and towering heights of the Rocky Mountains in their stride, along with the panthers and grizzlies. Jim Colter was the Mountain Man who was reputed to tell the tallest tales, but the tale got taller than Jim when he stumbled over those geysers, boiling mud springs, and glass mountains of the Yellowstone region. When he described these spectacles to the boys down on the Missouri, they just laughed at him and he couldn't get anybody to go and take a look.

And there were women among the vivid spirits whom I shall never forget. For instance, Mrs. Bennett and Mrs. Aroano lost in Death Valley along with their young children; they were the first white people to see that hell spot. Then there was that Shoshone Indian girl who, at sixteen years of age, carried her baby on her back across hundreds of miles of prairie and through the Rocky Mountains. She saved the lives of Captains Lewis and Clark who probably could not have made it to the Pacific coast without her help.

It was thanks to people like these that I discovered how big this continent of ours is. It is wide enough to contain within one land mountains as massive as the Rockies, Sierras, and Appalachians; deep enough to contain forests as vast as the Green Woods, North Pine, and Monster Mountain; plus five lakes that look like five oceans; rivers as mighty as the Mississippi, St. Lawrence, Mac-Kenzie, and Colorado; a prairie like the High Plains as a pasture for sixty million monster bison; deserts as immense as the Mojave, Sonora, and Great Basin where unearthly animals and plants live— and there was always another wilderness beyond!

Emerging now from these adventures I find myself in the vicinity of Fifth Avenue and Forty-second Street in New York, pushed around by a crowd that is hurrying somewhere. They have just voted themselves out of the last piece of unspoiled wilderness in the northeast, in the Adirondacks in New York State. They seem to want to cut it in two with a fast throughway, which will scare the animals and birds to death with pitilessly strident sounds, awful fumes, destroy the runways and trails, and change the water table that keeps the wilderness alive. I wonder why they didn't send that highway around. And I wonder why they are draining so many wet lands where heron must stand and ducks and geese feed. Is there no other spot for a lot o' little houses?

I wonder where the heath hens that danced on Martha's Vineyard have gone, and the magnificent great auks which dove for fish from the rocks along the Maine coast, and the beautiful passenger pigeons with the iridescent feathers, and the majestic ivory-billed woodpeckers who owned the cypress swamps, and the eagles float-ing over the Hudson River.

Somehow I can't get out of my mind and heart the pathetic lone-liness of the handful of whooping cranes who use their five-foot windpipes like French horns to bugle *kerloo, kerlee-oo*, and the little key deer, and the haughty old condor who, as this is written, is still floating in the winds over California, and the few buffaloes left over from those thundering herds, and the funny little prairie dogs. Do these lonely ones know that their ancestors lived in cities with multimillion populations where the antelope played?

I have seen in Hawaii bulldozers scooping up in a single afternoon tropical wilderness of great age and splendor. Can't they build their hotel in any other spot? I have heard the scream of power saws run through the heart of a giant tree in the northwest in three minutes that had taken five hundred years to create. Can't they grow enough wood in the tree farms? They are planning to lay wide strips of sterile, gray concrete along the last untouched dunes on Fire Island off the south shore of Long Island. Why isn't it better to continue to go there in boats to enjoy the swaying dune grasses and the wild shore birds?

I find myself holding a few fragments of a living wilderness that was the depth of our being and the wealth of our land—and these are slipping through my fingers.

R. P.

INDEX

301

INDEX

INDEX

INDEX

INDEX

INDEX

INDEX